John Donne

Richard Sugg

Long before I knew what a Renaissance or a university was, I was well acquainted with a poet who taught me how to write and how to live. This book is dedicated, accordingly, to the memory of my father, Frank John Sugg.

Contents

Acknowledgements

Acknowledgements

Tom Cain and Peter Howell kindly helped out with particular queries. Natasha Davies, Jason Draper, Roger Ellis, Daniel Hartley, Elizabeth Hudson, Paul Jump, Peter McCarthy, Christopher Marlow, Annabelle Mooney, Mareile Pfannebecker, Joel Rasbash and Kate Wallis all read one or more draft chapters and gave invaluable advice and generous encouragement.

As so often, the most important people are the hardest ones to adequately thank. I could not have written this book quite as it stands without the enthusiasm and acuity of many students at Cardiff University. The class involved in 'Adding to the World' in 2004 offered perhaps more than they realised at a time when a genuine passion for ideas was an especially precious thing. I have received much inspiration, help and generosity from Paul Hammond, Bob Cummings, Paul Innes, Jonathan Sawday, and John Peacock. Inga-Stina Ewbank offered an enviable example in both her life and her work. I still miss her. Many thanks for everything to my mother, to Chris and Danni, to Les and Douglas Fielding, and to Freya and Ellis.

Louise: many thanks for many true adventures.

Chapter One

Introduction

I

A young man is leaning out of a window. It is a warm night in late summer 1588, loud with bells, and made still warmer by the bonfires crackling up and down the length of every street, as far as his eyes can see. His expression, to any who can read it under the wavering light and shadow of the fires, or the torches brandished by streams of drunken revellers, is ambivalent. The Spanish Armada has just been defeated. A massive navy, the pride of by far the most powerful nation in the world, lies broken on the coasts of the small island nation which routed it, or is limping back to Spain. The terror of invasion which had haunted England – perhaps as intensely as it would later in the years of Napoleon or Hitler – has been at least temporarily banished. But not only that. While the Spanish might tell themselves that their military power and valour had merely been frustrated by bad weather, the Englishmen who sang and shouted beneath John Donne's window had very different feelings. Probably more important than the bare thrill of victory or liberation from fear was the sense that they – only quite recently confirmed among the few nations adhering to the new, reformed Protestant religion – had been undeniably marked as God's chosen people. Like so many events we would now understand as accidental, the storm that dashed the enemy fleet was no ordinary one for Donne's English contemporaries. As the commemorative medals stated, 'God blew and they were scattered.' The feelings that stirred the heart and mind of the sixteen-year old Cambridge student at this moment are hard to precisely imagine.[1] We can reasonably guess, however, that they were as complex and disturbing as the poetry that now survives him. Donne's country was England, his religion Catholicism. He might live for forty, for ten, for two more years in England: he would certainly spend eternity in heaven or hell.

By February 1602 Donne has been – nominally – Protestant for some years. But his troubles are by no means over. Sick, cold, and dismayed at the bleakness of his future prospects, he sits in the Fleet prison on the south bank of the Thames. Even here his grace, composure and eloquence do not fail him. Secretly married some two months since, he owes his imprisonment to the fury of his wife's father, Sir George More; and by the thin light seeping into his cell he now writes to More the kind of letter in which eloquence really earns its keep:

How little and how short the comfort and pleasure of destroying is, I know your wisdom and religion informs you. And though perchance you intend not utter destruction, yet the way through which I fall towards it is so headlong, that, being thus pushed, I shall soon be at bottom, for it pleaseth God, from whom I acknowledge the punishment to be just, to accompany my other ills with so much sickness as I have no refuge but that of mercy, which I beg of Him, my Lord, and you, which I hope you will not repent to have afforded me, since all my endeavours and the whole course of my life shall be bent to make myself worthy of your favour and her love, whose peace of conscience and quiet I know must be much wounded and violenced if your displeasure sever us.[2]

Whether for the sake of his daughter, or with some feeling also for his unexpected new son-in-law, More did eventually soften. Later that same month Donne was released from the Fleet. He remained, however, confined in his room in the Strand, and in a sense he was to suffer this kind of genteel imprisonment in varying degrees for the next thirteen years. While More – who seems to have been hot-tempered and proud rather than stubbornly vindictive – grew increasingly mild, Donne's no less

11

eminent employer, Sir Thomas Egerton, felt differently. Despite the appeals not only of Donne but of More himself, Egerton refused to restore the post of secretary which Donne had occupied since winter 1597-8. In a way very characteristic of Renaissance society, what seems to us a spirited romantic exploit (compare, for example, the similar secret marriage and dramatic elopement of Elizabeth Barrett and Robert Browning, centuries later) was to largely determine Donne's fate for well over a decade.

Ultimately, it may have determined his life. The third and last phase of this can be dated to one more pivotal moment, in November 1614. Aged forty two, Donne is pacing, with as much composure as he can muster, amid the ornate − if rather bare − surroundings of a Renaissance garden.[3] With not only a wife, but six children dependent on him, he has been without formal employment now since the harsh echo of a closing door welcomed him into the Fleet prison back at the turn of the century. Though presently in finer surroundings, he is once again waiting on the uncertain whims of the great. For he is about to enter the presence of the greatest man in the whole British Isles − a learned, bisexual, slightly bow-legged Scotsman whose tongue is too large for his mouth, and whose extravagance is too great even for the large resources that his position commands. Fortunately he has enough time, respect and money for John Donne. The latter's heart perhaps wavers as his patron, the Earl of Somerset, reappears in the garden of Theobalds, the Essex residence of King James I. He is hoping that Somerset has been able to secure him an administrative post in the royal household, one of the clerks of the Council having conveniently died just the previous night. In fact, Somerset has been over-ruled by James, into whose presence both men now go. Upon the king's insistent persuasion – as more than one account has it – Donne agrees to become a minister of the Church. In the remaining fifteen years of his life, he not only succeeds but excels as a London preacher, becoming Dean of St. Paul's in 1621, and delivering a last, famous sermon just over a month before his death in 1631.

In all of these three moments – and in the more general circumstances which flowed into and from them – we can discern the outlines of a triangular relationship. The points of that triangle are religion, the individual, and society. The lengths of respective sides may have shifted at different points in Donne's life: in 1614, for example, he as an individual seems to have had more power than he did in 1588 or 1602, and from the pulpit he was able to speak to the aristocracy and gentry as he could never have spoken to Sir George More. It is fair to say, though, that Donne could not break that triangle. Just as he depended on the forces of social and political power throughout his life, so he was powerfully saturated with a sense of identity derived first from the stubborn Catholicism of his family, and later from the Protestant faith which he seems genuinely – if not unproblematically – to have embraced. And Donne himself? T.S. Eliot stated that 'Donne would have been an individual at any time and place'.[4] Even the briefest glance at the substantial and varied body of writing Donne left seems to confirm this. A changing but forcefully recognisable voice persists across poetry, letters and sermons, just as certainly as the musical signature of Bach or Mozart stamps the numerous different forms in which they worked. At the same time, it is hard not to feel that much of Donne's distinctive energy and attraction comes from the peculiar pressures of both his personal life and his more general historical era. In what follows I will try to show how Donne reflected not only the more dominant religious attitudes and beliefs of his lifetime – towards women, the natural world, and to those strange, heathen peoples of the new Americas – but also how he ambivalently responded to the first stages of scientific, social and cultural change.

While I will look explicitly at Donne's problematic religious identity, and at the more secular forms of self-definition obliquely written into his poetry, it can be said that Donne's self, ultimately, is not easily fixed. Rather, all of

Donne's writings are his self. In one sense these are more reliable than biographical information. We are on the whole certain that they belong to Donne, as we are not always certain about the accounts of his wayward chronicler and sometime acquaintance, Isaac Walton.[5] Secondly, where even the most plausible facts of Donne's outer life are little more than a skeleton, his writings are the living blood, flesh and guts. Literature gives us life with a vibrancy, complexity and fineness equal to that of the living body itself. And thirdly – to return to the writer as an individual – Donne seems to have fused his self and his writing in a quite special way. He seems, indeed, to have been most fully himself only when he wrote or when he spoke. This was true of many of his contemporaries in a way that we can never quite recover. In an age without radio, photography or moving film, and when few people could easily afford paintings, literature had an authority, a cultural privilege, and a psychological value now hard to imagine. And the relationship between self and language seems in Donne's case to have been an especially strong one. Writing to his closest friend, Sir Henry Goodyer, in August 1607, he argues that 'letters have truly the same office as oaths'. Therefore,

> as I never authorised my servant to lie in my behalf ... so
> I allow my letters much less that civil dishonesty, both

because they go from me more considerately and because they are permanent; for in them I may speak to you in your chamber a year hence before I know not whom and *not hear my self*.[6]

Because both Donne's world, and his whole habit of thought, are in many ways immensely alien to us, it is necessary to reconstruct something of his life and his society in what follows: partly to guard us against misunderstanding the distinctive registers of Renaissance psychology, and partly because we need to see how certain basic details of everyday life conditioned the minds of Donne and his peers. But in doing so it is equally necessary to move carefully between life and literature, and to continually realise that the latter offers us truths and nuances that at once include and transcend those of documentary history.

To start, then, by shading some more colour and texture between those three stages of the life indicated above. Donne was raised as a Roman Catholic. His mother's family was descended from the Catholic martyr Sir Thomas More, who had died for the old faith under Henry VIII. While Donne's father died in 1576, his mother, Elizabeth, remained secretly faithful to Catholicism until her late death, just a few months before

Donne's own. Other members of the family incurred more than the minor embarrassment caused by Elizabeth. Donne's great-uncle, Thomas Heywood, was executed in 1574 for saying mass. Just under twenty years later, in 1593, Donne's brother, Henry, was arrested for harbouring a Catholic priest. This latter, tried under the rigorous anti-Catholic laws of the period, was 'hanged, cut down alive, struggled with the hang-man, but was [disem]bowelled, and quartered'.[7] Henry himself died in Newgate prison, a victim of the plague that blighted London severely in 1593. This loss must have marked Donne heavily: although no longer a child, he was still young enough to be impressionable. People matured early in the Renaissance. But at twelve Donne was unusually young to go up to Oxford. He did so, in 1584, because his youth allowed him to avoid subscribing to the 'Thirty-nine Articles' of the Protestant faith. Donne's College, Hart Hall, 'had the reputation of being a centre for Catholics' and conveniently had no chapel (meaning that he and his brother Henry could evade religious services without suspicion).[8] Again, Donne's fugitive religion caused him to leave Oxford in 1597 – without formally taking a degree – because longer attendance would have made him old enough to sign the Articles, and so precipitate a social and personal dilemma which as yet lay some years in the future.

During his Oxford days Donne may, indeed, have had an especially memorable brush with Catholic outlaws. Many years later (now writing on behalf of the Protestant king, James I) he tells of how 'at a consultation of Jesuits in the Tower, in the late Queen's time, I saw it resolved, that in a petition to be exhibited to her, she might not be styled Sacred'.[9] Some debate exists as to exactly when Donne visited these Jesuits (the most learned and often fearless intellectual élite of the Catholic religion) imprisoned in the Tower of London. If, as Dennis Flynn believes, it was in 1584, then it seems that the encounter was indeed an unhappy kind of family reunion: Donne was accompanying his mother, making a legitimate but undoubtedly oppressive visit to her captured brother, the Jesuit priest and missionary, Jasper Heywood.[10]   However, if, as R.C. Bald claims, the meeting occurred in 1591, family ties were not involved (the prisoners being the poet Robert Southwell and Henry Garnet), but the atmosphere must have been hardly less furtive and bleak.[11] And even at this later date, Donne himself was still a Catholic. Following a conventional path for an aspiring gentleman of the time, he began studying law, and the kind of sharp-witted, ambitious and fashionable milieu in which he lived between 1591 and 1594 survives not only in the tone and content of certain poems, but in his earliest portrait.[12] Here, dashingly clothed, with long hair and an ear-ring, and wearing a sword, he stands under a Spanish motto whose language alone has been viewed as a provocative assertion of his outlawed identity.[13] And the message – 'Sooner dead than changed' – is no less defiant than the medium.[14] Indeed, even the ear-ring, in the form of a cross, was an 'inconceivable' symbol for an English Protestant of this time.[15]

In some ways, and to some observers, Donne could have looked much like any other relatively privileged, talented young man of the 1590s. True, he had not taken a degree. But other students used Oxford or Cambridge in the same way – something hard to understand in our own age of obsessive validation – simply as a place to acquire cultivation and make useful social connections.[16] From 1591 he studied law at the Inns of Court, the legal training centres of London which have been said to more precisely resemble our own universities as places where education was completed.[17] Suave, charming, elegant, witty and – if the Lothian portrait is to be believed – good-looking, he seduced young women and captivated young men. He wrote poems that were passed to friends and acquaintances in manuscript form; attended comedies where he saw 'a comedian... turn over [his] shoulder, and whisper to the Devil', and tragedies where one could observe a character 'weltring, and surrounded in his own blood'.[18] He made friends. At once repelled and fascinated by the hard glitter of power, he attended the royal court, where he looked with contempt on the sham beauty of women and sham wit of the men who attempted to 'board' them as if they were 'weak ships fraught with cochineal'.[19] Most of all, perhaps, he read voraciously, 'coffined' in the 'standing wooden chest' of his tiny legal study with his friend Christopher Brooke, and overlooked by the 'grave divines', 'Nature's secretary, the Philosopher', 'jolly statesmen', 'gathering chroniclers', and the 'giddy fantastic poets' he refers to in a youthful poem.[20]

Even here, Donne must have acquired some of his unmistakable psychic edge from the ongoing friction between his soul and his society. But it was in the near future that the real crisis lay. He could train himself at Oxford, Cambridge and the legal Inns (where, indeed, he seems to have had Catholic tutors).[21] But he could not progress into the ordinary adult employment suited to someone of his background and abilities: 'As a Catholic the gates of preferment and success were barred to him ... his religion offered him nothing in this world but exile or the patient endurance of persecution.'[22] We must therefore surmise that at some time in the late 1590s he made the decision to formally abandon Catholicism and accept the Protestant faith of England. In chapter four I will argue at greater length that he did so with some degree of sincerity. For now, what we know is that by 1597, when he took a very promising post as secretary to the eminent state official, Sir Thomas Egerton, his employer would have wanted to be assured that Donne was no longer a Catholic. It is also possible that Donne may have privately made the decision to convert some months earlier. In 1596 and 1597 he sailed on military expeditions against the Spanish, and it might have been important to his conscience and his sense of personal integrity to feel that he was not aiming to sever the souls of his fellow believers from their bodies in the battles of Cadiz and the Azores.[23] Whatever the exact date and nature of this decision, Donne was to remain a Protestant – and in later years a very eminent Protestant – for the rest of his life.

Two broad points must be emphasised here. First: as the case of Donne's mother shows, English Catholics did not always surrender easily. Eamon Duffy has illustrated at persuasive length how the early switches of monarch and religion (Catholic-Protestant, Protestant-Catholic, Catholic-Protestant in just twenty two years, under Henry, Edward VI, Mary, and finally Elizabeth) allowed many of the Catholic faithful to view the new religion as a passing – if traumatic – aberration.[24] And Patrick Collinson claims that 'Protestant England was born' only 'some considerable time after' the accession of Elizabeth in 1558.[25] By the 1580s it must have been clear that Elizabeth and many senior churchmen were serious about Protestantism. Yet even then a number of powerful old aristocratic families were able to defy the state and the Church to a considerable extent – as they had explicitly and violently done back in 1571, the year of the Catholic rebellion known as the 'Pilgrimage of Grace'. In 1564 Donne's great uncle, William Rastell, left in his will a sum of money which could only be received so long as the beneficiary 'should not fall into heresy [Protestantism] or return to England until that land had been reconciled to the Catholic faith'.[26] The Pope had excommunicated Elizabeth I, and denied her legitimacy and therefore her status as monarch. Jesuit missionaries, acting as Catholic secret agents, were vigorously seeking to restore Catholicism to Britain, and in some cases to assassinate Elizabeth (these attempts persisting into the reign of James I, who narrowly escaped death in the abortive Gunpowder plot of November 1605).

Second: Donne himself must have developed a certain distinctive psychology as he became conscious of the strange and fraught atmosphere which uneasily charged both his home life and his experiences in the wider society of Oxford, Cambridge, and London. Before attending university he had private Catholic tutors. He apparently refers to them as well as to his family when he later admits,

I was first to blot out, certain impressions of the Roman religion, and to wrestle ... against some anticipations early laid upon my conscience, both by persons who by nature had a power and superiority over my will, and others who by their learning and good life, seemed to me justly to claim an interest for the guiding ... of mine understanding.[27]

At Oxford Donne had probably mixed with fellow Catholics. At the age of either 13 or 19 he had mingled with Jesuits in the Tower of London. In 1593 his brother had died for his faith. These and other experiences would have been enough to harden the stubborn resolve seemingly encoded in his Spanish motto of 1591. Added to these, however, was the early sense that his family must have conveyed, of Protestantism as a dangerous but merely transitory heresy.

If we match up these personal and historical circumstances with certain of Donne's writings we can gauge three things. One is the self-reliance of one who lives on wits, nerves and charm all ground and polished by the gritty frictions of life outside the recognised social world. The fact that Donne felt he *deserved* so much more would only have heightened this quality. A second result was a degree of religious and intellectual relativism: a lingering feeling that something else might be true, and that those who believed it might indeed have had good reasons and pure hearts in doing so. Thirdly, and perhaps most importantly, Donne imbibed a certain fundamental restlessness. The details and the expressions of what is often a positive force of mobile energy will be set out in all of the following chapters. To sum up one tough vital thread of that quality we might for now say that Donne never quite expected to be believed, or to be right. He never, perhaps, quite believed himself, raised as he was in one religious tradition, and forcibly repositioned in another. Had he done so, he might well have been yet another charming, graceful, yet essentially faceless and voiceless gentleman of the English Renaissance. But like Shakespeare, like Marlowe, Jonson, Nashe and Spenser, he came from somewhere else. He could not depend on existing family or social connections to secure his future career. And he knew, not only that the margins of society are cold and hard, but – a knowledge not available to everyone – quite simply that the margins are real.[28]

And he had plenty of time in which to absorb that knowledge. This phase of his life (1602-14), and that 'headlong' fall that brought him to it, give us a sharp insight into the harshness and rigidity of Renaissance social structure. Where Sir George More could ultimately allow personal resentment to fade appreciably,

Egerton remained immune to the pleas of both son and father-in-law not so much through hurt pride, but because – though in fact sympathetic to Donne as a fellow ex-Catholic – his own general reputation was at stake if he should relent and take back a disgraced employee. Here is Donne's assessment of the situation, in a letter to Egerton of 1 March 1602:

How soon my history is despatched! I was carefully and honestly bred; enjoyed an indifferent fortune: I had ... the sweetness and security of a freedom and independency, without marking out to my hopes any place of profit ... I was four years your Lordship's secretary, not dishonest nor greedy. The sickness of which I died is that I began in your Lordship's house this love. Where I shall be buried I know not ... To seek preferment here with any but your Lordship were a madness. Every great man ... will silently dispute and say, 'Would my Lord Keeper so disgraciously have imprisoned him and flung him away if he had not done some other great fault of which we hear not?' ... I know mine own necessity, out of which I humbly beg that your Lordship will so much intender your heart towards me, as to give me leave to come into your presence.

Affliction, misery, and destruction are not there; and everywhere else where I am they are.[29]

If this letter stands as one of the rare instances where the web of artifice and wit fails to hide the intensity of personal feeling, we need not be surprised. Donne was right. After his disastrous marriage of 1601 (someone, though probably not him, summed it up pithily in the line 'John Donne – Ann Donne – Undone') he spent years away from London, in relative isolation and poverty. From 1602-1606 he depended partly on the kindness of rich friends who let him stay on their estate at Pyrford in Surrey; and from 1606-1611 – gaining some independence and losing some comfort – languished in a small and humble cottage in Mitcham, surrounded by children who were often sick, and not infrequently dying. His prophecy about his own reputation seemed directly borne out on at least two occasions, when he unsuccessfully sought the posts of Secretary to Ireland in 1608, and to the Virginia Company in 1609.

Four hundred years ago, the countryside was not a pleasant retreat from the wild pressures of urban life – at least, not if you were poor. For Donne, a considerable ride out of London, it was an exile: 'all retirings into a shadowy life', he tells us, 'are ... alike subject to the barbarousness and insipid dullness of the country.'[30] In 1605 and early 1606 Donne broke the monotony by visiting Europe as a travelling companion to Sir Thomas Chute.[31] As Bald notes, he had lodgings in London from perhaps as early as 1607; and he and his friends did occasionally exchange visits.[32] But it has been plausibly claimed that even these were limited because – especially until 1609 – Donne's poverty prevented him from dressing with the grace and luxury thought essential to even making an appearance in certain circles.[33] In one important sense, though, Donne's loss in these years has proved our gain. While his poetic output is said to have been very low between 1602 and 1607, his letters are not only plentiful, but marked with a certain quality that those of more pressured years were to lose.[34] Donne's own claim, much later, that in poetry he 'did best when I had least truth for my subjects', might almost apply to the thin subject matter and effortlessly graceful style of his letters between 1602 and 1614.[35] Writing to Henry Goodyer, the closest of a network of influential friends who were vital in sustaining him in these years, he contrasts the dynamic blur of social activity with the 'insipid dullness' of his own home:

> To your life full of variety nothing is old, nor new to mine; and as to that life all stickings and hesitations seem stupid and stony, so to this, all fluid slipperinesses and transitory migrations seem giddy and feathery. In

that life one is ever in the porch or postern, going in or out, never within his house himself: it is a garment made of remnants, a life ravelled out into ends, a line discontinued, and a number of small wretched points, useless, because they concur not: a life built of past and future, not proposing any constant present; they have more pleasures than we, but not more pleasure; they joy oftener, we longer ...[36]

We notice here that the initial opposition between himself and Goodyer all but seamlessly shifts, with the two friends themselves ('we') coming to oppose a transient, illusory social froth. Donne's attitude to friendship will be considered in chapter three. What has to be admitted just now is that friendship was probably for Donne the greatest gain of this period. As for the stoic virtues and ascetic 'joys' of isolation and reflection: Donne may have believed that when he wrote it. But he may equally have been – as suggested – simply writing himself back to life once again, in any way he could. St Exupery's notion that 'it is what we are worth when motionless that counts' does not seem to have applied to Donne:

if I say that I have passed [the last week] without hurting any, so may the spider in my window ... I would fain do something, but that I cannot tell what is no wonder. For to choose is to do; but to be no part of any body is to be nothing.[37]

It has been remarked that Donne's writing a book in defence of suicide – his *Biathanatos* – at this time was no accident.[38] And images of death do indeed sound a dull refrain throughout the letters up to 1609 in particular.

Relief came just in time. Finally, in autumn 1608, Donne's father-in-law granted the dowry which had so long been withheld.[39] From now Donne's life becomes easier and more varied. We are still in some danger, though, of over-estimating his own sense of security and direction. We, of course, have hindsight. Donne did not know that in 1615 he would be made a royal chaplain and an honorary doctor of divinity. Hence, as late as May 1614 he explains to his friend Sir Robert Ker that, while 'others may have told you, that I am relapsed into my fever', rather 'that which I must entreat you to condole with me, is that I am relapsed into good degrees of health ... and ... am fallen from fair hopes, of ending all'.[40] In general terms, though, his prospects had been steadily advancing since late 1610, when he was commissioned by Sir Robert Drury to write a memorial poem for his prematurely deceased daughter, Elizabeth.[41] Ultimately, Donne in fact wrote two long memorials, *An Anatomy of the World*, and a companion-piece, *Of the Progress of the Soul* (1611 and 1612). Tellingly, he did not produce his best work in this case. In a sense it is a kind of tribute to Donne's independence and self-integrity that he wrote badly to order. Indeed, the poems seem not to have been any more popular on their first publication than in later centuries. Most famously, Ben Jonson stated that they were 'profane and full of blasphemies', and (perhaps tellingly) that 'if it [*sic*] had been written of ye Virgin Mary it were something'.[42] Yet the poems are also interesting just because Donne, a little off his guard, talks revealingly about so many other things beside his dead subject. Thanks to Robert Drury he now finally moves back to London (in 1612) after travelling with that family on the continent earlier in the same year. In 1614 he briefly acts as a Member of Parliament, and – as seen above – is finally brought back into public life and prosperity by Somerset and by James (though not, it would seem, before he had been compelled to write with evident resentment to the former).[43] We will hear more about Donne's later life (1615-31) and the transition from secular obscurity to ecclesiastical eminence in further chapters, and especially in the conclusion. As we will see, security did not destroy either Donne's restless creativity, or his peculiar ambivalence.

For now, the life summarised here can be broadly split into three parts. There is, first, Donne's bright and promising youth – a brilliant career shattered and darkened by the results of his rash marriage in 1601. Within that first phase itself, his relatively late rupture from his native religion is one of the most important events. From 1602-1614 Donne existed in varying degrees of obscurity and poverty. Long as that period was (and perhaps especially so in an era when average life expectancy was around forty), the nadir appears to have fallen some time around its centre. From the time of the dowry to his meeting with James I, Donne was slowly but increasingly moving outward and upward. And it is important to remember that throughout those twelve-odd years Donne retained and acquired many influential friends. Finally, we have Donne the preacher: a more successful and worldly figure, but one who seems never to have forgotten his friends or his own older selves as he delivered the words of God to ever more attentive and eminent London audiences.

This triptych is, of course, partly convenient and artificial. To the person living it, life does not feel so neatly structured. But it is also artificial in another way. Donne's life was lived in pre-scientific, pre-industrial world whose notions of social order, politics and justice would now strike many as intolerable, and at times barbaric. To fully appreciate his writings, we need to set them in this context, and to restore some of the living drama of that environment. Let us spare just a few moments, then, to spill those painstakingly recovered and isolated drops of biography back into the rich, disorderly and simmering froth from which they were extracted. What might we have seen, some four hundred years ago, in Elizabethan London?

II

Bells are ringing. The buildings are timbered, plastered not white but a softer, muted shade of pale beige. The glass in the windows is rough, heavily-textured. As far as you can see, the air is filled with spires – perhaps a hundred, and effortlessly the tallest things that pierce the sky, save perhaps one or two of the thick forest of masts swaying gently down on the Thames. The streets are filled with mud. At certain points, with no warning whatsoever, the air is clotted with an indescribable stench of decaying human waste. Impossible as this is to avoid, the mud soon proves no less so. A thin strip of relatively clean space runs along each wall of the street (though even there carriages can flick one's clothes easily). But this sacred zone, it transpires, is reserved for others than yourself. A large man – not so much fat as impressively bulky – makes this forcefully clear as he approaches you, brow darkened, hand reaching for the hilt of a sword that gleams against the deep pile of a gorgeously crimson-lined cloak. (Well, he can have the wall if it means that much to him.[44])

There is, after all, sufficient distraction to compensate for mud and stench. Perhaps the best way to sum it up in a single word is this: contrast. Little flurries of filthy and underfed children break like human surf around your knees; women carrying baskets of oranges cry their wares in an accent resembling nothing you have ever quite heard. Beggars rot in the mouths of alleyways.[45] An occasional pig is seen snuffling through the mud. Ragged youths stoop under long wooden chutes of water. People's clothing varies: sometimes plain but clean, rough but pure linen; sometimes shredded, unimaginably soaked with the blood, mucous, dirt and excrement of ages; but generally, colourless or very muted. And amidst all this vital yet humble traffic of London life there suddenly appears a wild vision of something all but otherworldly: horses whose very sweat seems to shine and varnish their beautiful coats like the gleaming panels of the coach they draw; an immaculately uniformed driver, occasionally flicking a whip at a slow pedestrian. Within, behind flawlessly shining glass, a glimpse of unusually pale skin, a flash of jewellery, the soft gleam of a velvet glove: a countenance so staggeringly, effortlessly arrogant that it might belong not so much a to a different class as a different species ...

It is perhaps some slight comfort, briefly mingling with the crowd outside St Paul's, to listen to the austere but luridly compelling denunciations of the preacher, spitting chill breath and hot damnation on such luxuries. (Nor does he seem keen on the bright new theatres to which he gestures across the water.) Instinctively breaking away from the intensely monochrome figure (all black in the body and tautly white about the lips and jaw) you glance quickly into the church itself. For a moment, subconsciously linking its neglected rough exterior with the oddly busy, irreverent atmosphere within, you indeed wonder if it is a working church at all. The water-carriers are here again, and seem undeniably as they pass one another briskly, whistling and singing, to be using it as a short-cut. Groups of people whisper in a businesslike rather than awed manner against the pillars, certain of which are blotched by what can only be advertisements. The combined mass of all these hushed voices imparts a restless aural pressure, a kind of bee-swarm filling the air. A weary verger is swiping at the head of a small boy to discourage him from stoning pigeons. And that faintly steaming dark patch there is ... yes – undeniably – urine.[46]

Threading between rolling barrels and the shouts of labourers you head east along the waterside. Little rowing-boats nip bravely across the crowded river between cargo ships; passengers flow in varying degrees of colour and haste up and down the steps cut into the bank. Reaching Tower Bridge you are pleasantly surprised at the nearness of green spaces to north and south of you, bounding in the tight boisterous little network of streets and churches. The bridge itself, once entered, is largely a city in its own right. Looking back from the south side you see rotting and discoloured heads jammed onto poles, here and there crowned by a raven or kite briskly jabbing at the jelly of a sightless eye. No one else seems to have noticed this - nor, for that matter, the skeletons in ragged coats of flesh which hang suspended over the river (pirates, you later learn). There again, an awful lot of people do seem to be drunk, or much less than sober. This is clear not only from their gait but from the ubiquitous bursts of song brightening the air above the rushing water. And so you stagger on, sword clinking on your side, through this city whose stinking gutters suddenly open on unexpected visions of heaven. A bear roaring, bloodied, wild with rage and pain, is torn at by dogs darting toward the stake that binds it. Angelic voices rise and fuse against the stone vaulting of a nearby church. The plaintive chords of a lute rise, in the strangely blank, open soundscape, through a tavern window.

Amidst this riot of gorgeous luxury, unimaginable poverty, violence, cruelty and hunger Donne moved from day to day. His world is a lost country into which we can only make rapid brief forays – and even then, not without a strenuous effort of imagination.[47] As much of the above indicates, we would probably not want to live there. And it may well have been partly because much of life was so uncertain, harsh, and difficult that the Renaissance so doggedly wove between itself and these grim realities innumerable screens of delicacy, wit, and beauty – often seeming to strike the canvas or the page or the keyboard with the kind of brisk precise exactness of people who had not the time, patience or temperament for half-measures.

With Donne in particular we are especially fortunate. He left us love poems and religious poems, satires that jolt impatiently through the sights and sounds of the city streets, elegies of youthful scorn, furtive midnight debauchery, and gleeful obscenity; the carelessly elegant prose of the letters, and the poise, balance and weight of his sermons, that 'massive music' which sounded through the churches of London for just over fifteen years.[48] The different forms in which Donne wrote are important, as are the rhetorical traditions which surrounded him. But the influence of these as constraining factors on his independence or originality can be exaggerated: at times critics appear to claim that neither Donne nor anyone else could say anything new at all.[49] By contrast, Ben Jonson – though himself far from uncritical – was ready to recognise Donne as 'the first poet in the world in some things'. Jonson also said that 'Donne for not keeping accent deserved hanging'; and that 'for not being understood [he] would perish'.[50] The first comment, on the oft-noted lack of smoothness in Donne's versification, has a wider range of implications than might at first appear. And the second, for some decades, almost seemed to have come true. Recent critical views of Donne are incorporated into the next six chapters. I will close the present one by briefly examining how different ages understood, or sometimes failed to understand, Donne's poetry.

III

How, then, did different eras variously create and recreate Donne in their own images? Donne's early influence was evidently powerful. An edition of his *Poems* was published in 1633, eighty of his sermons in 1640, and even some of his letters (including the telling advertisement 'to several persons of honour') in 1651. Certain Cavalier poets in particular worshipped Donne, with Thomas Carew writing an elegy on his death and paraphrasing him closely in his own work.[51]

Katherine Philips was influenced by Donne, and the notoriously risqué playwright Thomas Killigrew clearly alludes to Donne's 'Lecture on the Shadow' when a character notes 'this sad truth in Love; the first minute after noon is night'.[52] Donne's followers seem in particular to have admired his wit and ingenuity. But even here a faintly ambiguous note already creeps in. Carew's elegy is clear enough in its praise for Donne ('the lazy seeds/Of servile imitation thrown away,/And fresh invention planted'), but his echo of Jonson is intriguingly complicated when we are told not only that,

> ... to the awe of thy imperious wit
> Our stubborn language bends

but that Donne's poems had 'Committed holy rapes upon our will'.[53] The phrase 'holy rapes' stands out a little oddly in the context of Carew's eulogistic lines. The period used 'rape' in the sense of 'violently seizing' as well as that of sexual assault. Yet in either case aggression and violence seem to be at stake. And these are present, if more subtly, in the notion of Donne making language 'bend' to his 'imperious wit'. A question which follows on from this is: how far can a writer bend language before it breaks?

By the late eighteenth century Donne's popularity was very low. In a sense, this was indeed 'for not being understood'. Yet the lack of understanding was more interesting and more fundamental than a simple inability to keep up with the workings of a brilliant and agile mind. The best (and best-known) summary of the period's attitude to Donne comes from one of its most influential and archetypal literary figures – the lexicographer, critic and (nominal) poet, Dr Samuel Johnson. Writing not just on Donne, but on 'the metaphysical poets' with whom Donne was then grouped, Johnson claimed that in their poetry,

> The most heterogeneous ideas are yoked by violence together; nature and art are ransacked for illustrations, comparisons, and allusions; their learning instructs, and their subtlety surprises; but the reader commonly thinks his improvement dearly bought, and though he sometimes admires is seldom pleased.[54]

Johnson's analysis echoes Carew's emphasis on violence and ingenuity. Yet it also sharply contrasts with the earlier poet's fervent admiration. For Carew a degree of intellectual and linguistic 'violence' was a good thing; for Johnson it was bad. We can already sense, then, that what we are witnessing is not only a divergence of personal taste, but the reflections of a more absolute cultural shift. To put this a little more precisely: we can say that Johnson and Carew have very different notions of what language and metaphor can and cannot do. Carew, remember, talks about '*holy* rapes'. Donne is not, to him, ransacking nature and art in acts of senseless violence: rather, he is effectively finding something out, revealing something. As Donne's contemporary and probable acquaintance, John Hoskins, put it, in defining the rhetorical mode of 'hyperbole', a certain metaphoric exaggeration was legitimate, in order 'that rather you may conceive the unspeakableness, than the untruth' of what is related.[55] Donne can move so swiftly and yet so successfully between seemingly incongruous images because in the end the universe is convincingly, densely meaningful in a way that it had ceased to be for the late eighteenth century.

We can elaborate this by looking further at Johnson's criticisms. He goes on to explain that 'Great thoughts are always general, and consist ... in descriptions not descending to minuteness'. The 'metaphysicals' therefore failed just because

> Their attempts were always analytic; they broke every image into fragments; and could no more represent, by their slender conceits and laboured particularities, the prospect of nature, or the scenes of life, than he, who

dissects a sun-beam with a prism, can exhibit the wide effulgence of a summer noon.[56]

Just after this Johnson confirms his distance (and misunderstanding) by deriding the metaphysicals' use of that 'hyperbole' which Hoskins and his peers understood so differently. Most importantly, Johnson here all but explicitly admits that his antagonism is founded on a radical change of culture and belief. The nature of 'Great thoughts' is to him as axiomatic and indisputable as Newton's law of gravity. He and his age are no longer able to conceive of the 'descent to minuteness' as a process of discovery or of distillation – the poetic alchemy of a period when many still believed that alchemists could in theory strip away surface dross to reveal the minute secret essence within. Again, Donne's era accepted a religiously-based notion of general truths expressed in miniature: the 'microcosm' of humanity, with its hair, blood and bones reflected the 'macrocosm' of nature, with its grass, rivers and rocks. Indeed, vapours flowing down from the stars were held responsible for numerous everyday phenomena.

It is easy, now, to attack Johnson; and in an obvious sense unnecessary to do so, given that many still read Donne's poetry, and very few that of the learned Doctor. Having acknowledged our own natural distance from Johnson's position, we should perhaps try all the harder to understand where he may be right, as well as wrong. If we add that one source of our alienation from him is the maddeningly bland self-satisfaction of those weighty cadences, we are not merely noting a matter of temperament. Can we also claim that Johnson is in a certain unintentional sense *accurate* in his complaints about Donne's violence? Donne lived in a culture which placed more cosmic value on language than we do. He was able in good faith to talk about small things and universal things, transient things and eternal things, in one breath. But he also lived in a time when that older view of meaning and truth was beginning slowly to erode. New discoveries in medicine and astronomy, and the revelation of a whole massive continent, undocumented across centuries of written history, clearly shook educated Christians in his lifetime. And they seem, as chapters five and six in particular will show, to have especially troubled Donne, with his all but involuntary desire to admit that an opposite perspective might equally be true. Was Donne at times not also trying to create meaning through language, depending on it as a substitute for beliefs to which emotion still clung, although the intellect increasingly began to doubt? To do justice to Donne as a complex and credible writer and individual, we need to see that his creative skills could have more than one side to them. They certainly did extend the range of human feeling and thought. Yet they also (and sometimes in the same breath) said many interesting things that Donne's conscious mind would have violently denied. Donne is interesting both for his times and for the temperament with which he responded to them. There were, of course, men just as complacent as Johnson in the English Renaissance. But Donne allowed the cultural changes and anxieties of his time to affect him in a way that the Johnsons of the world did not.

It was not until the earlier twentieth century that Donne was effectively canonised. And the ecclesiastical overtones of the word are especially apt in this case. Donne's champion was T.S. Eliot. Eliot is famous in the obscure world of literary criticism not only for his poetry, but for some attractive yet highly-disputed comments about the distinctive qualities of Donne and his peers. Eliot found in Donne 'a direct sensuous apprehension of thought, or a recreation of thought into feeling'. Contrasted with Donne, Victorian poets such as Tennyson and Browning did not 'feel their thought as immediately as the odour of a rose. A thought to Donne was an experience; it modified his sensibility.' Eliot goes on to broaden these comments by stating that

The poets of the seventeenth century ... possessed a mechanism of sensibility which could devour any kind of experience. In the seventeenth century a dissociation of sensibility set in, from which we have never recovered ... [57]

Eliot later offered a slightly different version of his theory:

If such a dissociation did take place, I suspect that the causes are too complex and too profound to justify our accounting for the change in terms of literary criticism. All we can say is, that something like this did happen; that it had something to do with the Civil War [and]... that it is a consequence of the same causes which brought about the Civil War ... [58]

That second statement was made twenty years after the first, and over a year into World War Two. Its shift is interesting, in that Eliot now admits that politics (the Civil War of 1642-49) was chiefly to blame for that cultural trauma he had identified in the seventeenth century. And yet Eliot's notion of the cultural difference between the Renaissance and the Victorians remains oddly quaint. He has managed to admit politics into his argument, but still omits something that to us may seem to be staring him grimly in the face. That factor is, of course, religion. When we say that the Renaissance believed in God far more forcefully than did the Victorians we can be quite precise about it. People probably did die voluntarily for Christianity in the nineteenth century; but those people were not senior members of the Church or politicians such as Sir Thomas More, Thomas Cranmer, Nicholas Ridley, and Hugh Latimer.[59]

It may be that this seemingly curious omission on Eliot's part has prompted much of the antagonism to a theory which is in fact quite plausible. (Eliot effectively claims that the seventeenth century witnessed a massive cultural shift; compare the paraphrase, 'they felt differently because they believed in God'.) He is indeed rightly cautious in his argument about the Civil War, refusing to crudely determine the exact nature of political cause and psychological effect. But it was probably Eliot's political stance which irritated many. This is evident even in little details such as 'we have never recovered' (who are 'we'? and have the poor and a great many women not indeed 'recovered' considerably since the seventeenth century?). Elsewhere he attributes the shift, with delightfully grandiose apolitical mysticism, to 'something which had happened to the mind of England'.[60] Eliot's attitude to Donne alone is itself intriguingly ambivalent, as we will see later. For now, let us part company from him by just noting what seems to have been especially attractive to him about Donne (or a certain version of

Donne as he saw him). Embedded in Eliot's theory of the 'dissociation of sensibility' is this reflection on poetry:

> When a poet's mind is perfectly equipped for its work, it is constantly amalgamating disparate experience; the ordinary man's experience is chaotic, irregular, fragmentary. The latter falls in love, or reads Spinoza, and these two experiences have nothing to do with each other ... in the mind of the poet these experiences are always forming new wholes.[61]

In a narrow sense this claim is true enough. But if we contextualise it carefully alongside Eliot's nostalgia for the age of Donne, and his odd failure to admit the colossal changes in religious outlook, we realise in fact that Eliot wants not so much to understand Donne, as to *be* him. Faced with the social, intellectual and religious disintegration of his own era he yearns for a 'new whole' and for just that 'mechanism of sensibility which could devour any kind of experience' (or, perhaps, bend it to one's imperious wit or will).

Eliot's analysis of Donne, then, so neatly contradicts that of Johnson because the religious and social erosion which Johnson could still ignore was now sufficiently pronounced to produce an urgent longing for some past wholeness in the later critic. Like Donne, Eliot seems to have suffered from a conflict between his formidable intellectual integrity, and his emotional desire to believe in God. In 1922, in *The Waste Land*, the former clearly dominates; in the *Four Quartets* of 1946, the latter. And Eliot would ultimately convert to Catholicism (the parallels or inverse parallels indeed tempt one to believe in reincarnation). It is fair to say, perhaps, that when Eliot talks about the 'poet's mind' he is really talking about the mind of God; or unconsciously wishing that the poet was God – wishing, at any rate, that the harmonious order of that creative mind was meaningfully reflected in the world as a whole.

This brief survey of critical responses should help to show the danger of insisting on any definitive version of either Donne or his writings. Our interpretations are in some sense always creations. It would be rash to say that Carew, or Johnson, or Eliot were plainly wrong. Rather, the cultural oxygen of our times gives us a certain voice, or – if you like – tints the ink we write with. Yet this relative interpretative position does not prevent us from assessing just how Donne's own era conditioned his writing. In his book *The Order of Things*, Michel Foucault identifies what he terms a 'discontinuity' between the *episteme* of the sixteenth-century, and that which succeeded in 'the first half of the seventeenth-century'.[62]

Epistemology is the theory of knowledge, and Foucault's use of the term *epistemé* reflects his desire to study not history, or history of ideas, but something which he sees as more primary: the basic conditions governing 'knowledge itself' – what was recognisable as knowledge and what was not.[63] 'Discontinuities' are those periods in which, 'within the space of a few years', epistemological conditions have changed 'at that archaic level which makes possible both knowledge itself and the being of what is to be known'.[64] To summarise briefly for now: Foucault's ideas warn us that Donne could only think and feel according to the peculiar assumptions and beliefs of his society. We might add, conversely, that he could think and feel in ways no longer available to us. We need, then, to bear in mind that Donne is a distinctive author, but one who in many ways has far more in common with his contemporaries than he has with a modern writer (Eliot, for example) of ostensibly similar qualities. Yet, as we will find, Donne's own age was itself an increasingly divided one. Both he and it occasionally looked forward to certain things which they would have preferred not to see, as a once unified religious truth increasingly fractured and disintegrated around them.

Chapter Two

Self

Be then thine own home, and in thy self dwell.[65]

I

Ben Jonson, as we have seen, admitted that Donne was 'the first poet in the world in some things'. And this insistent delight in shock and novelty is swiftly evident to anyone just glancing through the collection of poems known as 'Songs and Sonnets'. The openings are irresistibly compelling:

> I long to talk with some old lover's ghost,
> Who died before the god of love was born
>
> ('Love's Deity')

> For God's sake hold your tongue, and let me love
>
> ('The Canonization')

I wonder, by my troth, what thou, and I

Did, till we loved?

                                                                 ('The Good Morrow')

Or, again:

When my grave is broke up again

Some second guest to entertain

                                         ('The Relic')

Go, and catch a falling star,

Get with child a mandrake root

                                              ('Song')

When I am dead, and doctors know not why ...

                                         ('The Damp').[66]

Sometimes startling, sometimes briskly conversational or imperative, not infrequently all three, the poems have a quickly recognisable and unforgettable voice. We cannot quite say that this is the voice of Donne himself. What we can confidently claim is that the sharp impatience with convention which so roughly seizes our attention is an adroit and effective form of self-construction. No one had ever quite done this before, and afterwards those who attempted to do it again would necessarily be at least tinged with convention themselves.

Before engaging directly with Donne's poems, we need briefly to tackle one important point. It has for some time been argued that the 'self', in anything like the sense generally recognised now, was still a relatively new entity in Donne's lifetime.[67] Those notions of individual identity which have since become as seemingly indispensable to human beings as their hearts or brains scarcely existed in the Medieval period, and were still in process of development in the Renaissance. Perhaps the most important thing to understand, first, is that the seemingly axiomatic notions of 'trusting oneself' or 'believing in oneself' were – at least in theory – incomprehensible to Renaissance Christians. Rather, the self was most commonly understood in negative terms, as that part of one's consciousness likely to be swayed by the Devil, or at least to turn from the God whose presence should ideally condition one's inner life. The self, then, was constrained and tabooed at the most basic metaphysical level.

Secondly, it was heavily shaped by the stubbornly rigid social barriers we glimpsed in chapter one. In one sense, social hierarchy encouraged a forceful awareness of one's self (and perhaps especially for the privileged). But at the same time, belief in the absolute necessity of these social divisions meant that individuals tended to be subordinated to a social whole understood as greater than the sum of its parts. Time and again in Renaissance literature, we meet the image of the 'social body'. This, with its implications of health or disease, and its organic hierarchy of parts and roles (some essential, others disposable), was not merely a metaphor. So, ironically, to be sure of yourself (as, say, an educated if not very rich gentleman) was to be sure of society itself, and therefore to necessarily limit one's own independence from larger structural forces.[68] Chapter four will show that Donne was in some ways very much conditioned by Christian notions of personal identity. As we have already seen, however, neither his religious nor his social status were straightforward or stable. In the following pages I will argue that certain of his poems offer us glimpses of a self-hood still waiting to be formally invented or acknowledged by society as a whole.

The form of self-definition examined in this opening section can be broadly classified as anti-Petrarchan. Francesco Petrarch (1304-74) was a highly influential figure in the rise of Italian humanist and Renaissance culture.[69] Our interest at present is with his love poetry. Petrarch wrote numerous sonnets inspired by a woman called Laura. One uses the phrase 'inspired by' advisedly: it has been claimed that Petrarch in fact never actually met Laura, or that if he did it was only once. She was already married, and Petrarch was apparently resigned to the hopelessness of any intimate relationship between them. The poems, then, are not exactly 'about' Laura in any sense we would recognise. Rather, they had for Petrarch something of a religious function. In keeping with the persistently idealising, abstract descriptions of Laura (her hair is like gold wire, her cheeks like snow, her eyes like the sun), Laura serves almost as a kind of Catholic icon – a focus for contemplation of the highest reality of all, God himself. While these poems do often have a considerable intimacy of tone, they are therefore far from intimate or personal in the sense of being a depiction of love, or of the beloved. An important feature of what came to be known as 'Petrarchan love' was indeed the intrinsic hopelessness of it. The female beloved was always unobtainable. Futile and paradoxical as this might seem at first glance, it had certain useful consequences for Petrarch and his numerous imitators. The love necessarily then becomes more abstractive and unreal. To quote the much later but very apt summary of Scott Fitzgerald in *The Great Gatsby* (a tale which owes much to Medieval and Renaissance traditions of courtly love): 'no amount of fire or freshness can challenge what a man can store up in his ghostly heart.'[70] Conveniently, Petrarch does not risk the kind of disappointment which Jay Gatsby is said to suffer finally on (almost) obtaining the fantastically hypostatised Daisy. Immune to worldly disillusion, the Petrarchan lover's vision retains a kind of melancholy perfection, distant but always immaculate. Besides being essentially religious in its abstraction, the Petrarchan 'relationship' also clearly involves a certain self-denying and obsessive faith: he will never turn to another, despite the impossibility of it all.

We will find Donne occasionally writing poems (and arguably some of his best) not entirely alien to those of Petrarch. Perhaps most obviously, in 'Air and Angels' and 'The Ecstasy', he views women or love as mediums through which he can experience the divine, elevating one to a higher state in the way that Petrarch's mesmerised contemplation of Laura seemed to give him some partial glimpse of the ultimate reality of the next world. But there is little doubt that when he wishes to be, Donne is the most gleefully anti-Petrarchan poet of his day. The Petrarchan mode was first imported into Britain back in the 1530s, via translations made by Sir Thomas Wyatt and the Earl of Surrey, and further perpetuated when certain of these English poems were anthologised in a collection known as *Tottel's Miscellany* (1557). While Donne was still little more than a child, Sir Philip Sidney had already begun to shift away from the Petrarchan love poem, in his long sonnet sequence, *Astrophil and Stella*. Sidney's ironic reference to 'poor

Petrarch's long-deceasèd woes' was presently underwritten more forcefully in Shakespeare's famous sonnet 130:

> My mistress' eyes are nothing like the sun;
> Coral is far more red than her lips' red;
> If snow be white, why then her breasts are dun;
> If hairs be wires, black wires grow on her head.[71]

The implication of this – that the speaker indeed loves his mistress *because* she is real and distinctive – is already an important statement of a new conception of intimacy. Again, in *Twelfth Night* we meet Count Orsino, a figure for whom love seems to begin and end with his own narcissistically over-indulged sentiments of aesthetic whimsy and self-pity. The very fact that Orsino is so comic and so unsympathetic from an audience's point of view similarly indicates the new stance toward the Petrarchan lover.

Donne had almost certainly written some of his Songs and Sonnets before 1601, when *Twelfth Night* was performed.[72] But even if all of Shakespeare's swipes at Petrarchanism had preceded those of Donne, the latter would still retain a certain unsurpassable edge. For a prime example, consider this:

Mark but this flea, and mark in this,

How little that which thou deny'st me is;

Me it sucked first, and now sucks thee,

And in this flea, our two bloods mingled be;

Confess it, this cannot be said

A sin, or shame, or loss of maidenhead,

Yet this enjoys before it woo,

And pampered swells with one blood made of two,

And this, alas, is more than we would do.

('The Flea').

Donne's contemporaries would have been less easily shocked by the poem's sexuality than were the Victorians or Edwardians. Indeed, we know that, unlike some of the most overtly licentious Elegies, 'The Flea' was not excluded by the censors from the 1633 edition of Donne's poems. At the same time, Donne was undoubtedly well aware of what he was writing. A number of what look like his most conspicuously youthful poems were probably composed while he was at the legal Inns of Court in the early 1590s. As we have seen, Donne had not taken a degree at either university, and in a broadly similar way, it was a mark of one's genteel sophistication not to do anything so vulgar and crudely self-advertising as actually *publishing* one's poetry. Ben Jonson was mocked when he published a collected edition of his plays in 1616; and Donne himself in 1612 was unable to forgive his own 'descent in printing anything in verse'.[73] Rather, poems would be circulated in manuscript amongst an élite – and almost certainly male – group of friends and acquaintances (and often copied by those suitably impressed). In poems such as the 'The Flea' Donne is seeking to establish his reputation as a wit not with the general public, but with a handful of highly self-conscious young men who have far higher standards. Indeed, Arthur Marotti, viewing Donne as a quite specifically 'coterie poet' during the relatively ambitious and optimistic years of the 1590s, has argued that the content of such poems was moulded by a serious desire for social advancement.[74]

As we will see, Donne adds to the general disdain for print his own personal form of self-construction. This is all the more effective just because it is so obliquely and subtly impressed upon the reader. Even in manuscript, a clumsy poet could commit the horrible solecism of advertising his talents too overtly. The jaunty confidence of the accomplished seducer, able to suavely talk round the most resistant young woman, is one element of Donne's anti-Petrarchan persona. Less obvious, but no less important, is the carefully balanced mixture of absurd ingenuity and mock-rigorous logic in the argument of 'The Flea' itself. To copulate is to do no more than mingle bloods; these are already mingled in the flea; therefore ...[75] And with typical resourcefulness the poet can also twist his argument to fit any situation. The woman threatens to crush the invading insect, prompting from the speaker the plea

> Oh stay, three lives in one flea spare,
> Where we almost, nay more than married are.
> This flea is you and I, and this
> Our marriage bed, and marriage temple is;
> Though parents grudge, and you, we'are met,
> And cloistered in these living walls of jet.

Despite Donne's going on to claim that this killing would indeed be 'sacrilege, three sins in killing three', no mercy is shown. And so, with the flea dead ('hast thou since/Purpled thy nail, in blood of innocence?'), he goes on to shift the emphasis of his argument yet again:

> Yet thou triumph'st, and say'st that thou
> Find'st not thyself, nor me the weaker now;
> 'Tis true, then learn how false, fears be;
> Just so much honour, when thou yield'st to me,
> Will waste, as this flea's death took life from thee.

We can imagine the Victorians being especially outraged at the 'marriage bed' ingeniously telescoped into the body of a flea. By contrast, those for whom Donne wrote were likely to be struck by his resourceful inventiveness, that ability of 'making the familiar strange, and the strange familiar', which Coleridge thought so essential to good poetry.[76] To take a less complementary critical stance, we might seem to find in 'The Flea' just what Johnson lamented, 'the most heterogeneous ideas ... yoked by violence together', and 'combinations ... that not only could not be credited, but could not be imagined'.[77] But here as elsewhere the 'violence' is in fact just the point. A limited degree of violence is intrinsic to novelty, as Carew seemed to recognise when he celebrated Donne's 'holy rapes'. As for combinations which 'could not be imagined', that of the flea and the marriage bed clearly could, and was. The ability to do so is forcefully attested by the way that Donne does not merely conceptualise the idea (that is, assert at the abstract level of his argument) but also perceptualises it in the minute but vibrant 'living walls of jet'.

More will be said in chapter four about the seemingly odd mingling not only of marriage beds and fleas, but of fleas, sex, and Christianity ('cloistered', 'sacrilege', 'purpled thy *nail* in blood of innocence'). How else, though, does Donne succeed in defining a certain poetic persona in that poem? Much of his success depends on the force of novelty and invention. These traits would have been the more conspicuous because 'flea poems' were in fact themselves already a recognised form, at which various people had tried their hands for some time. It was all the harder, therefore, to be new and impressive. Donne rises to this challenge partly by the sheer deftness with which he manoeuvres his argument and glides between reality and metaphor (a flea becomes a room). But his achievement is not simply limited to the content of his novel imaginings. His tone is no less effective. The piece is strikingly economical in its brisk air of assured command ('Mark but this flea' – note how the emphatic stress of the first word jolts us to attention), elegant yet convincing in its mimesis of colloquial speech, and inflected with the skills of a veteran dramatist in the way it shifts us from the voice of the speaker, to the realisation that he is addressing his reluctant lover. We move all but seamlessly, in a bare few lines, from an evidently staged performance to a kind of eavesdropping, as if a bedroom door swings open quietly, voices rising into audibility from within, upon the hinge of these first lines.

That voice is, of course, still staged. The writer knows this, and expects the reader to know it. But this does not prevent it deftly announcing its creator, any more than Donne's ability to ventriloquise a range of voices – including, very occasionally, female ones – ultimately masks the single figure behind the varying styles. In 'Community' we find one facet of 'The Flea' rewritten a little more single-mindedly:

> Good we must love, and must hate ill,
>
> For ill is ill, and good good still,
>
> But there are things indifferent,
>
> Which we may neither hate, nor love,
>
> But one, and then another prove,
>
> As we shall find our fancy bent.
>
> If then at first wise Nature had
>
> Made women either good or bad,
>
> Then some we might hate, and some choose,
>
> But since she did them so create,
>
> That we may neither love, nor hate,
>
> Only this rests, All, all may use

'The Flea' offers a kind of dramatic encounter and debate. In the stanzas above the tone has become more muted, less conversational, and gives us an impression of general address. Its measured, at times almost overly compressed structure is in keeping with the careful, but dense, logical progress of the argument. One can, indeed, see the influence of Donne's legal milieu here, with its habits of supposedly rational persuasion veering between the plain statement of unanswerable truths, and the kind of self-serving casuistry for which lawyers were so proverbially notorious. That tension is accentuated in the fourth and final stanza, when Donne concludes

> But they are ours as fruits are ours,
> He that but tastes, he that devours,
> And he that leaves all, doth as well:
> Changed loves are but changed sorts of meat,
> And when he hath the kernel eat,
> Who doth not fling away the shell?

The calmly detached, axiomatic way in which this formula is derived perhaps makes its bad taste all the sourer. And we are, as chapters three and six in particular will show, right to sense that the very control and assurance of this philosophically-based misogyny is more sinister and more fundamental than some merely local burst of anger or frustration at the supposed failings of the female sex. The second stanza's seeming insistence that women – not either 'good or bad' – lack the same level of human ethical responsibility as men is one version of a gender-theory which plunged deep and tenacious roots through the foundations of Renaissance thought and religion. We already catch some glimpse of that pervasively structural prejudice in the line 'But they are ours as fruits are ours': it is not a question of whether women 'belong' to men; only a question of *how* they belong.

Does Donne believe this? Without wholly denying that he and his peers certainly could believe such statements, what is perhaps more telling in this case is that neither he nor his readers are really *expected* to believe it. Part of the persona of the poem derives from that tone of off-handed, airy sophistry which crucially implies that all this is a game. Its end is not some unshakeable general truth – good or bad – but the successful self-creation of a young man able to convincingly hint at his learning, wit, sophistication and licentious opportunism - the creation, that is, of a persona which is also, ambiguously, a kind of self.

By way of recompense, let us listen to Donne seemingly worsted in the battle of the sexes:

> When I am dead, and doctors know not why,
> And my friends' curiosity
> Will have me cut up to survey each part,
> When they shall find your picture in my heart,
> You think a sudden damp of love
> Will through all their senses move,

And work on them as me, and so prefer

Your murder, to the name of massacre.

('The Damp')

This opening stanza can certainly be viewed as anti-Petrarchan. Yet that effect is itself achieved by pushing the claims of Petrarchanism just that little bit too far. Donne once again takes a longstanding concept or fancy (here, the notion of the beloved as 'pictured' in one's heart) and mischievously undermines it by thrusting it into a startlingly physical context. At first, we might feel that the old idea is not so much subverted as powerfully revivified. By just happening to find this picture in the course of a post-mortem autopsy, the surgeons – holding it up curiously in a pair of forceps and wiping the blood from it – render it all the more strikingly visible. And Donne was undoubtedly making shrewd use, in these lines, of a very new and jarring phenomenon. From around the mid- or later-1580s – a period when Donne himself was just sufficiently mature both to appreciate such things and, in his relatively blank youthfulness, be the more impressed by them – public anatomies gained a new prestige and prominence in Elizabethan London. The fullest significance of this movement toward modern medical science will be discussed in chapter five. What we need to appreciate just now is how fiercely novel and modish anatomical conceits were. Donne is effectively pinning a badge of knowingly topical savoir faire to himself in the very act of writing this first stanza.[78]

And it may well be that in 'The Damp' he is partly indulging in novelty for its own sake. For the piece certainly appears to shift tack a little disorientatingly in its second and its final stanzas:

> Poor victories; but if you dare be brave,
> And pleasure in your conquest have,
> First kill th'enormous giant, your Disdain,
> And let th'enchantress Honour, next be slain,
> And like a Goth and Vandal rise,
> Deface records, and histories
> Of your own arts and triumphs over men,
> And without such advantage kill me then.
>
> For I could muster up as well as you
> My giants, and my witches too,
> Which are vast Constancy, and Secretness,
> But these I neither look for, nor profess;
> Kill me as woman, let me die
> As a mere man; do you but try
> Your passive valour, and you shall find then,

Naked you have odds enough of any man.

In moving so swiftly from that dramatic set-piece of the dissecting slab to the mythic generality of personified 'Disdain' and 'Honour' (and the hardly less mythic 'Goths and Vandals', the famed destroyers and barbarians of Ancient civilisation), we feel at first faintly cheated. And it is fair to recognise that if Johnson ever has a valid point about Donne's lack of imagistic cohesion, he may do so here. Yet somehow the piece still holds together. Most obviously, it does so again through its unmistakable voice. Notice how, for example, the dismissive 'Poor victories ...' punctuates the change of tone, with its plosive and heavily-stressed first word signalling the drop from breathless wonder to the tough realism of Donne's argumentative and conversational mode. What, though, is this voice saying? It is here that we need to work a little harder to unearth the more buried structural level of cohesion that underpins the poem. If we start with the 'damp' of the title, we find that it refers to a kind of poisonous mist emanating from the woman's picture. The Petrarchan motif of the male lover dying for his love is here playfully amplified into the 'massacre' accomplished upon the surgeons and witnesses, through a kind of amorous witchcraft.[79] Notice, however, the pivotal phrase 'you think'. The mythical potency of the 'damp of love' is in fact just that: no more than an outworn rhetorical convention, due for burial along with other of 'poor Petrarch's long deceasèd woes'.

It is for this reason that we then meet the mock-figurings of 'Disdain' and 'Honour' in the following stanza. If they look out of place, it is because they are. So the speaker impatiently rips down these grand but insubstantial effigies in order to assert a more limited yet more satisfyingly immediate and intimate relationship. The woman is asked to imitate the Goths and Vandals in order to destroy not simply cultural achievements per se, but the stagnant culture of Petrarchanism: one which understands women and love only through a sterile and de-sensitising screen of dead concepts. Those 'victories' of a powerfully destructive female persona are 'poor' just because they are unreal, and because they obscure the human reality of the beloved. It would be rash to view 'The Damp' as a plea for equal sexual relations. Indeed, there seems at least a touch of the old male sophistry in that final persuasion to nakedness. But it can be said that the poem is at least ambiguous. The nakedness here has an edge of liberation to it, the clothes being the worn and dusty ones of a past culture. And similarly the sex itself, while not without implicit power relations, is ultimately subversive when seen as a reaction against Petrarchanism and the broader culture of abstraction from which it arose.

Donne can often be seen as *playing* with such outworn traditional concepts, rather than outrightly destroying them. At the same time, such play is itself quite as serious as the playing of children. It involves finding out something about a world that is still beautifully, exhilaratingly fresh, plunging clean hands into the mud, and bringing out treasures whose precise outlines remain uncertain. Donne's treasure, in this case, is the self. And its novelty is attested in part precisely by his playful creation and recreation of this strange new entity. It resurfaces, for example, in 'Love's Alchemy':

> Some that have deeper digged love's mine than I,
> Say, where his centric happiness doth lie:
> I have loved, and got, and told,
> But should I love, get, tell, till I were old,
> I should not find that hidden mystery;
> Oh, tis imposture all:
> And as no chemic yet the elixir got,
> But glorifies his pregnant pot,
> If by the way to him befall,
> Some odoriferous thing, or medicinal,
> So, lovers dream a rich and long delight,
> But get a winter-seeming summer's night.

The opening couplet offers us a faint sound of mock-solemnity, countered by a drily sceptical undertone ('so I'm told'...). In a few more lines this stance breaks down entirely in the weary expostulation, 'Oh, tis imposture all.' Just as the alchemists have consistently failed to get at that fundamental chemical essence which would transform lead into gold, so there is no glittering and immortal gem at the heart of 'love's mine'. Any benefits, rather, are far more transient and accidental. Donne thus denies the rhetoric of depth and the absolute in love. And this is followed up emphatically in the second, closing stanza. The speaker rhetorically demands whether or not the best of life ('ease ... thrift ... honour') should be sacrificed to such a chimaerical quest, before going on to ask:

> Ends love in this, that my man,
> Can be as happy as I can; if he can
> Endure the short scorn of a bridegroom's play?

We notice quickly an irritation at the supposed democracy of this quasi-sacred amorous experience – available even, God forbid, to one's servants. What we might also register is that the Petrarchan delusions mocked there are shunned precisely because they are tarnished by their allegedly wide general currency. The rigorous and disdainful élitism of this stance is one more way of defining one's self. Donne is no more going to marry himself to this cheap, promiscuously available version of love than he would accept a popular form of religion based on faith without intellect. Just in case that exclusively demanding persona should be in any doubt, he closes by further distancing himself from women. One is foolish to imagine that 'Tis not the bodies marry, but the minds', because women indeed *have* no minds:

> Hope not for mind in women; at their best
> Sweetness and wit, they are but mummy, possessed.

The notion of clasping a mummified body in erotic embrace is fairly repellent to most modern tastes. In Donne's lifetime, though, the word 'mummy' had another sense which may have made it still more so. Medical theory posited a kind of human life-force or 'balm' which was supposed to be somehow preserved in various corpses. Those from Egypt or Arabia, suspended in costly embalming fluids and the fabulously dry climate, were especially prized. But such was the demand for this alleged panacea that certain doctors set out recipes supposed to guarantee similar efficacy from 'the corpse of a red-haired man of twenty-four', perished of a violent death, sprinkled with 'myrrh and aloes' and 'rubbed with vinegar'.[80] The very precision of this shows us that we are not dealing with any lingering myth. Indeed, mummy was part of a hard-headed trade, one of various exotic commodities with a high price. But the most important thing about this balm is that to imbibe it one frequently had to *eat* human flesh. While Donne is not proposing to devour the degraded woman here, the associations of mummy clearly stick to her unpleasantly. And it may even be that the parallel is all the more grimly effective for its precision. 'Mummy' was not exactly 'dead' in the same way as an ordinary corpse. Similarly, the woman has a kind of spiritual principle in her, but one that no more makes her human than the remaining 'balm' of mummy flesh makes it alive (or, for that matter, a congenial bedfellow).[81] The careful nuancing of Donne's comparison thus renders it more piercingly negative than any wild hyperbole could ever be.[82]

Perhaps it is as well, at this especially low point in male-female relations, to turn to the fresher and more innocent world of comedy. As we have seen, in *Twelfth Night* the Count Orsino stands as an especially pronounced type of the ridiculously exaggerated Petrarchan lover. He is rich, leisured, and idle. And his resourceful constructions of Olivia into the stock types of the genre ('marble-breasted tyrant' and so forth) can be all the more easily conjured just because Orsino has no conception of her as a real human being. Even his wooing, indeed, is done by his servant – a strategy for which he is aptly punished when Olivia falls in love with messenger rather than master.[83] All this is well summed-up in the general character Orsino unwittingly betrays in the play's opening lines:

> If music be the food of love, play on,
> Give me excess of it that, surfeiting,
> The appetite may sicken and so die ...

As with any dramatic comedy, one could of course play this speech for varying degrees of laughter. But the undoubted keynote of it, however delivered, is self-indulgence. The indulgence, moreover, is passive. Entirely dependent upon others, Orsino displays a selfishness which is hopelessly sealed (solipsistic, to use the philosophical term) – as sterile, disengaged, and neurotic as a kind of emotional bulimic, caught in their own caged cycle of gorging and vomiting.

Donne, predictably, has very different ideas about love:

> To what a cumbersome unwieldiness
> And burdenous corpulence my love had grown,
> But that I did, to make it less,
> And keep it in proportion,

Give it a diet, made it feed upon
That which love worst endures, discretion.

('Love's Diet')

This characteristically metaphysical version of love as a separate entity which eats and grows is consequently disciplined and disillusioned in following lines. All the minute scraps which amorous fantasy could transform into a banquet are wryly degraded. If this creature – a bird, we finally learn – gets

A she sigh from my mistress' heart,
And thought to feast on that, I let him see
'Twas neither very sound, nor meant to me.

Tears, moreover, are proven to be no food or drink for a lover, and with that all but scientific rigour we have met elsewhere:

His drink was counterfeit, as was his meat;
For, eyes which roll towards all, weep not, but sweat.

By this and other means Donne reclaims

... my buzzard love, to fly

At what, and when, and how, and where I choose;

Now negligent of sport I lie,

And now as other falconers use,

I spring a mistress, swear, write, sigh and weep:

And the game killed, or lost, go talk, and sleep.

Once more the sharply but lightly-chiselled outlines of the self (it has, surely, high cheekbones and a coolly amused stare) are all visible – or rather, visible and audible. The assured, faintly indolent poise of one who acts only at his own convenience and without dangerous impulse is felt in the second and fifth lines especially; but arguably no less in the final, typically insouciant throwaway style of 'the game killed, or lost, go talk, and sleep'. Something of the tone of Andrew Marvell is heard in those last four words, adumbrating the exquisitely balanced drollery of 'The grave's a fine and private place/But none, I think, do there embrace.'[84] The genteel sport of falconry shades in further outlines of the rakish persona, to whom hawking, and the trapping or 'springing' of women are equally fine but trivial forms of entertainment. We might infer, too, that the setting and tone of the poem are markedly those of an élite male community – something so distinctive to the period as to have been classified not just in terms of the coterie, but as 'homosocial'.[85]

If asked to isolate a single quality of 'Love's Diet' one must surely choose that of control. Most obviously, the issue is *self*-control. But implicit in that is also control of women. In Shakespeare's embittered sonnet 129, perhaps most famously, we find male sexual experience jarringly offset by regret and dismay at the temporary loss of self-composure and independence.[86] Donne clearly sketches a different, calmer version of such disillusionment. But perhaps a still greater difference is this: the carefully starved and trained bird of the poem is not just a figure of love, but a figure of the self. In the precise associations of the hawk or falcon – aloft in its majestic isolation, swift, exact and unsparing in its sudden deadly swoop and puncture of the soft flesh – we have a remarkably accurate encapsulation of the youthful Donne. As we will see in just a moment, that attractive self-construction can be viewed from other, less flattering angles. What should also be added before leaving the Songs and Sonnets for the present is that, details aside, 'Love's Diet' has achieved something quite remarkable in the very act of embodying and externalising that seemingly whimsical version of the nascent ego. It is here that we see the distinctive possibilities of the metaphysical style written most forcibly: 'let us find out what happens if we take that old rhetorical screw, and twist it further, and more violently ...'. What happens is that the independent human ego – an entity whose radicalism, at this point, cannot be overstated – suddenly breaks out, and begins, still blinking dazedly, to look about for ways to feed itself. To state Donne's achievement a little more broadly: he is part of an avant-garde that has managed to liberate, transform and relocate a psychic energy long frozen in the distant wastes of heaven, and only now pulsing through the veins of just a rare, brave handful of adventurers in this new territory of the self. It is, of course, no accident that we can only recognise that achievement with hindsight. Anything like a modern or post-Romantic concept of the self was heavily shadowed and continually reined back by a deep-seated religious mistrust, making the self tentative, oblique or problematic in its literary manifestations.

In such cases, then, we can discern the lineaments of a self at once radical and oppositional, actively defining its traits against tradition, inertia, and the herd. The role of the coterie might of course seem to limit that fundamental independence. But our impression must surely be that Donne sets the rules rather than following them. He is part of a male coterie, but not contained or wholly defined by it. To put it a little differently, in his own words: 'I can allow myself to be *animal sociale*, appliable to my company, but not *gregale*, to herd myself in every troop.'[87] This motto seems to apply with a vengeance in the context of the Elegies and the Satires.

II

Several of Donne's Elegies offer us a distinctive amorous persona: a young man elegant, dashing, charming, yet also furtive and perhaps nervous as he negotiates creaking stairs in the house of his young mistress' parents, or cuckolds a dreary old husband in the man's own bed. Let us start with the former case:

> Once, and but once found in thy company,
> All thy supposed escapes are laid on me;
> And as a thief at bar, is questioned there
> By all the men, that have been robbed that year,
> So am I, (by this traitorous means surprised)
> By thy hydroptic father catechized.
>
> ...
>
> Though thy immortal mother which doth lie
> Still buried in her bed, yet will not die,
> Takes this advantage to sleep out day-light,
> And watch thy entries, and returns all night,
> And, when she takes thy hand, and would seem kind,
> Doth search what rings, and armlets she can find,
> And kissing notes the colour of thy face,

And fearing lest thou art swoll'n, doth thee embrace;

...

And politicly will to thee confess

The sins of her own youth's rank lustiness;

Yet love these sorceries did remove, and move

Thee to gull thine own mother for my love.

('The Perfume')

Tread softly, then, for you tread in the furtive backstair world of Elizabethan adultery and the poaching of prized daughters. Fortunately, Donne is good at it. Although

Thy little brethren, which like fairy sprites

Oft skipped into our chamber, those sweet nights ...

were later bribed by the parents, yet not they, nor even

The grim eight-foot-high iron-bound serving man,

That oft names God in oaths, and only then

...

Which, if in hell no other pains there were,

Makes me fear hell, because he must be there:

Though by thy father he were hired to this,

Could never witness any touch or kiss.

Yet finally – although 'I taught my silks, their whistling to forbear', and 'even my oppressed shoes, dumb and speechless were' – the game is up. And it was indeed the perfume that finished it:

> A loud perfume, which at my entrance cried
> Even at thy father's nose, so we were spied,
> When, like a tyrant king, that in his bed
> Smelt gunpowder, the pale wretch shivered.
> Had it been some bad smell, he would have thought
> That his own feet, or breath the smell had wrought.

Proceeding to curse the offending scent at some length, the speaker closes on a suddenly optimistic note:

> All my perfumes, I give most willingly
> To embalm thy father's corse; What? will he die?

The fourth of Donne's Elegies, this poem is quite simple in its basic narrative: a suave and presumably attractive young man seduces a young woman – one who, under the rigid patriarchal laws of the Renaissance family, would evidently be denied to him. Accordingly, he enters her house secretly, night after night. Adept in the arts of stealth, he is yet finally detected not by a sound, but by a scent. His own perfume is too fine a smell to go unnoticed in the parents' house – perhaps particularly so in an age with such basic sanitation, and when most people considered frequent washing unhealthy.[88] From this basic material, Donne produces another piece of highly-adroit self-definition. Much of its success lies in its fiercely single-minded pursuit of one effect: that of the daring young lovers weaving brilliantly between a set of obstacles and strategies that are themselves vividly and neatly conjured into verse. Notice, for example, how lightly Donne touches in details. The 'silks' that do not so much as whistle provide an oblique signal of elegance and social status. And we find that even the couple's undoing is to Donne's credit: had he smelled as bad as the father, he would have gone undetected a little longer. The final couplet, with its deftly-vocalised mimesis of sudden interruption and possible 'good news' ('What? will he die?'), adroitly captures not just the irresistible and agile narrative voice of so many Elegies, but also their implicit motto: 'If you can't say anything nasty, don't say anything at all.'

Other Elegies do little to dispel this impression:

Fond woman, which wouldst have thy husband die,
And yet complain'st of his great jealousy;

If swoll'n with poison, he lay in his last bed,

His body with a sere-bark covered,

Drawing his breath, as thick and short, as can

The nimblest crotcheting musician,

Ready with loathesome vomiting to spew

His soul out of one hell, into a new,

Made deaf with his poor kindred's howling cries,

Begging with few feigned tears, great legacies,

Thou wouldst not weep ...

('Jealousy')

The opening of this first elegy again strikes us by its unrelenting and surely-targeted aggression against a creature not simply repellent, but – through Donne's vicious ingenuity – far more abhorrent than any actual person could be. The aged and tormented husband is not merely sick, but 'swoll'n with poison', his skin crusted over like the trunk of an ancient tree. Where lovers in Donne's poems are frequently imagined as exchanging the rarefied spirit of the soul in kisses[89], the cuckold is about to 'vomit' his soul from the hell of this life into the next (ll. 3, 7-8). Moreover, he is despised not only by Donne and the (slightly more ambivalent) wife, but by his relatives, who value him for purely selfish material reasons.

Needless to say, then, our sympathies are manipulated very effectively in a bare few lines. Most readers are likely to identify with Donne and the lover against the luckless husband. Thus, we enter willingly into the gleeful mischief not merely of sexual adventure, but of an especially brash affair, hinted at table via 'scoffing riddles', and underlined by the couple's hurrying upstairs when the old man, 'swoll'n, and pampered with great fare,/Sits down, and snorts, caged in his basket chair' (ll. 18, 21-2). By comparison with this gluttonous and slothful animal the suspicious parents of 'The Perfume' look relatively attractive. And Donne does not easily tire of his theme, re-playing it with variations in elegies 12 and 14. In both those cases we find the speaker and a bored wife covertly signalling mutual desire under the very nose of a dull and credulous husband.[90]

Anyone who has read just a reasonably broad scattering of lyric poetry from the same period will see that the precise dramatic realism of such sexual adventures is a remarkable achievement on Donne's part. Indeed, it seems so far ahead of its time that we must exercise some caution if we are not to collapse it too misleadingly with our own modern senses of love, youth, justice and self-hood.[91] As ever, Donne had pre-existing frames in which to exercise his talents. In terms of rhetorical theory, a certain kind of ethical neutrality supported him.[92] Rhetorical modes such as 'amplification' indicated that, once you had chosen your theme, your only duty was to succeed at it as forcibly and persuasively as you could. More precisely, the Elegies owe their heaviest debt to Ovid, the Roman poet who penned not only the influential mythic transformations of love known as *Metamorphoses*, but a number of verses which have a similarly knowing, wry cynicism and suavity to those of Donne at his most licentiously exuberant and defiant.[93] To gain a little perspective as to the influence of Ovid, however, we need also to bear in mind that many others were similarly dazzled by him (Marlowe and George Chapman, as well as Shakespeare) without producing anything remotely like 'The Perfume'.

Might we, then, identify its male persona with other, self-consciously roguish seducers since become far more familiar to us? Is this dashing young Elizabethan, snatching female prey with foxlike stealth, that different from (say) an illicit lover of the 1990s, insisting that we should take him seriously, very seriously indeed...?[94] In some limited sense this kind of parallel is useful. Donne evidently *was* making virtue from necessity in such portrayals, painting the swift, resourceful and beautiful image of a fox where others might have seen a lamed and hunted dog. The enforced outsider has become a dangerous and brilliant law-unto-himself, whose personal talents are all the more sharply evident in face of the obstacles set against them. And there must have been some who were ready to take the side of nimble, handsome youth against stagnant, aged wealth.

But it was many decades before the implicit moral or cultural hierarchy encoded in that preference would find its fullest expression. We would radically underestimate the power, solidity and durability of the Renaissance social structure if we tried to push the parallel too far. This was a society in which recalcitrant daughters of the gentry or aristocracy would be beaten, locked up and half-starved into agreement about arranged marriages to rich aged men. (Donne's own daughter, Constance, was married at age twenty to the fifty-eight year old actor-manager, Edward Alleyn.[95]) The authority of fathers, though already – to paraphrase Donne – 'tyrannical' in the earlier sixteenth century, is said to have become still more so as Protestantism gave the family head a semi-priestly religious authority over his household.[96] And parents as a whole had an authority now startling to us. Men and women of forty would kneel before their mothers and fathers; would not sit down until given permission; and would address them as 'Sir' or 'Madam'.[97] Nobody knew about the sharp end of all this so well as Donne, come late 1601. Indeed, in one of his letters to the irate George More he acknowledged the rakish reputation of the

Elegies just as he disclaimed it, asking More to believe that 'that fault which was laid to me of having deceived some gentlewomen before, and that of loving a corrupt religion, are vanished and smoked away (as I assure myself, out of their weakness they are)'.[98] It is far from coincidental that Donne here splices together those two facets of his supposedly 'vanished' youth. And in fact he has effectively juxtaposed his outlawed Catholicism, and his libertine adventures, in the Elegies themselves. As suggested above, these poems offer us a self constructed for Donne's élite male peers. But beyond that, the Elegies also allow him to recreate his own perilously oppositional situation of the 1590s. The poems provide a kind of amorous playground, and a space where Donne can safely act out a successful rebellion and revenge denied to him in his years of social insecurity and secret defiance. In this fantasy world charm, looks, grace and cunning all triumph over a rigid grey conformity. With that covert function of the Elegies in mind, let us now look at the rather different oppositions presented in a further set of youthful poems: the Satires Donne wrote between 1593 and 1598.

III

In Donne's Satires we move from a relatively private realm to a
conspicuously public one. The first of these five poems opens
with a scene of reluctant transition, as a young student tries to
resist an invitation for a walk through the London streets:

> Away thou fondling motley humorist,
>
> Leave me, and in this standing wooden chest,
>
> Consorted with these few books, let me lie
>
> In prison, and here be coffined, when I die;
>
> ...
>
> Shall I leave all this constant company,
>
> And follow headlong, wild uncertain thee?
>
> First swear by thy best love in earnest
>
> (If thou which lov'st all, canst love any best)
>
> Thou wilt not leave me in the middle street,
>
> Though some more spruce companion thou dost meet,
>
> ...
>
> For better or for worse take me, or leave me:
>
> To take, and leave me is adultery.
>
> (Satire 1)

Believing, however, that his wayward acquaintance has repented of 'these vanities', Donne presently rises:

> ... lo
> I shut my chamber door, and come, let's go.

And indeed his companion at least keeps to his side (albeit, conveniently, the side by the street wall, furthest from the splash of the famous London mud). But he is certainly not able to ignore the more conspicuous passers-by:

> Every fine silken fool we meet,
> He them to him with amorous smiles allures,
> And grins, smacks, shrugs ...
> And as fiddlers stop lowest, at highest sound,
> So to the most brave, stoops he nigh'st the ground
> ...
> Now leaps he upright, jogs me, and cries, 'Do you see
> Yonder well-favoured youth?' 'Which?' 'Oh, 'tis he
> That dances so divinely'; 'Oh,' said I,
> 'Stand still, must you dance here for company?'

A combination of social butterfly and chameleon, Donne's companion has a self which is fluidly amorphous and unanchored, wavering unstably from one fashionable figure to the next, and notably oblivious of any 'grave man' (l. 79) who must pass unacknowledged. This obsequious bobbing and flattering is so skilfully conveyed as to almost physically irritate the reader – perhaps most especially when they feel themself 'jogged' at the elbow only so that they might appreciate a gaudy courtier, reeking of the fashionable new vice of tobacco. Again, then, we swiftly – if not immediately – identify with the speaker. Accordingly, this latter figure acquires a personal outline which is as effective as it is (in one sense) self-effacing. Aloof, dry, contemptuous, and – perhaps above all – stable and independent, he wearily pushes through this scattering froth of London vanity with the certain path of one who already knows their way. The persistent contrast is most vividly exemplified when the butterfly spies his mistress at a window:

> And like light dew exhaled, he flings from me
> Violently ravished to his lechery.
> Many were there, he could command no more;
> He quarrelled, fought, bled; and turned out of door
> Directly came to me hanging the head,
> And constantly a while must keep his bed.

The companion's flimsy lack of substance is here brilliantly conveyed by the image of evaporating dew, and further pointed by the fact that he can neither fight very well, nor rely on the physical valour of 'friends' who are probably as fickle and as cowardly as he.

In the Satires, then, identity is once more oppositional, while notably combining moments of personal opposition with a general antipathy to the transient and over-blown follies of city and court life. But Donne is not simply outside of all this. As I have argued above, he depends on it in one sense, knowing who he is by quietly but effectively showing who he is not. Even when he states that independence quite openly, he backs up his assertion by the wit with which he does so. Take, for example, the second Satire:

> But he is worst, who (beggarly) doth chaw
> Others' wits fruits, and in his ravenous maw
> Rankly digested, doth those things out spew,
> As his own things; and they are his own, 'tis true,
> For if one eat my meat, though it be known
> The meat was mine, th'excrement is his own.
>
> (Satire 2)

We find here the same adroit mixture of logical rigour, contempt, and aloofness encountered in certain Sonnets or Elegies. From that poem, with its especially forthright opening ('Sir; though (I thank God for it) I do hate/Perfectly all this town') we progress to more lightly effected touches of mockery, as in number four, when another vain companion praises his skills as a linguist so shamelessly that

> ... I was fain to say, 'If you had lived, Sir,
> Time enough to have been interpreter
> To Babel's bricklayers, sure the Tower had stood.'[99]
>
> > (Satire 4)

Similarly, a familiar lack of gravity is conveyed even at the level of vocal pitch: 'He, like to a high stretched lute string squeaked, "O Sir,/'Tis sweet to talk of kings"' (ll. 73-4) Donne kindly suggests that this can be best achieved in discussion with the keeper of the royal tombs at Westminster Abbey:

> Your ears shall hear naught, but kings; your eyes meet
> Kings only; The way to it, is King Street.
>
> > (Satire 4)

Here and elsewhere in the poem the poised, wearily amused superiority of tone is arguably more effective a form of self-construction than the lines' actual content. And Donne is, of course, further outlined (a kind of dark photographic negative of the overbright courtier) by the man's inability to even register this and other slights, the narrator indeed being obliged to presently 'belch, spew, spit,/Look pale, and sickly, like a patient' – albeit still with no greater success.

At another level, the Satires also assert identity by their sheer innovation and formal boldness. Once again, Donne certainly had precedents. In good Renaissance fashion his broad models were the Roman satires of Horace and Juvenal. Yet it was a characteristic irony of this Renaissance drive back to a purer, truer version of the Classical past that it often produced wholly new forms of art and of knowledge. And we know that satire in general was a subject of considerable public scandal and anxiety in the late 1590s. In 1599, two prominent bishops issued an edict against the recently published satires of John Marston, Joseph Hall, Christopher Marlowe, Thomas Nashe, Thomas Middleton and five others.[100] As Lynda E. Boose has argued, there is some ambiguity as to why satire provoked this response. Was the issue political, given satire's supposed licence to scourge or whip social abuses and corruptions? Or was it – as Boose herself believes – in fact sexual?[101] The question does not directly concern us here, as Donne's Satires were not published during his lifetime, and therefore escaped the ban, which (in yet another of Christianity's innumerable contributions to cultural freedom) included the burning of offending volumes, as well as their exclusion from further publication. What is important is that Donne was once more at the forefront of a novel and subversive mode of expression. Indeed, if critics are right to date composition of the Satires between 1593 and 1598, then Donne was especially alert in his exploitation of a nominally classical genre which now mutated into something quite new.[102]

Donne's Satires are remarkable for their brashly dynamic replication of London life in all its colour, luxury, squalor, violence and instability. To fully appreciate this one has to work patiently through the poems themselves, in a well-annotated edition: the most ingenious and alert of readers cannot possibly understand their numerous glancing allusions to contemporary sights and events unless they happen also to be a formidable Renaissance scholar.[103] What can be said briefly is that Donne's achievement in these pieces is essentially twofold. First, he conveys a remarkable amount of exact sensuous detail in a relatively short space – using local colour not merely in his witnessed narrative, but also for his illustrations and metaphors (see, for example, the horse, ape and elephant of Satire one.) This style itself – a kind of low particularity – is a characteristic of satire, and one which makes the genre especially valuable to us, given how rare concrete precision is in Renaissance literature. Our impression that Donne excels at this aspect is confirmed by the similar eye and ear for local nuance which so brilliantly animates many Elegies. But that exactitude is also cemented by its alliance with a second broad feature. The Satires are intensely dramatic. We realise that all the more if we contrast them with (say) Joseph Hall's efforts in this genre, which are again rich in immediate detail, but tend to drag and weary us as they accumulate layers of imagery which gather inertly, unrelieved by the rough uncertain momentum of Donne's lines.[104]

We do not need Hall, though, to appreciate the skill with which Donne whisks us among the flashing surfaces of Elizabethan London. Reading these poems in a post-cinematic age it is hard not to feel as if the speaker is jolting down the uneven streets with a handheld video camera on his shoulder (or perhaps, indeed, poking secretly from the mouth of a bag). What we might not recognise so easily is how *vocally* accomplished these pieces are. Particularly when characters rap out quick bursts of speech in and across lines we feel that Donne had not only been fruitfully attentive to the 'new plays', but that in his mimesis of dialogue he occasionally surpasses them.[105] Speech in the London streets may well have been an especially important social medium. The city, while hardly quiet, was largely empty of mechanical noise, and – as Bruce R. Smith has ingeniously shown – most especially of continuous noise, or of anything approaching the volumes to which we have become more or less accustomed.[106] At one level, this alerts us to the fact that people could be heard far more clearly and across greater distances – a crucial point in a context where conspicuous display and public self-awareness are such central elements. More subtly, we may even wonder if the very rhythm and force of speech sounding through these lines is moulded by the different aural environment of the period: as if the staccato ripostes and sharply aimed vocal blows owe some precise debt to the clarity of London bells or the hard echo of hoofbeats.[107]

The remarkable compression of living energy and variety kaleidoscoped across the Satires at times threatens to give way, as the lines strain and buckle under the intense dramatic pressure. Thus it was that Alexander Pope, typifying that pseudo-classical desire for balance we saw in Johnson, notoriously rewrote two of these pieces with the pointed word 'versified' in his title.[108] But while Pope's complacent and mannered efforts missed the point with dazzling ease, others were more appreciative. The Earl of Rochester's violent

Restoration satires, though in some ways unique, probably owe much to Donne's. More certainly, Robert Browning developed the distinctive speaking voice of the poems into the 'dramatic monologue' so famously associated with him (compare especially the opening of 'Fra Lippo Lippi'); while T.S. Eliot used it to great effect in 'Prufrock ...', whose 'Let us go then, you and I' recalls Donne's more energetic 'come, let's go'. Perhaps Eliot of all people valued the rough chiselled monuments of Donne's Satires, pushing verse to its furthest dramatic limits just as other poems pushed ideas. For these poems matched his explicit insistence that the modern poet should try to 'force, to dislocate if necessary, language into his meaning'.[109]

IV

Our examination of the Satires should help us to readdress the questions asked about the rakish youthful persona of the Elegies. We speculated as to how far Donne might be aligned with a more modern image of the heroic outsider or underdog. What we can add to the previous general cautions urged by Renaissance society are certain telling hints dropped in the Satires. In the fourth especially Donne clashes with our basic notions of social justice when expressing what would now be seen as fairly crude snobbery. His trying acquaintance asserts that 'I of this mind am/Your only wearing is your grogaram', and Donne deliberately mistakes this preference for a type of cloth, taking it to mean that the speaker has no other clothes.[110] Indeed, that criticism has already been made far more forcefully at the man's first appearance:

> ... towards me did run
>
> A thing more strange than on Nile's slime the sun
>
> E'er bred ...
>
> Than Afric's monsters, Guiana's rarities
>
> ...
>
> His clothes were strange, though coarse; and black, though bare;
>
> Sleeveless his jerkin was, and it had been
>
> Velvet, but 'twas now (so much ground was seen)
>
> Become tufftaffaty; and our children shall
>
> See it plain rash awhile, then naught at all.
>
> (Satire 4)

The bizarre appearance upon which Donne insists at such length appears to be chiefly a matter of dress. To put it plainly, one can scarcely tell who or what this is because his clothes are so old and worn as to resemble no recognised material that a gentleman should own. For us, there is something of a gap between that creative evocation of the exotic and monstrous, and the more mundane fact of old clothes. What we are registering is the immense force, rigidity, and detailed degrees of the period's social pyramid as it was both formally and informally known. Offer someone a thousand pounds today to tell you the ranking order of earl, baron, viscount and marquis, and they probably could not do so. In Donne's time such distinctions were at once easily familiar and intensely meaningful. And these titles themselves were merely the most obvious features of a far more pervasive and complex web of social semiotics. In theory, people were obliged to *dress* in a certain way according to their status. Those beneath a particular level were forbidden to wear various colours or styles of clothing.[111] What is especially interesting about these rules (known as the 'sumptuary laws') is that, although they were not easily enforceable, they were based not on mere income, but on title. Donne's period had what we might call an organic notion of a rigidly and permanently structured society. In theory, earls and their sons just *were* earls, as one simply was tall or short, male or female: one could not buy one's way into such positions. As Lawrence Stone notes, 'in 1641 the titular rank of the earls of Bath and Strafford was identical, although their gross incomes from all sources differed by a factor of 25'.[112] At the same time, however, society was apparently becoming genuinely more unstable. A class of newly-wealthy untitled merchants was growing, and this change was aggravated by economic factors, as well as by occasionally excessive creations of knights.[113] By James I's time titles were being outrightly sold to fund the wild extravagance of the Jacobean court.

Where does this leave Donne, and his seeming snobbery? It suggests, first, that many of his peers might well have found the shabbily dressed upstart quite as 'monstrous' as Donne claimed him to be. For the Renaissance, a monster was an error of nature which often spilled across accepted natural categories (a hermaphrodite, for example, violated ordinary gender divisions).[114] Similarly, the satire attacks something almost literally 'unknowable', because it does not fit into an accepted social category, while implying that such categories *should* have been as generally absolute and rigid as those of the natural order. As I have implied, however, this was increasingly not the case. Donne's society had no overt conception of anything like meritocracy, with many viewing upward mobility as a negative rather than positive phenomenon.[115] Yet there does seem to have been a covert appreciation of the success of those who began life with relatively slight advantages. Donne's sometime employer Egerton was one such example, having originally been of illegitimate birth.[116] And Donne, whose illegitimacy was of a different and effectively more serious kind, was for a time another instance of talent, charm and industry triumphing over circumstance.[117] We might then draw a second inference about Donne's social élitism by asking: are his occasional jabs at the socially inferior in part a reflection of a certain lingering insecurity? Does he feel the need to state the codes of the social élite a little *too* obviously?

We should not overstate this tendency to assert social divisions. As we have seen, the more representative persona of both Donne's Satires and Elegies is an effortless, lightly-worn grace, learning and worldliness – perhaps, indeed, an early version of a general English persona associated with the public schoolboy, whose greatest horror is of vulgar boasting or laboured show. But there is also one other, fundamental reason *why* Donne might have now and then tried a little too hard to stake his social claims. This is his Catholicism. The date range of the Satires (1593-98) falls precisely across the period at which Donne's anxieties about this were most acute. We have seen that he must have resigned himself to a change of religion by 1597, in order to gain his post with Egerton. And the detail of the Satires offers us numerous scattered clues to Donne's religious and social anxiety. In the second poem, the claim that the social status of poets is 'poor, disarmed, like papists, not worth hate' (l. 10) can be read both as an admission of felt persecution, and an oblique plea for relief. At the end of that poem Donne compounds the sense of oppression by referring to 'the vast reach of the huge statute laws' (l. 112), and in Satire four more vividly imagines '... I saw/One of our own giant statutes ope his jaw/To suck me in' (ll. 131-3). Leaving the royal court at the close of the fourth Satire he acknowledges the overt, highly visible threat of State power when he passes the gigantic guards of the 'great chamber' – 'men big enough to throw/Charing Cross for a bar', in whose presence, 'I shook like a spied spy' (ll. 231-7). One could, surely, have found many other comparisons for the tremor of fear. The point is that Donne *feels* like a 'spied spy' – fugitive, unwanted and out of place.[118] And a few lines earlier he has glanced at a less conspicuous but effectively more unnerving agent of power, when a contemptible courtier has

> ... whispered 'By Jesu', so often, that a
> Pursuivant would have ravished him away
> For saying of our Lady's psalter.

We can detect in this a glimpse of the kind of oppressive, at times paranoid unease of one who has internalised a fear of surveillance to the degree that they effectively survey themself. And that kind of self-censorship is explicitly apparent when the above lines are compared with certain manuscript versions of the poem. There 'pursuivant' (a crown officer enforcing religious laws) read 'Topcliffe'. As A.J. Smith notes, Topcliffe was the most notorious persecutor of English Catholics in these years, responsible for spying, and for the arrest and torture of suspected Catholic agents. Donne's suppressed lines thus indicate not only a very genuine fear, but his more precise awareness of just *who* he should fear.[119] In Satire two, we find a comically persistent lawyer making clumsy protestations of love to a young woman, in an endless torrent of words:

> More, more ...
> Than when winds in our ruined abbeys roar.

From another writer the depiction of the abandoned monasteries disempowered and plundered by Henry VIII might be unremarkable. They were certainly conspicuous, after all, and Shakespeare mentions their 'bare ruined choirs' in sonnet 73.[120] But Donne's statements need to be treated with more suspicion. Given the context of the image, indeed, we might ask: is there an implicit sense of corrupted power (the lawyer, standing for law in general) tyrannising over a helpless and feminised religion? We certainly know that Donne was aware of the awful physical penalties of anti-Catholic legislation. As John Carey has ingeniously shown, the seemingly descriptive 'silence' of the 'oppressed shoes' in 'The Perfume' in fact encodes a reference to the stubborn silence of certain English Catholics. In 1586, for example, one Margaret Clitheroe was legally and publicly (op)pressed to death with rocks - a sentence prompted not merely by her having harboured Jesuit priests, but by her 'silent' refusal to plead.[121] All in all – as Carey has again emphasised – we can certainly not take at face value Donne's striking rhetorical question at the end of elegy 6: 'What hurts it me to be excommunicate?'

This elegy is no straightforward tale of amorous conquest. It seems rather to conflate love, politics, and religion. In doing so, it makes more explicit the religious and political undercurrents simmering through Donne's other Elegies and Satires. The speaker begins by comparing his servitude as a lover to that of a courtly flatterer. Having immediately entwined amorous and social ambition, he imagines himself as the bed of a stream, and his mistress as the current flowing through it. At first the two are 'wedded' harmoniously and smoothly together. But before long

> She rusheth violently, and doth divorce
> Her from her native, and her long-kept course,
> And roars, and braves it, and in gallant scorn,

In flattering eddies promising return,

She flouts the channel, who thenceforth is dry;

Then say I: that is she, and this am I.

$$(\text{Elegy } 6)$$

These pivotal lines offer us a key to the implicit sexual politics of the Elegies discussed above. For the image of the helpless lover gives us not just a sense of amorous passivity, but of *social* insecurity. At one level, the turbulent instability and inexorable rush of water seems to neatly capture those powerful and hostile currents against which Donne fought as a young Elizabethan Catholic. In the face of this, he might at least have consoled himself that he, the underlying channel, retained a certain constancy. But what use is this – he implies – when the animating forces of life abandon you? For the dry and sterile channel is a neatly accurate portrayal of Donne's general worldly prospects at certain points in the 1590s. Just how bleak these appeared, and how crushing his environment was, is emphasised by the way that the passage unmistakably feminises him: he is the passive, empty channel of the stream, his harsh social mistress the powerful, unpredictable force of active (and implicitly male) life rushing through it. It is in this context that Donne decides to fall 'from Rome', and asks the ambiguous question so rightly suspected by Carey.

This slippage between sexual and social abandonment is by no means limited to Elegy six. Recall the wary student, initially resisting a social invitation in Satire one. He suspects not merely that he will be abandoned, but that he will be temporarily 'married' and then deserted:

For better or for worse take me, or leave me:
To take, and leave me is adultery.

The general sense of disempowerment and of insecurity there coalesces into a moment of particular social 'jilting' in which the feminised, relatively helpless party is snubbed in a very public way.

Given these various signs of alienation and frustration, we might go on to wonder if the persona of the rakish Elegies (1, 4, 12 and 14 most notably) is serving a quite precise function in response to a sense of more or less urgent social crisis. It has already been suggested that the edges of that figure are cut the more sharply by the frictions which its creator suffered in his teens and twenties. Can we also ask if the revenge he seems to take on the society implicitly denied to him is unconsciously a very just one? That is: the elegies, with their repellently corrupt and unsympathetic figures of greed, stasis and power, offer Donne a delightful playground in which the far more serious and tangible corruption and injustice of the Elizabethan state can be thwarted by a heroically astute and fearless individual. That broad impression is convincingly demonstrated in the amorous strategy upon which he and the mistress hit in 'Jealousy'. They will, finally, have to take their pleasure in another house, given that the husband is now taking them very seriously indeed:

> ... if, as envious men, which would revile
> Their prince, or coin his gold, themselves exile
> Into another country, and do it there,
> We play in another house, what should we fear?

From the lips of Donne – whose relatives were forced abroad in far less easy or voluntary ways – the word 'exile' has an unhappy resonance. What really betrays him, though, is his boast that

> There we will scorn his household policies,
> His silly plots, and pensionary spies,
> As the inhabitants of Thames' right side
> Do London's Mayor; or Germans, the Pope's pride.

'Thames' right side' refers to the south bank of the river, where various low pleasures such as those of the brothels, bear-baiting, and theatre were tolerated by the State, and castigated by Puritans.[122] Donne is thus already setting himself on the margins in order to live a full and satisfying existence. But the notion of the Protestant Germans is the most glaring signal. That nation certainly did defy the Pope; yet if Donne is trying to evoke a comparison with *assured* defiance, why pick Germany, which was naturally less well-defended than an island nation considerably farther north? The answer would seem to be that, unlike the many English Protestants who – especially after 1588 – saw their country as the chief barrier against Rome, Donne has necessarily mixed feelings about England's religious status.

It would finally be not just reckless but futile to try and state absolutely how Donne felt about his position in the 1590s, or about the persona which arose from his early alienation. His feelings, like those of many interesting and talented people in a difficult situation, were as shifting, complex and uncertain as the fluid and at times encoded stances of the Satires and Elegies. As Smith shrewdly argues, the wayward caller who pulls Donne from his book-lined cell could indeed be an aspect of the poet's own self as much (or as well as) a separate person. Satire four echoes that possibility, with its weary self-reproach at the desire to go to court. He has, he implies, only himself to blame. Perhaps Donne at times attacked society because – according to the formula of another outsider who both succeeded and suffered in English public life – he could not get fully into it. Perhaps at other times he genuinely believed that 'Not alone/My loneness is ...' (ll. 67-8), as the speaker of Satire four stated in response to praise of the court; or that his true role was found when

> At home in wholesome solitariness
> My precious soul began, the wretchedness
> Of suitors at Court to mourn.

Some might like to feel that the 'true voice' was that which suddenly breaks out, with surprising directness and candour, in Satire four:

> Shall I, none's slave, of high-born, or raised men
> Fear frowns? And, my mistress Truth, betray thee
> To th'huffing braggart, puffed nobility?

But even with mention of the 'mistress Truth' the picture grows more uncertain. On the one hand Donne evokes an anchorage of absolute religious certainty. On the other, he prompts us to recall the less legitimate secular mistresses celebrated in numerous poems and Elegies. Accordingly, the phrase leads us back to the complex re-creations of actual existence offered in these self-consciously mischievous pieces. There Donne's mistresses are ostensibly very different, yet in fact similarly valuable as sites of control, power and refuge. Poems such as 'Jealousy' or 'The Perfume' present us with varying degrees of alienation, from furtive secrecy to outright exile. While Donne's oppositional self-hood shifts and alters subtly in different poems, what we can say is that some kind of opposition is his preferred mode of self-definition. He might oppose himself to tradition; to the herd; to women; to the foolish; the vain; or the corrupt. Perhaps in all these cases part of his adroit self-presentation in fact stems from an underlying need to fully believe in one definite or stable foundation of his personal identity. The following chapter builds on this complex oppositional self-hood, considering how Donne both allies himself to and distances himself from women; and how male friendship, for the Renaissance, is at times as peculiarly intimate as heterosexual love.

Chapter Three

Men and Women

> Women have served all these centuries as looking-glasses possessing the magic and delicious power of reflecting the figure of man at twice its natural size.
>
> (Virginia Woolf)

I

At ten o'clock one morning while a servant was lighting the fire, Donne wrote to his closest friend, Sir Henry Goodyer. Apparently referring to an unknown document written by himself, and enclosed with his letter, he stated that this work had been

> I cannot say the weightiest, but truly ... the saddest lucubration and night's passage that ever I had. For it exercised those hours, which, with extreme danger of her, who I should hardly have abstained from recompensing for her company in this world, with accompanying her out of it, increased my family with a son.[123]

The initial effect here is typical of that produced by some of Donne's most compressed and tortuously phrased poems. At first glance we are unsure quite what is being said. Yet the lines are also representative, not simply of Donne, but of the relations between men and women during his lifetime. For the second sentence, on closer examination, refers to a particularly difficult child-birth. It is already telling that what is (to us) the most important information in the letter should be so oddly obscured. Three other implications are perhaps still more striking. First, there is the sheer grace and lightly expressed wit of Donne's construction: the peculiar agonies and perils of an early-seventeenth-century child-birth are dissolved, flattened and re-expressed as a characteristically artful and dense piece of wordplay. Second, the exact structure of the sentence drops us with an abrupt gasp into the alien world of Renaissance gender relations, in a way that no bare piece of documentary history ever could. Look closely: the second sentence opens with the unnamed document ('it') and closes with the successful delivery of a male child. The sufferings of Donne's wife, Ann, are doubly buried between those two points.[124] Already veiled by the obscure wit of Donne's phrasing, they are also effectively enclosed within brackets. Indeed, in strict grammatical terms, the birth is credited not to Ann Donne, but to 'those hours' of her labour. If we object that the last, most obvious feature of the lines is the birth of 'a son', we find that this basic fact is crucially inflected by the social assumptions of the time. The child is male, and therefore worthy of mention. Not only that, but the birth has increased 'my' rather than 'our' family.[125] Thirdly – in keeping with that parenthetical, sealed experience of (evidently prolonged) labour – it appears that Donne was writing or reading in a separate room during his wife's ordeal. While the relevant words are perhaps just slightly ambiguous, the more general sociology of birth in the period shows us that he was almost certainly not with her. The time preceding, during and after child delivery was remarkable for its almost exclusive dominance by women: a community of female friends (perhaps not so readily available in Ann Donne's case) and a female midwife.[126] That situation alone, as historians and literary critics have noted, tells us a good deal about the period's distinctive attitudes to women and to female sexuality.

Elsewhere we find Donne writing not to a man, but to one of the women whose role in his life may have partially rivalled that of Ann Donne:

Madam,
Man to God's image, Eve, to man's was made,
Nor find we that God breathed a soul in her,

Canons will not Church functions you invade,
Nor laws to civil office you prefer.

Who vagrant transitory comets sees,
Wonders, because they are rare; but a new star
Whose motion with the firmament agrees,
Is miracle; for, there no new things are;

In woman so perchance mild innocence
A seldom comet is, but active good
A miracle, which reason 'scapes, and sense;
For, art and nature this in them withstood. [127]

To paraphrase this very briefly: comets are rare enough, but an entirely new, permanent star, in a cosmos supposed to have been fully, absolutely mapped centuries ago, is a miracle. Passive female goodness matches the comets in its uncommonness; but *active* good' (of which more later) lies beyond the realm of 'reason', being fundamentally alien to the most basic unchangeable nature of the female sex. Although these arguments appear initially to be part of a poem, they are in fact the opening of one of several 'verse letters', written and sent by Donne to various friends. The general artifice of that form and the particular invention of the above conceit echo the effect of the Goodyer letter, in that we are more aware of *Donne*, in either case, than of his traumatised wife or his female friend and patron, the Countess of Huntingdon. What, though, of the very first stanza? This seems to place the whole status – even existence – of the female soul in doubt. If we look at the relevant passage from Genesis we find that it is conveniently ambiguous on this point: although it does not state that Eve was *not* in-spired with a soul, it fails to make specific mention of God breathing his spirit into her, as He does into Adam.[128] Notice how Donne then 'proves' his opening claim by adding in lines 3 and 4 that women are universally excluded from religious or state employment. Perhaps nothing pitches us back into the extraordinary gender assumptions of the time better than that seemingly comic inversion of cause and effect. 'Yes', we would say, 'religion supports the oppression of women: justify that.' For Donne and his peers, church and state law (in this area at least) were no more accidental or political than the unalterable generic nature of women, as devised by God. Women were just *like* that, and so, obviously enough, they could not be priests or lawyers.

We will learn more about the divinely created natures of both men and women below. For now, we have two instances of Donne's relationship to his wife, and to a woman who was in some sense his friend. Perhaps inevitably, we are prompted to ask two questions. Did Donne love his wife? Did he like (or respect) his friend? From the point of view of cultural history or literary criticism these questions could be seen as overly-polemical or misleading. Some might argue that such queries simply would not have occurred to Donne or his peers. To argue from evidence in these precise cases themselves, we could also claim that Donne loved Ann enough to be imprisoned and all but ruined for her; and that he was not so stupid as to misunderstand the conventions of a complementary [*sic*] letter to an aristocratic woman (who, indeed, clearly remained on good terms with him). But these questions can, nevertheless, be used as frames in which to explore issues of gender, love, and personal identity. In addressing these topics, sections two and three look first at poems which seem to offer us a resounding 'no', and show how women's inferiority was understood to be rooted in their most basic material and spiritual composition. My concluding section examines some of Donne's most enlightened, forward-looking images of love and of women. In between these two poles (the negative and positive) I will try to contextualise Donne's seemingly intimate love poetry by discussion of something often no less intimate, and arguably quite as radical: namely, male friendship.

II

As Achsah Guibbory has emphasised, it is in Donne's Elegies that we find the clearest and most jarring symptoms of Renaissance misogyny.[129] Guibbory further argues that these poems in particular reflect a prevailing male discomfort with the country's female ruler, Elizabeth.[130] This belief is disputable. My own view is not that the Elegies are not intrinsically misogynistic, but that the clarity and force of their misogyny does not make them any more disturbing or remarkable than the more casual, habitual and implied gender attitudes of numerous other poems - including, as we have just seen, ones personally addressed to women. The Elegies may well betray the need (strongest, as I have argued, during the 1590s) to over-assertively define identity via opposition; and they almost certainly stand as products of the tight-knit male coterie for whom they were written. But the kind of beliefs encoded in them are ultimately far more longstanding, pervasive and deep-seated: so much so that, as already hinted, they substantially determined English Christian attitudes to the bewildering appearance of the Americas.

In 'Community' we encountered a rakish male persona who presented women as 'fruits' to be consumed and used by men.[131] And Donne's third Elegy, 'Change', seems initially to echo the notion of women as communal property:

> Foxes and goats, all beasts change when they please,
> Shall women, more hot, wily, wild than these,
> Be bound to one man ...?

But in fact the argument of this elegy is a little different. For the poem has begun by hoping that speaker and mistress are closely bonded. It then goes on to admit, 'yet much, much I fear thee'. What the speaker fears is just that supposed law of communal sexual property invoked in 'Confined Love'. As he explains:

> Women are like the arts, forced unto none,
> Open unto all searchers, unprized, if unknown.
> If I have caught a bird, and let him fly,
> Another fowler using these means, as I,
> May catch the same bird; and, as these things be,
> Women are made for men, not him, nor me.
> ...
> Who hath a plough-land, casts all his seed corn there,
> And yet allows his ground more corn should bear ...

Donne here plays three variations on the same theme. Most obviously, women are a kind of sporting prey (as we saw in the case of the carefully trained bird in 'Love's Diet'). They are also likened to fertile land. What we note there is not just the familiar motif of female property, but the implication of a passive material substratum, one whose fertility is only potential and dormant until activated by male intervention. The same note recurs in the simile of 'the arts'. While 'open to all searchers', these are crucially 'unprized, if unknown'. And once again, the arts are just one of various gentlemanly pursuits or diversions – to be taken up or laid down at pleasure, just as the hawk of 'Love's Diet' flies 'at what, and when, and how, and where I choose'.[132]

Important and central as these implications are, it is notable that 'Change' is relatively compromising when compared to other rakish elegies. It decides presently on a kind of happy medium:

> To live in one land, is captivity,
> To run all countries, a wild roguery

One should, accordingly, love neither just one woman, nor an unlimited number. Perhaps this (again, only relatively) balanced attitude is linked to the piece's conclusion – the kind of lines one can imagine lovingly quoted or anthologised well out of context:

> ... change is the nursery
> Of music, joy, life and eternity.

In one sense that statement could stand as an epitaph for a life and a mind variously surprised by, or seeking for, change and difference – states which prompt a persistently febrile wavering between excitement and fear.

For the latter, we know that many Renaissance men had a deep-seated fear of women: a kind of ironic unease at a mysterious otherness which they themselves had largely created. Did Donne fear women? Elegy seven – a poem addressed to a woman – certainly suggests a need to keep them at a careful and well-defined distance:

> Nature's lay idiot, I taught thee to love,
> ...
> Remember since all thy words used to be
> To every suitor, *Ay, if my friends agree*;
> ...
> And since, an hour's discourse could scarce have made

One answer in thee, and that ill arrayed

In broken proverbs, and torn sentences.

The tone and general drift of this poem are clear enough. Donne has shaped, instructed, and sophisticated this female mistress. Indeed, he seems to have given her a basic individuality which she lacked in the days when any decisions would be lamely referred to 'my friends'. That new sense of self-hood is typically Donnean, characterised by subtlety of manners and elegance of expression. And in fact he considers her so much his peculiar creature that he ends by (somewhat impatiently) outlining his rights to ownership over those of her husband:

Thou art not by so many duties his,

That from the world's common having severed thee,

Inlaid thee, neither to be seen, nor see,

As mine: who have with amorous delicacies

Refined thee into a blissful paradise.

Thy graces and good words my creatures be;

I planted knowledge and life's tree in thee,

Which oh, shall strangers taste? Must I alas

Frame and enamel plate, and drink in glass?

Chafe wax for others' seals? break a colt's force

And leave him then, being made a ready horse?

The husband, we are told, has done no more than crudely fence off ('inlaid') this female territory. Donne by contrast has made a garden of rare and subtle delights. Typically, he cannot resist sharpening this general metaphor into the precise innuendo of 'love's tree' – 'planted', one may infer, more than once in this receptive soil. Along with the image of fallow or dormant land, the sense of women as food ('ours as fruits are ours') returns in the anxiety that 'strangers' shall 'taste' of the consequent harvest. Again, if one has troubled to acquire silver goblets ('plate') one should not have to drink from humble glasses. The horse is perhaps for us the most glaring comparison. For Donne, however, it is sufficient to stand as a kind of axiomatic rhetorical question, ending the argument beyond all dispute and closing the poem. Its individual will must be broken and harnessed (notice how fragments of the metaphor survive) before it is fit for its proper use and purpose. Horsemanship was a particularly important mark of genteel and aristocratic identity; and while horses were objects of pride and status, attitudes to them as living creatures were arguably less sentimental than the imbecilic affection which some modern men now expend on cars. What of the wax? As we will see, this had a vital, since buried resonance as precise and authoritative as modern laws of science. On the surface it perhaps more readily suggests a kind of general male currency: one heated wax to seal a letter, stamping it with a distinctive metal image that in some degree acted as one's signature (especially so, in a period when it would have been more uniformly recognisable than the creatively varied spelling of one's own name).

It would, of course, be foolish to overlook the crude assertion of sexual possession coded in that metaphor. The woman stands as a kind of formless, malleable substance waiting to be imprinted with the subtle but definite identity of conquest, just as she has been more generally formed and refined through her amorous and social 'education'.[133] But is there also something more ambiguous and complex signalled here? Recall how Donne stated the distinctively tight relationship between his own identity and those letters that were both part of him, and separate from him once they presented his self in another's private room ('in them I may speak to you in your chamber ... and not hear my self').[134] Is he in fact anxious not just at a simple loss of sexual pleasure and waste of careful labours, but rather at losing something into which he has put him*self*? From his writing as a whole we certainly know that Donne could often force himself on his subject, displaying his immense learning with a persistence that has prompted his sermon editor, Evelyn Simpson, to lament his 'too evident desire to be learned and ingenious'.[135] To be reluctant in *omitting* instances of self-assertion or demonstration in that way is broadly the same as the fear of losing what one has so distinctively created ('my creatures'). Just posing, rather than answering, the question now, we might wonder: is there in that poem a certain – admittedly tainted – edge of personal and intellectual rigour? Donne once said that he would have no such readers as he could teach.[136] In case he probably meant male readers. Did he also feel, at least sometimes, that he wanted no such mistresses as could not appreciate his teaching, and thus – crucially – be drawn closer to him?

Lest we grow too headily optimistic with the (limited) shift of tone and balance those questions suggest, let us turn our attention to the very lowest points of the Elegies' conception of gender. In number eight, 'The Comparison', Donne follows a convention of parallels between his own and another man's mistress. The former is eulogised in the highest possible terms, while the latter is degraded with vicious ingenuity. So, Donne first insists on his own mistress' perspiration being like the 'sweet sweat of roses in a still' or the first dew of 'th'early east'. And the other?

> Rank sweaty froth thy mistress' brow defiles,
> Like spermatic issue of ripe menstruous boils,
> Or like that scum, which, by need's lawless law

> Enforced, Sanserra's starved men did draw
>
> From parboiled shoes, and boots ...

Like a kind of verbal and imaginative blow in the face, the unrelentingly forceful stresses of those opening three words punch back the speaker's opponent by sheer muscle as much as by detail of insult. But the detail is itself impressive. The rival's beloved is imagined as sweating not only pus, but, still more creatively, a liquid like the boot tar that starved soldiers were obliged to feed from in the siege of Sancerre. (That they certainly did so is confirmed by credible reports of still more desperate citizens turning to cannibalism during the same crisis.[137]) Again: the favoured mistress has a head 'round as the world's ... on every side' (l. 15) – an image, presumably, of conceptual perfection, as no one's head is precisely round - while the other's is

> like a rough-hewn statue of jet,
>
> Where marks for eyes, nose, mouth, are yet scarce set;
>
> Like the first Chaos ...

The former has a breast resembling 'Proserpine's white beauty-keeping chest' (l. 23), while the latter's calls up

> ...rough-barked elmboughs, or the russet skin
>
> Of men late scourged for madness, or for sin,
>
> [and] sun-parched quarters on the city gate ...[138]

Not only were both the latter sights familiar enough in London, but the quartered bodies of traitors, impaled as visible warnings, were evidently browned by the sun – a skin-tone which for the period connoted not health or holidays but the degradation of outdoor manual labour. The worst, however, is yet to come. Donne's mistress has a 'best loved part' like 'the limbeck's warm womb' (ll. 38, 35) – the vessel in which alchemists sought to derive the essential spirit of gold – whereas

> Thine's like the dread mouth of a fired gun,
>
> Or like hot liquid metals newly run
>
> Into clay moulds, or like to that Etna
>
> Where round about the grass is burnt away.

There is something here of that fearful uncertainty implied (and perpetuated by) the whole secret world of birth and midwifery, rendered vividly in *King Lear* with the claim that

But to the girdle do the gods inherit,

Beneath is all the fiend's; there's hell, there's darkness,

There's the sulphurous pit, burning, scalding,

Stench, consumption!

The same ambiguous conferral of dark power (a suitably riven acknowledgement of the female capacity for generation) comes through in Donne's evocation of 'hot liquid metals' and the deathly smoke of the 'fired gun'. On the other hand, although such power is again present in the massive subterranean energies of a volcano (all the more formidable in an age lacking modern bomb technologies), it is sharply undercut by the low, precisely visualised detail of charred grass, supposedly resembling pubic hair.

If this body is grimly repellent in itself, its activities hardly beautify it. The kisses of the luckless couple are

... as filthy, and more,

As a worm sucking an envemomed sore ...

And the undertone of male fear returns when Donne asks

Doth not thy fearful hand in feeling quake,

As one which gathering flowers, still fears a snake?

> Is not your last act harsh, and violent,
>
> As when a plough a stony ground doth rent?

That assault is subverted a little, we might feel, when Donne opposes his own embraces – as delicate, he claims, as a surgeon 'searching wounds' (l. 51). Does this conceit really offer a very attractive contrast? Surgeons, of course, had to be very delicate in these days before anaesthetics. But we may well frown a little and remain unconvinced. If so, we are probably registering our surprise at an image which betrays the period's lack of vocabulary and of feeling for acts whose intimate nuances still remained largely undeveloped. There may also be a more precise note of control favoured over passion. At any rate, Donne feels justified, now, in concluding with a faint but significant shift of tone:

> Leave her, and I will leave comparing thus,
>
> She, and comparisons are odious.

A broadly similar attitude and conceit underpin the second Elegy, 'The Anagram'. The joke of the poem is a 'praise of ugliness', here slanted to the whimsical idea that the addressee's mistress has the 'anagram of a good face'. That is,

> ... though her eyes be small, her mouth is great,
> Though they be ivory, yet her teeth are jet
>
> ...
>
> If red and white and each good quality
> Be in thy wench, ne'er ask where it doth lie.[139]

If this were not sufficient consolation, the male acquaintance can also be thankful that

> Beauty is barren oft; best husbands say
> There is best land, where there is foulest way.[140]

Similarly, think how little one need fear adultery from her

> Who, though seven years, she in the stews had laid,
> A nunnery durst receive, and think a maid,
>
> ...
>
> Whom, if she accuse herself, I credit less
> Than witches, which impossibles confess,
> Whom dildoes, bedstaves, and her velvet glass,
> Would be as loth to touch as Joseph was.[141]

In both 'The Comparison' and 'The Anagram', Donne is again following popular conventions; as Smith reminds us, both the 'praise of ugliness' and harsh comparisons were fashionable poetic themes in the sixteenth century.[142] And, once more, Donne is probably following a general rhetorical device in relentlessly seeking to outdo his predecessors or peers by the foulest and lowest means to hand. He seems to have succeeded with 'The Anagram', as this piece was apparently popular in the personal miscellanies which people kept in their own handwritten versions.[143] One hardly needs to draw attention to the generally sour feeling these two Elegies in particular now give us. But there are three closely related implications perhaps less obvious on a brief reading.

First: as with the mock-serious argument of a poem such as 'Community', it is not a certain truth which is aimed at. The aim is again largely one of self-construction and announcement, achieved in part via ingenuity, and more indirectly by coolness and suavity of tone. To put it a little differently: those two poems are exercises. What is arguably most discomforting about them is not the writer's antipathy to women, but his exploitation of them as indifferent materials for successful abusive creations. If Donne had instead held up a (supposedly accurate) painting of *one* particular woman and insisted precisely on how ugly she was, we might actually be less uneasy. We are hit hardest, rather, by the sense that women in general simply *do not matter* in the way that men do. To develop that claim in a little more detail: the second key point is that the two women in question (almost certainly fictitious ones, as the stock Latin name 'Flavia' further hints) are as malleable and insubstantial as the waxen creature of Elegy seven. A woman can be broken up and reassembled by a sharp-witted poet just as easily as shuffled letters in different combinations.[144] The final couplet of 'The Comparison' – with its telling note of man-to-man advice retained even there – obliquely underscores that aspect. It is in effect a gentle boast of imaginative resource. We might read it equally as 'I'm not saying she's that ugly, but if you don't find someone else, I'll convince everyone she's uglier still'; or 'You didn't realise, did you, how ugly she really was until I showed you?'

Thirdly, it is absolutely taken for granted in both poems that the poet is attacking the most – if not the only – valuable qualities of a mistress. One could simply not write such effective pieces about men in this period. Indeed, the vigorous creative energy of the poems, and the strikingly repellent visual products, combine to give an ironic illustration of what the art critic, John Berger, neatly captures as the 'different social presence' of the sexes: 'Men *act* and women *appear*.'[145] While affluent Renaissance men were arguably more apt to use flamboyant sartorial display as a means of self-assertion than those of later centuries, the broad distinction undoubtedly holds good. Women are not defined by their wisdom, their ethical status or their industry (recall the 'active good' which so startled Donne elsewhere). This kind of misogyny persisted for centuries after Donne's death. But in his era it had a special foundation which would later be progressively eroded. Women were *made* in a fundamentally different way from men. This notion was encoded in medical theory. But it was also enshrined in theology: women's very souls (as we began to suspect from Donne's verse letter to the Countess) were different from those of men. The following section sets out the origins of this belief, and shows how Donne echoed it time and again throughout his writings.

III

The basis of this distinctive female nature is hinted at frequently by repeated motifs in Donne's poems. Women are understood to be naturally more passive and more simple than men. To state that second point a little differently: they seem to be less rigid and less well-defined in terms of the *form* of their identity (recall the notion of the wax and seal). It is implied that men can and indeed should, almost by way of ethical duty, make use of them for the purposes their nature allows: hence Donne's images of the horse and the soil. In Elegy seven especially, Donne has an effectively godlike relation to the mistress, developing and 'refining' a kind of crude basic material. These scattered hints are far more than mere sexist metaphors. When Donne lived, such notions were securely embedded within the most basic (we might say archaeological) fabric of common belief and behaviour. For many people they had the axiomatic, solid certainty that scientific laws would later acquire.

The best way to understand those now faded and discredited (though not wholly vanished) ideas is through the Renaissance conception of the human soul. After the seventeenth century, the soul increasingly became understood as something incorporeal. It was defined by its opposition to matter. Donne and his contemporaries would have found this a very unsatisfying, dilute, vague, and limited substitute for what they knew in their lifetimes. Christianity had inherited and adapted a Greek idea of the soul. Borrowing this pre-Christian theory had certain potential dangers, as we will see in chapter five. But for many centuries the synthesis of Classical and Christian ideas held together. The soul was closely associated with blood, and in certain senses pervaded the entire living body. Its nature was three-fold: in the liver there was a soul of growth, in the heart a soul of sense, in the brain a soul of thought or reason (vegetable, sensitive, rational – compare Donne in his 'Valediction: Of My Name in the Window': 'all my souls ... understand, and grow, and see'.[146]) Thus plants had the first kind of soul (they merely grew); animals, which could grow and feel pleasure or pain, had the first and second; while humans, who were fundamentally rational beings, had all three, and were (ideally) dominated by the third and most noble or divine. Neither the Greeks nor the Christians of the Renaissance had anything resembling modern scientific notions of complex biology and physiology. The soul, therefore, had a physiological function, explaining the integrity of the body as a single living organism. Sensation, will-power, and voluntary movement are now explained in terms of electrical impulses and brain chemistry. In Donne's time they were all dependent on the power of the rational soul, as it charged and recharged the body by the continuous transmission of a nimble, light, rarefied vapour derived from 'the thin and active part of the blood'.[147] Consider the word 'animate': it derives from 'anima', the Latin term for 'soul'. Hence a plant is inanimate and a human animated. This intriguing pervasiveness and precision of the soul, the inextricable character of ordinary body function and the most divine immortal principle (as if the breath of God did indeed thrillingly whisper through one's veins, fibre and tissue) was a vital part of Christian theology.[148]

This, then, is the general nature of the soul, and of body-soul unity: a typically indivisible blend of elements that only later separated out into the scientific and the religious. But there was also a distinct version of this theory for women. Medical theory was heavily coloured in various ways by the differing physical and spiritual natures of men and women. Men were hotter, drier, more active; women cooler, moist, and relatively passive. Unsurprisingly, these distinctions were hierarchically perceived. Women were in fact creatures who had failed to develop as fully as men. This was no vague prejudice, but a medical notion reflected in analogies between male and female bodies (ovaries and testicles, for example). All foetuses were potentially male, but if they lacked sufficient heat they would not progress that far. This was evident partly in the interior location of female genitals, which greater male heat pushed outward. It has even been argued that the period in fact recognised only one sex, of which women were an inferior variant.[149] It was not usually claimed that women did not have rational souls (although this was not unknown). Rather, as compared with men they were far more heavily dominated by the souls of growth and sense, and far less by that of reason. In conception male seed supplied form (associated with reason and spirituality) and female seed provided matter.

If we look again at Donne's image of the wax and the seal we can begin to understand it more fully and precisely. Aristotle, the Greek philosopher chiefly responsible for the above ideas, had famously explained body-soul unity via the following comparison:

> we can wholly dismiss as unnecessary the question whether the soul and the body are one: it is as meaningless as to ask whether the wax and the shape given it by the stamp are one.[150]

The stamp, that is, gives a high degree of organisation and living vigour to a body: without it there is only formless, undefined and more or less inert matter. It was God who gave this at once divine and fundamentally human imprint (notwithstanding the mediating role of male semen). But, as we might guess, he gave it more fully to men than to women.

We can now better appreciate Donne's claim to have refined, organised and essentially improved (to have all but created) the woman of Elegy seven. And we can also begin to see what lay behind that seemingly very odd letter to the Countess. Women were indeed less 'animated' than men: less rational, less active, less spiritual and less virtuous (the prejudice is knotted up in the very root of that last word, 'vir',

Latin for 'man' – compare 'virile'). It has to be admitted that it is not easy to pin down *exactly* what men thought about this. (Indeed, that very uncertainty probably reflects the fact that women were generally unable to press men to a more rigorous and stable expression of this conveniently misty attitude.) But in practice the imprint of the idea is seen time and again in Renaissance literature. It is probably as pervasive as the modern cultural vocabulary of evolution. Donne wrote a paradox which wondered 'why have the common opinion afforded women souls?'. In it he included a comparison between women and animals – one which other evidence from the period obliges us to take quite seriously.[151] He may have grown a little embarrassed about this in later years. But in a sermon of 5 November 1622 we find him restating the claim of the verse letter:

> [Although] we are sure women have souls as well as men ... yet it is not so expressed, that God breathed a soul into Woman, as he did into Man; all forms of government have this soul, but yet God infuseth it more manifestly, and more effectually ... in a kingdom ... this form of a monarchy, of a kingdom, is a more lively, and a more masculine organ, and instrument of this soul of sovereignty, then the other forms are.[152]

It is hard not to suspect at least a faint echo of some wider debate behind even that opening assertion. But most important are the close associations between the 'masculine' and a political body which is 'lively' because its soul has been (let us say) more tightly fused into it, activating and firing it more dynamically and 'effectually'. Versions of this fundamental gender division are numerous. Praising the unusual virtue of his friend, Mrs Magdalen Herbert, Donne talks of 'your manlier active part of doing good'.[153] He notes to Goodyer 'how fertile and abundant the understanding is, if she hath a good father'.[154] In his poem 'The Curse', he wishes the malediction to fall on whichever man has attempted to name his mistress – but adds, 'if it be a she/Nature before hand hath out-cursed me' (ll. 31-2).[155]

In giving this necessarily brief sketch of an extremely durable, well-integrated theory which included and exceeded misogyny, my aim has been to show just how massively pervasive and structural gender prejudice was. It must certainly have been complicated by the presence of Elizabeth as monarch (notice, above, Donne's preference for 'a kingdom' – he is speaking in the reign of James I). But ultimately the most important thing about Renaissance misogyny was its religious character. The remainder of this chapter looks at Donne's more positive evocations of intimate human relationships. Although broadly divided into two categories (those between men, and between men and women) these images of intimacy ultimately appear to share certain interesting features.

IV

> Meet me at London, then,
> Twenty days hence, and thou shalt see
> Me fresher, and more fat, by being with men
> ('The Blossom')

Let us consider something strange. People in the sixteenth century did not have friends. To be a little more precise: they did not have friends in anything like the sense which we now take for granted. This, at any rate, is the contention of historians such as Lawrence Stone.[156] What can such a claim mean? As a rule, people are supposed in this period to have been intrinsically more distant and cool towards one another than we would naturally expect. We have glimpsed this already in terms of parent-child relations, and we will meet the issue again in the context of religious belief. There is good reason for believing that this kind of lower emotional or sentimental pressure was partly produced by distinctive Renaissance child-rearing habits. Babies, for example, were swaddled. At least since Freud, and arguably since the Romantics, with their insistence on play and youthful freedom, European culture has accepted that early impressions have a special and lasting force on the human individual. Moreover, that early environment should involve a certain basic space for the psychic growth and exploration of the slowly flowering consciousness. Imagine, by contrast, how loose, relaxed, and emotionally open you are likely to be if you have been rigidly bandaged up like a mummy for the very first months of your life. Again, it now seems similarly axiomatic to many that a baby or infant should have a close and stable relationship with its mother. But in the Renaissance, under the long-established and widespread system of wet-nursing, reasonably affluent parents paid a professional nurse to breast-feed and care for their children. These and other practices must have psychically conditioned the receptive minds and bodies of both children and adults. And they were, of course, also reflections of fundamentally different attitudes, as well as causes of them.

Later, on entering the brutalising milieu of the Renaissance school, boys would be routinely beaten. Striking children across the lips or the buttocks (and frequently drawing blood) was not just a standard means of pragmatic control.

Once again, such violence had ideological roots. Children were not so much budding plants that should be nurtured, as wayward animals which must be broken and tamed into submission, kept from the lures of the devil to whom they were especially easy prey. What was the result of these practices? Perhaps not surprisingly, men in general appear to have been far more aggressive than those of later centuries. Both Ben Jonson and the Italian sculptor Benvenuto Cellini (two men now known chiefly for their love of art, beauty and religion) committed homicides. Legal records, Stone tells us, are full of cases of violent assault over seemingly trivial matters – a habit probably aggravated by the convention of carrying a knife, if only in theory to cut meat.[157] Donne's contemporary, Sir Germander Pool, had his nose bitten off during a fight in March 1613.[158] Donne himself was clearly mild-tempered by comparison with many of his peers. But we must bear in mind that he sailed twice on military expeditions; and that he was also indirectly conditioned by the standard attitudes of his time. He seems, for example, to show an intrinsic respect for physical courage and military skills when contemptuously describing the public tournaments of the French during a visit to Paris in 1612: 'there were no personal rencounters ... and for their bravery no true stuff.'[159]

This last point brings us to the wider, underlying social code which powerfully licensed and encouraged aggressive male behaviour: namely, honour. Honour also involved issues such as the reliability of promises and personal integrity. But its most conspicuous expression was violence. Ironically by our standards, honourable violence increased in broad proportion to one's education and status. Gentle and titled men fought duels to defend their reputations. So, in *Twelfth Night*, Sir Andrew's sham gentility is underscored by his cowardice – a failing highlighted by contrast with the ready swordsmanship of Sir Toby. Perhaps most memorably, we find Donne's friend, Edward, Lord Herbert of Cherbury, sat in a tavern in Brussels, where he overhears foreign soldiers speaking ill of his king, James I. After musing for a moment that, if he had been merely 'a base fellow' he could have tolerated this abuse without revealing his nationality, Cherbury takes the only honourable course. Rising with a flourish and 'putting off my hat', he announces ringingly to the assembled company: 'Sono Inglesi.'[160]

All these factors would have conditioned those same sex relations (here we are necessarily concerned only with men) that we now describe as friendships. The very word 'friend' had distinctive registers since lost. It commonly meant something like 'protector' or 'associate', encoding a sense of friendship that seems to us discomfortingly pragmatic, unsentimental and self-seeking. In Stone's words, 'it was ... frequently used to mean not a person to whom one had some special emotional attachment, but someone who could help one on in life'. One could only be sure that it had its modern emotional sense if clarified as '"a choice special friend"', with this register not becoming dominant until the mid-eighteenth century.[161] 'In certain respects', we are told, 'friendship was like an arranged marriage, whose success was guaranteed not by personal feelings but by objective factors such as status, wealth, family strategy, and parental approval.'[162] Donne seems to glance at the common self-interest or pragmatism of such relations when he admits that he is 'not of the best stuff for friendship, which men of warm and durable fortunes only are'.[163] He cannot be a 'true friend' precisely because he cannot help his friends *materially*. Francis Bacon's essay 'Of Followers and Friends' is revealing by its title alone. And even its apparent recognition of a more modern altruistic human association is contained in the reflection that 'there is little friendship in the world'.[164]

But existing social and emotional habits do seem to have been changing – at least slowly – during Donne's lifetime. In terms of friendship in particular, the late Alan Bray has suggested that 'the stance of an intimate and altruistic

143

friendship is everywhere evident in ... the new humanist learning of the sixteenth century', and that this stance was opposed to those older 'obligations that were frequently irksome and always dangerous'.[165] It is, of course, Donne's personal letters which allow us to see him in the vanguard of such changes. In the broadest terms we recognise something like our own modern views of friendship when he notes 'with how much desire we read the papers of any living now (especially friends) which we would scarce allow a box in our cabinet ... if they were dead'. This, he says, is because 'the writings and words of men present we may examine, control, and expostulate, and receive satisfaction from the authors; but the other we must believe, or discredit; they present no mean'.[166] In the same passage Donne gives a further idea of the active power of letters, praising them because 'the Evangels and Acts teach us what to believe, but the Epistles of the Apostles what to do'. 'No other kind of conveyance', he decides, 'is better for knowledge, or love.' Anyone who has ever scrolled through old e-mails to find, with a start, that it was over a year since they last wrote to (let alone saw) an old friend will feel the weight and truth of Donne's claim that 'when we think of a friend, we do not count that a lost thought, though that friend never knew of it'.[167] Again, the common belief that there are certain things only a friend can say is apparent when he hopes he can advise Goodyer (with what we might consider a certain edge of moral superiority) because that 'is pardonable in a friend'.[168]

One broad element linking these various facets is the memorable human voice of the letters. 'Speech', Donne observes elsewhere, 'is the glue, the cement, the soul of conversation'; and it is in the letters that we come closest to hearing Donne in conversation.[169] We can, of course, never be quite sure *how* close. But we should bear in mind that he was certainly capable of speaking balanced, elaborate and ingenious sentences which we would now typically expect to hear only from professional actors.[170] Moreover, the tradition of 'familiar letters' as defined by the influential Humanist writer Erasmus (1466-1536) stated precisely that such writings should 'resemble a conversation between friends' and be 'neither unpolished, rough, or artificial'.[171] Indeed, one Robert Langham had in the late sixteenth century attempted to devise a phonetic alphabet in order to capture the human voice more exactly on paper.[172]

Beyond these general echoes, we find that Donne values friendship in ways that aptly reflect his temperament and times. Let us take just three of the most important of these here. First: he explicitly refers at one point to 'my second religion, friendship'.[173] Elsewhere he develops the implications of that parallel a little more fully: 'in the offices of so spiritual a thing as friendship, so momentary a thing as time must have no consideration.'[174] On the surface the idea of friendship as above time is just a whimsical extempore creation. But other echoes of that motif show it to be far from accidental. Friendship, for Donne, is at once 'religious' and somehow pitched out of the transient, mundane world, because it is again a centre of stability. What we must also note once more is that Donne is helping to create and outline that aspect of it, intensifying it through the metaphor of an extra-temporal relationship. If there is some similarity between those sentiments, and our own surviving notion of friendship as 'sacred', it must be admitted that there is also considerable difference. What we might say is that Donne confers on friendship the emotional value and pressure of a *religious* feeling which would later distil itself more tightly into an individual sentiment of personal affection.

A second strand in the mesh of Donne's attitudes to friendship is perhaps now still more alien than the density and pervasiveness of seventeenth-century religion. It has been convincingly argued that gender divisions at this time were so strong as to effectively divert into male friendships the emotional and intimate habits that later became exclusive to heterosexual romance and marriage. This does not mean that all male friendships were homosexual. Rather, it means that homosexuality as we know it did not exist:

> The Renaissance male was brought up within a society where many of his most important relationships were with other men, and within this masculine culture the bonds of affection, loyalty and obligation were often passionate. 'Love' was what bonded friends, neighbours, kinsmen and households ... men in Renaissance England ... freely shared beds, embraced and kissed, and used highly-charged language for their bonds of friendship and social obligation. Perhaps a range of emotion and erotic feeling was allowed, and seen as enhancing rather than endangering the masculine milieu.[175]

As noted, James I himself was nominally bisexual. But the Renaissance did not explicitly recognise that label or concept. The peculiarly exclusive and self-consciously male community Paul Hammond describes here has been usefully captured under the term 'homosocial'. As Eve Kosofsky Sedgwick puts it in her pioneering study of this topic, homosociality implies 'the potential unbrokenness of a continuum between homosocial and homosexual'.[176] Within this social sphere, friendships could include seemingly erotic habits or expressions that did not necessarily imply a fully homosexual love. Bray's book *The Friend* has shown that male friends were known to assert that camaraderie by rituals remarkably like those of marriage. Later, they would sometimes be buried together, or have shared tomb monuments (as proposed, but never realised, in the case of Sir Philip Sidney and his lifelong friend Fulke Greville).[177] Indeed, Donne's curious 'For better or for worse take me, or leave me' in Satire one may betray something broadly similar, notwithstanding its roots in a genuine personal insecurity.[178]

Conversely, same-sex love, where it did exist, was importantly different from later versions of homosexuality just because that homosocial culture was so pervasive and influential. Later definitions of homosexuality were different because the heterosexual intimacy to which they were opposed had itself changed. In one sense that tightly enclosed male world – experienced by Donne at university, in the law schools, and in warfare – forms another component in the whole negative structuring of women who simply do not exist on the same level as men. (In terms of universities, indeed, it is worth noting that the Oxford of *Brideshead Revisited* still looks in some ways remarkably like the homosocial world of the Renaissance.[179]) We glimpse this when, at the close of the 'birth letter', Donne admits, 'Thus much more than needed I have told you ...'. His apologetic aside excuses reference to humble domestic matters – a trait seen more strikingly when he relates his son's premature death to his friend Sir Robert Ker, before explaining, 'Because I loved it well, I make account that I dignify the memory of it, by mentioning of it to you, else I should not be so homely.'[180] Note the faint but undeniable peculiarity here: he has not privileged his friend by conferring this personal news, but – he says – 'dignified' his son's death by putting it in Ker's presence.

Without forgetting that telling marginalisation of the 'homely' world of family and marriage we can also identify homosocial elements in friendship which, when taken alone, look more positive. 'Strong is this love which ties our hearts in one' – this line is in fact not from an ordinary love poem, but from a verse letter to Christopher Brooke.[181] Similarly, Donne tells Henry Wotton that

> ... more than kisses, letters mingle souls;
> For, thus friends absent speak.[182]

He explains to another friend that, 'if I owed you not a great many thanks for every particular part of [your letter], I should yet thank you for the length; and love it as my mistress's face, every line and feature, but best all together'.[183] He closes a letter to Goodyer with the statement, 'I kiss your hands; and deliver to you an entire and clear heart, which shall ever when I am with you be in my face and tongue'.[184] Again, if we had no addressee, we might well guess the recipient to be a woman; and even the unusually plain final words, 'yours very affectionately', convey a notable degree of sincere intimacy. These kind of phrases indeed make us wonder a little when Donne cautiously admits that 'new loves ... of other men' are consistent with 'true friendship' as this latter is 'not a marrying'.[185] When he tells Goodyer, after an illness, that 'I made no doubt but my ... pain ... affected you also', they being 'so much towards one [another], that one part cannot escape the distemper of the other', we seem remarkably close to the metaphysically inextricable lovers of 'A Valediction: Forbidding Mourning'. And throughout the letters Donne frequently signs himself as 'your friend and servant and lover'. As Hammond again points out, this last term was an ambiguous one for the period. It often simply meant '"well-wisher"'. Hammond also suggests, however, that there was an uncertain potential overlap between that sense of the word and its heterosexual usage – a possibility which would match the (to us) ambiguous behaviour of the homosocial communities of the time.[186]

Thirdly and finally, we find that the letters frequently bring us back to the question of self-hood. Donne's parallel between letters and kisses clearly has both religious and erotic overtones. But the mention of the soul also necessarily connotes the self. Writing from Mitcham to Sir Thomas Lucy, Donne stated that 'the writing of letters, when it is with any seriousness, is a kind of ecstasy, and a departure and secession and suspension of the soul, which doth then communicate itself to two bodies'.[187] As so often, Donne is at his most revealing when seemingly most careless (here the conceit is part of an elaborate joke about letters written but unsent). Donne really feels that he is imparting something of himself in a letter, and his notion of self-hood is fundamentally inflected by the relationship between earthly self and immortal soul. Elsewhere he returns to the entanglement of self and self-expression, telling George Gerrard that 'our letters are ourselves, and in them absent friends meet'.[188] We certainly find an edge of self-presence and immediacy when he closes a communication 'whilst my fire was lighting at Tricombs [at] ten o' clock'– this was me, at that time, there.[189] Elsewhere he re-states the powerful bond between self and self-expression when punning on 'leaves' of paper and of trees. 'Wheresoever these leaves fall', he claims, 'the root is in my heart'. Moreover: 'thus much information is in leaves, that they can tell you what the tree is, and these can tell you I am a friend and an honest man.'[190] Within that remarkably precise evocation (leaves are detachable, yet grown from oneself and still somehow part of oneself) we might detect a characteristic pride in his own uniqueness. That quality is amplified when he admits that 'your man's haste and mine to Mitcham cuts off this letter here; yet, as in little patterns torn from a whole piece, this may tell you what I am'.[191] Dr Johnson might well disagree; but for Donne fragments can distil truth.

To some degree friendship and self were linked because – at least in Donne's more isolated years – letters were often his only form of homosocial self-expression besides poetry or formal prose (such as his *Biathanatos*). Hence we find him explaining that letters 'mingle souls' just because 'this ease' (the relief of writing) 'controls'

> The tediousness of my life; but for these
> I could ideate nothing, which could please,
> But I should wither in one day ...[192]

I should wither ... Anybody who has felt themselves somehow constrained or diminished when cut off from intimate company will appreciate this only too well. To put it another way: can we be entirely ourselves without speaking, or without speaking fully and freely?

Perhaps the subtle ties between friendship, self and self-expression can be best summed up in the claim of Cicero, whose letters were not only praised by Donne, but were generally instrumental in promoting a new, Humanistic vogue for personal communications. For the Roman philosopher, 'a true friend' was 'as it were, another self'.[193] Or, in Donne's version of this sentiment, 'if we write to a friend, we must not call it a lost letter, though it never find him to whom it was addressed, for *we owe ourselves* that office to be mindful of our friends'.[194] We can therefore understand Donne's relatively avant-garde, intimately enclosed style of friendship as in part another version of his equally advanced self-hood. There is no doubt that that self remains relatively distant to us. In his remarkable autobiography Cellini tells of how, locked in a Roman dungeon, he sat singing to himself to keep up his spirits.[195] At rare moments such as this the thick crust of history melts open and drops us into the presence of a human being who is not only recognisable but loveable. We occasionally have the same kind of experience with Samuel Pepys; or, much later, with Dr Johnson's friend, James Boswell. In many ways those three men are loveable for their faults as much as their virtues. Donne, of course, is frequently defined precisely by his self-control, his artful – rather than beguilingly childlike – self-revelation. This side of his identity may derive in part from the general emotional rigidity of Renaissance life. But it also derives from his persistent need for sources of stability. To be able to control oneself, or the presentation of oneself, is in a sense to control one's world. We have seen that Donne could derive stability from his books, that 'constant company' which he was reluctant to leave for the fickle caller of satire one. It seems, too, that he could derive it from a friendship which managed to a surprising degree to assert the self against the world. Let us look finally at a drive toward stability and self-enclosure which involved not men, but women.

V

The highest degree of other love, is the love of woman
... rightly placed upon one woman.[196]

We began by asking the provisional question: did Donne love his wife? Before returning to this, let us for now ask another. Could he write love poems? The answer is not only 'yes', but also that he wrote a new kind of love poem. I will look here at three broad elements within a handful of such pieces. 'The Good Morrow', 'The Sun Rising', and 'The Canonization' deftly entwine and manipulate philosophical notions of reality; the relatively recent growth of personal and amorous privacy; and Donne's own circumstances as an energetic, ambitious, yet constrained individual living in imposed isolation after 1601. Considerations of space largely exclude Donne's 'Valediction' poems from this discussion. Two pieces which can also be classed as love poems – 'The Ecstasy' and 'A Nocturnal upon St. Lucy's Day' – will be examined in other contexts. We might also be tempted to include poems such as 'The Bait', or the 'Song' which begins 'Sweetest love, I do not go ...'. The accomplished metrical flow of such pieces is certainly a useful weapon against those critics who have varied Jonson's old complaint as to Donne's supposedly rough poetic style. We may indeed imagine, whimsically, that they are deliberate responses to that same weighty contemporary of Donne's, who one night in The Mermaid tavern frowned for a few intent moments over a manuscript draft of (say) 'The Good Morrow', laid it down with a respectful nod and then, after a long swallow of ale, asked Donne: 'But can you write a straight line? Something we could sing?' By next week, let us imagine, Donne had. And it is important to see that Donne's iconoclasm was of a certain kind. When art critics wonder if modern *enfants terrible* such as Damien Hirst *et al* 'can draw a straight line', they often cite those older experimenters, such as Picasso, who certainly could. And yes, Donne could write a straight line. But for present purposes those rare instances are most useful as contrasts. It is hard not to feel that they constitute something like adroit formal exercises by comparison with the rigorously self-demanding and self-expressive poems under discussion here.

We can cement that argument by noting that Donne appears to have prized certain poems, or certain precise conceits, over others. 'The Damp' and 'The Legacy' are variations on one very distinctive theme, as are 'The Relic' and 'The Funeral'. The image of 'gold to airy thinness beat' is found not only in 'A Valediction: Forbidding Mourning', but reappears in varying forms in certain of Donne's sermons.[197] And it can be said that Donne returns most frequently – and most convincingly – to the evocation of lovers whose relationship is defined against the world in general. In 'The Good Morrow' the initial note is one of fairly measured, almost offhand conversational reflection:

> I wonder by my troth, what thou, and I
> Did, till we loved? were we not weaned till then,
> But sucked on country pleasures, childishly?
> Or snorted we in the seven sleepers' den?
> 'Twas so; but this, all pleasures fancies be.

If ever any beauty I did see,

Which I desired, and got, 'twas but a dream of thee.

Within this deceptively brisk speech certain now long-vanished notions of reality and illusion are more or less clearly evident. As often with Donne, phrasing requires us to halt and unpick its knots. The second part of the fifth line means 'except for this love, all pleasures are mere illusion'. Nominally, the 'sleepers' den' is a reference to a miraculous incident from ancient Christian history, where seven members of the persecuted new faith survived their imprisonment by somehow sleeping for 187 years.[198] Before their love, then (Donne suggests to the woman) all past life had been a kind of illusory dream. Modern lovers, by contrast, are more likely to praise their union by saying that it *is* a kind of dream. The Renaissance tended not to value actual night-time dreams; but what is most important here is the more general notion that life itself is only a passing dream by comparison with the full, ultimate reality of the life to come, in the heavenly kingdom of the Christian God. Here Donne transposes that widely-held notion into the private realm of sexual love.

We need also to recognise that the Christian sense of worldly unreality or transience was itself based on earlier philosophy. For Donne seems to glance obliquely at an older,

Greek notion of 'reality', of which Christians made wide and varied use. He talks not only of a false 'dream' of true love, but of being previously sealed into a kind of cave. The philosopher Plato – whose influence in the Renaissance increasingly began to rival that of Aristotle – had illustrated the relation between human life and divine truth by imagining prisoners in a cave, bound so that they could only stare at its inner wall. A fire was burning behind them, allowing them to see their own and other objects' shadows on the cave wall before them. Knowing nothing else, they took these secondary reflections for reality, unaware of the actual objects from which they derived. For Plato, this epitomised human experience of divine Truth, something which could be perceived only partially and indirectly. A vast leap of imagination or ingenuity is hardly required to see how Christianity borrowed this idea of a final reality which on earth could only be viewed 'through a glass darkly'.[199]

Donne could undoubtedly have expected his contemporary readers to catch such an allusion with minimal prompting, especially given the poem's central emphasis on awakening to a new awareness of truth. What is interesting about this changed psychic state is that Donne and his lover do not simply escape from cave or den into some expansive and clear open space. Rather, they voluntarily re-enclose themselves:

> And now good morrow to our waking souls,
> Which watch not one another out of fear;
> For love, all love of other sights controls,
> And makes one little room, an every where.
> Let sea-discoverers to new worlds have gone,
> Let maps to others, worlds on worlds have shown,
> Let us possess one world, each hath one, and is one.

> My face in thine eye, thine in mine appears,
> And true plain hearts do in the faces rest,
> Where can we find two better hemispheres
> Without sharp north, without declining west?
> What ever dies, was not mixed equally;
> If our two loves be one, or, thou and I
> Love so alike, that none do slacken, none can die.

Three elements are particularly important in these two final stanzas. One is a union whose fullest power and uniqueness derives from a fusion or balance of two souls. That union is presented in terms of two lovers gazing into one another's eyes, and of two souls which 'watch not one another out of fear'. The philosopher Bertrand Russell once said that human life would be vastly improved if people could learn to love rather than fear one another. The idea is at once simple and remarkably difficult in practice. What is easier is to suspend or transform routine fear or caution in relation to just one other human being. Anyone who has had that experience of seeing their own reflection in a lover's eyes – and usually for an extended time – can begin to appreciate what Donne is evoking here. Such experience is intrinsically intimate. It requires the kind of physical proximity which implies a kiss – either just partaken or imminent. In a certain precisely anthropological sense one has therefore already overcome ordinary fear by breaking the usual conventions of personal space. But what is arguably most distinctive about these moments is their peculiar transformation of self-hood. They depend upon a voluntary yielding of self-control and self-enclosure which can indeed give the feeling of being some strange new composite entity, pitched beyond oneself into that highly-charged fragment of space between two rapt and hardly blinking pairs of eyes.

First of all, then, the poem insists on a love which overcomes fear, and which suffuses all experience to the degree that the lovers become a world unto themselves. To put that another way: the love is defined by enclosure and by privacy. It is this which forms the second element of the poem. To us, the idea of sexual love as private may seem relatively axiomatic. We need to realise, however, that within Donne's poem in particular, and his society in general, the issue of privacy is complicated by distinctive social factors. In the earlier sixteenth century, people's lives were far less private than those of later eras. The situation necessarily varied across social classes, but there are reasons for thinking that the richest and poorest suffered from the problem to a similar degree. The former were continually surrounded by servants, and the latter could often share a two- or even one-room house with several other family members.[200] But the very word 'suffer' may in fact misrepresent people's actual experience of what to us appears an uncomfortable lack of personal space. At one level, it is clear that human beings can still adapt successfully to a continuously public lifestyle. Public schools are a good example. Not only are they are more or less voluntarily endured, but they seem to produce a type of person who often shows a much less marked division between private and public selves throughout their life. As we have seen, in the Renaissance people were generally far more distant and cool in their habitual relations, both in public and in what we would consider 'private' life. That factor must also have been important in determining how people responded to a sense of actual, possible, or implicit observation during the most intimate moments of their lives. Once again, however, a new degree of privacy seems to have been slowly emerging. As Hammond notes, some (albeit relatively limited) private spaces became available to the privileged: 'small chambers or closets, secret alcoves, large window recesses, seats and bowers within the gardens.'[201] What privacy there was, therefore, was still novel. As such, we can well imagine that it might have specially attracted Donne's poetic imagination.

We now need to consider the third element of the poem. Just what kind of private space is here created and inhabited by Donne and his lover? At first it seems to be one which dismisses and defies not only the outside world as ordinarily known, but the strange *new* worlds now explored by 'sea-discoverers'. That emphasis heightens the strategy of self-enclosure, because it is far more difficult to shut out something so novel and uncharted, and because that novelty would also revitalise the conceit for readers intensely aware of the exotic wonders and cultural strangeness of the new Americas. And in fact, here as elsewhere, Donne is *not* fully or straightforwardly shutting these new lands out of the charmed circle in which the lovers work their silent blissful spells. Rather, by merely implying these vibrantly uncertain, fascinating regions he necessarily includes them to some degree. For contemporary readers especially this presents one more powerful trick of self-construction via opposition. The two lovers are already quite remarkable and advanced in their assertion of a still nascent, only partially-developed form of more private sexual relationship. But in typically Donnean fashion that privacy is forcefully heightened by the implied presence not only of the world per se, but of a new world which – always threatening to invade or overwhelm the minds of European Christians – here shimmers potently just outside the lovers' own special domain.

Donne is, then, undeniably using this world even as he seems to deny it. Is he also using the individual reader in another, more precise way? William Shullenberger has argued that certain of Donne's love poems are distinctive in their novel assertion of privacy. Following Stone's view that the Renaissance 'social structure' was one which 'inhibited the expression and satisfaction of private longing', Shullenberger claims that Donne nevertheless manages to create intimacy by using a third person, whose implicit or explicit gaze helps define private amorous space.[202] That outsider therefore acts in a broadly similar way to the at once present and excluded 'new worlds'. By extension, the reader of such poems also becomes a kind of voyeur, throwing onto the privileged lovers a kind of emotional spotlight. Interesting as Shullenberger's argument is, it is also necessarily problematic in the context of Renaissance society. Can you really talk of voyeurism in a society which is so pervasively public? In a realm where privacy itself is so partial and novel, people have probably internalised a sense of surveillance which renders them at least partly immune to voyeurism. It would therefore seem that Donne's intended reader could not easily occupy the role Shullenberger describes. In a certain important sense, however, they do. For the privacy of this poem is of a quite special kind: not physical, but metaphysical. The voyeurs looking in on the magic circle are at once vital agents of definition, and necessarily frustrated observers, in that they finally *cannot* 'see'. That is, they cannot understand something whose most inviolable core of intimacy is spiritual and emotional – the uniquely exalted state of two purified lovers who first lose themselves in each other, and then lose that third, intermediate self in awareness of an ultimate spiritual reality only dimly glimpsed by ordinary mortals.

Something similar is clearly at stake in 'The Sun Rising':

> Busy old fool, unruly sun,
>
> Why dost thou thus,
>
> Through windows, and through curtains call on us?

The opening is abrupt for any reader, but especially so for those of Donne's contemporaries who knew the traditional convention of the 'dawn poem' or *aubade* – one usually characterised by a far more reverent, quasi-religious address to the sun at its first appearance. And this break with convention is no mere surface trick. For Donne once more announces a whole philosophy of love and self through his seemingly colloquial outburst. As in 'The Good Morrow', where the general tone of the first stanza, and the particular pun on 'c(o)untry pleasures' could co-exist with an immensely rarefied emotional state, so here we glide seamlessly from the jolts of mock-abuse to the thinnest heights of a love which now defies not only space, but time:

> Love, all alike, no season knows, nor clime,
>
> Nor hours, days, months, which are the rags of time.

Again, Donne is here alluding to Plato, for whom human, earthly time was just a flawed version of eternity.[203]

Space itself has already been discreetly insinuated. Not only have the lovers shut out the rude business of 'late school-boys' and 'court-huntsmen', but the mention of 'curtains' slyly hints at private pleasures, and at a further defiant screening out of this common bustle of a new day. In the next stanza Donne reasserts that private, supposedly independent world by telling the sun that a wink would shut him out, and offering a further challenge:

> If her eyes have not blinded thine,
>
> Look, and tomorrow late, tell me,
>
> Whether both th'Indias of spice and mine
>
> Be where thou left'st them, or lie here with me.

'Indias' (or 'Indies') was the Renaissance's tellingly loose term for the non-Christian lands of East and West: the great spice-trading realms of China and Asia on the one hand, and the fabulously wealthy treasures of mineral resource synonymous with the newly-found Americas on the other. The parallel between the woman and these material treasures is important, as we will see more fully in chapter six. For now we need only note that it neatly cements the evocation of general space by filling it with material treasure. And that strategy is underscored when the following lines command the sun:

> Ask for those kings whom thou saw'st yesterday,
>
> And thou shalt hear, All here in one bed lay.

To us this may seem like vague hyperbole. It must have been far more startling when kings were a real political force (on which, as we have seen, Donne himself depended), presented by some as having divinely-given powers over their subjects.

The weighty and elaborate social pyramid of social distinctions distilled and hinged in the person of the monarch is here gleefully collapsed into the most private space available to the period, as the world's kings impossibly meet in the poet's bed. The piece ends by telling the sun,

> Shine here to us, and thou art everywhere;
> This bed thy centre is, these walls, thy sphere.

As Smith has shrewdly emphasised, this conceit has a certain powerful charge to it, effectively firing the boiling energies of the sun through the veins of the lovers who, importantly, *feel* as if they are the centre of the world, and as if nothing could be more vital, energetic or valuable than the astonishing new experience in which they are caught.[204] The theft of cosmic power is, then, as legitimate as the unstoppably vigorous self-belief that motivates it. Insisting (against Johnson) that one can indeed condense the wide effulgence of a summer noon through the prism of a bedroom window, 'The Good Morrow' offers a potent reassertion of something all the more compelling because it seems never to have happened to anyone else before, and necessarily cannot happen again to one's self.

It would be an impossible task to say from just where that kind of energy comes. Clearly much of it belongs to the restless self whose unstable manifestations we met in the previous chapter. Does at least some of it also derive from the beloved? We need to be cautious and realistic here. No recognisable woman is conveyed by these poems – we can infer the 'she' of the present piece only through the effects for which she appears partially responsible. Even then we must note the repeated hierarchy of 'She is all states, and all princes, I' (l. 21). But if we return to the issues of public and private life sketched out above, we can again argue that by its very insistence on the value of a private relation between a man and woman, the poem is unusual, if not radical. 'Compared to this/All honour's mimic' (ll. 23-4), we are told. As indicated above, honour was a component of male identity so valuable to educated and privileged men that they were prepared to risk their lives for it in warfare, duels, or spontaneous violence. Donne's brief statement therefore had a peculiar charge when it was made. If we now turn to 'The Canonization', we might be able to see just *why* he should want to say it in the first place.

'The Good Morrow' and 'The Sun Rising' can be seen as anti-Petrarchan. We saw that Petrarch and the Petrarchans used the distant contemplation of a single woman as a focal point which might help them shift beyond the human to the divine. In both of Donne's poems, by contrast, that transcendence is achieved by a real and evidently physical relation to an actual person. Moreover, there is a vital tension between this concrete relationship and the ultimate truth it figures. Donne, we might say, cannot bring himself to lose and simply degrade the physical and personal side of the whole process. Similarly, those two poems feel able to comprehend a range of tones which do not compromise their final seriousness. Both qualities are writ large in 'The Canonization':

> For God's sake hold your tongue, and let me love,
> Or chide my palsy, or my gout,
> My five grey hairs, or ruined fortune flout ...

Stanza two makes the same attack from a slightly different angle:

> Alas, alas, who's injured by my love?
> What merchant's ships have my sighs drowned?
> Who says my tears have overflowed his ground?

These and other seemingly whimsical queries are an indirect swipe at Petrarchanism, insofar as they effectively deny the cosmic significance of love. Yet, once again, Donne has little trouble getting his fingers round a startling change of key:

169

Call us what you will, we are made such by love;

...

The phoenix riddle hath more wit

By us; we two being one, are it.

So to one neutral thing both sexes fit

We die and rise the same, and prove

Mysterious by this love.

A vital motif is introduced here, with the effectual 'third state' of the two lovers as a unity being explicitly signalled by the 'neutral thing', in which 'both sexes fit'. Once more, that special product is, we can infer, immune to change. And, as the word 'mysterious' indicates, it is also beyond ordinary comprehension.

The fourth stanza appears to offer another, slightly more subtle change of emphasis:

We can die by it, if not live by love,

And if unfit for tombs and hearse

Our legend be, it will be fit for verse;

And if no piece of chronicle we prove,

We'll build in sonnets pretty rooms;

As well a well wrought urn becomes

The greatest ashes, as half-acre tombs,
And by these hymns, all shall approve
Us canonized for love:

'Die' may again have the old punning sense of orgasm, but clearly has that of actual death most of all. Accordingly, the poem now sets out the details of a retreat and an enclosure from which the grand spaces of the new world or of the cosmos are markedly absent. But the tone is evidently not straightforwardly negative, as we realise most certainly in the closing stanza:

And thus invoke us; 'You whom reverend love
Made one another's hermitage;
You, to whom love was peace, that now is rage;
Who did the whole world's soul contract, and drove
Into the glasses of your eyes
(So made such mirrors, and such spies,
That they did all to you epitomize,)
Countries, towns, courts: beg from above
A pattern of your love!'

Perhaps only Donne could successfully insert parentheses into a climax as involved and powerful as this one. In those nine lines the arguments of 'The Good Morrow' and 'The Sun Rising' (perhaps also of 'The Ecstasy') are energetically compacted with a rigorous intellectual craftsmanship that tightens the metaphoric screws to the last twist without quite splintering the whole creation. The energy is forcefully present in the active power of the mythical lovers who 'did the whole world's soul contract, and drove/Into the glasses of your eyes ... /Countries, towns, courts ...'. The intellectual toughness and certainty are again partly derived from the philosophy of Plato and his followers. The 'pattern' refers to Plato's notion of the ideal, unique forms of all entities and states contained somewhere in heaven. Once more, earthly life showed only flawed copies of those immaculate originals. Donne and his beloved, however, convince the admiring multitudes that such a union must have been as transcendental and perfect as the heavenly 'forms' or 'ideals' of Plato.

'The Canonization' shows us Donne at his most defiantly inimitable. It somehow welds together the staged colloquial impatience and wit of the first two stanzas, the partly offhand ('Call us what you will'), partly sacralising tone of the third, and the steadily rising crescendo of the final two verses. Dr Johnson might have shaken his head wearily; T.S. Eliot perhaps sighed with wistful and nostalgic envy: once it could be done in good faith, with conviction, but (alas!) no longer ... While Eliot was still very young, another critic, Edmund Gosse, claimed the piece to be a love poem to Ann Donne. Much of Gosse's criticism of Donne is wayward or limited. But in this case Gosse is not alone: a number of more recent (and more rigorous) critics have taken a broadly similar view.[205] And certain hints in the poem already offer support for such a context. The first stanza refers to 'the King's ... face'. Like 'The Sun Rising', with its glance at James I's notorious love of hunting, it must therefore date from late 1603 or after (but could plausibly be seen as composed early in James' time – hence the eagerness to see his still novel face). Additionally, there is Donne's admission of 'ruined fortune' – a state about which we are all too certain. Without being over-confident, we can say that a date not many months after the marriage – when love was still fresh, but the extent of damage was now forcefully clear – would be a plausible inference.

It seems very likely that all three poems postdate Donne's meeting with Ann More, if not his marriage to her (two clearly do). Seen in this context, the brusque demand 'who's injured by my love?' looks grimly ironic. We know that Donne and his wife were injured most seriously, but can also detect a deliberate glance at the excessive punishments visited on him by the unreasonably 'injured' More and Egerton. Does it matter that Donne is writing in the aftermath of his disastrous marriage? At one level, it does if we reconsider our opening question. We might now say that Donne clearly loved Ann More enough to write a poem like this one. In a letter of 1614 he stresses that he must not deny his wife company. When he adds, 'we had not one another at so cheap a rate, as that we should ever be weary of one another', he implies that his love has grown all the more stubbornly powerful because of the hardship it has brought.[206] Again, telling Goodyer of recently dark moods, he suddenly fears that 'if I melt into a melancholy whilst I write, I shall be taken in the manner' and therefore give 'sad apprehensions' to Ann ('one too tender towards these impressions') as she sits besides him.[207] Even such hints as this must be included in the admittedly fragmentary picture of Donne's marriage now left to us.

But the most important reason for situating 'The Canonization' in this way is that we cannot fully understand it otherwise. Donne has experienced a kind of social death, as he implies in his sardonic 'we can die by it, if not live by love'. The defiant retreat he then describes is therefore not simply imagined. It is a response to a social and personal catastrophe now hard to conceive. We would be naive and misguided to imagine that Donne manages to transmute his bleak condition purely through a romantic feeling for his wife. That feeling *was* evidently strong enough to inspire the reckless behaviour of late

1601 - although excessive self-confidence and ambition should also be considered. But ultimately the diverse colours and textures of this poem hold together so well just because they are riveted by a tough (indeed, immortal) skeleton which is essentially religious. And, notwithstanding the implied jokes and irony, it is important that the religion in question is Catholicism. As we have seen, the derisive and detached persona of the Elegies and Satires was in part a product of Donne's alienated and dangerous religion. Without attempting to fully analyse his state of mind after 1603, we can confidently suggest that he may have been all the more angry and ambivalent to have found himself still socially marginalised, despite the apostasy that should have let him in to the centre of his society. It is appropriate, then, that he draws in part on Catholicism for his oblique revenge. While this is obvious enough in the implication of two 'saintly' lovers, what is perhaps yet more telling is the subtle, perhaps even unconscious, Catholicism of the piece. Donne's abandoned faith was one which invested small objects (saintly relics, religious icons, rosary beads) with immense spiritual potency. Equally, 'The Canonization' offers a highly-charged, religiously potent space (the 'pretty rooms' or 'well wrought urn') which effectively bounds infinity in a nutshell.

In one vital sense 'The Canonization' is more extraordinary than its companion pieces, in that it so openly signals Donne's bleak situation, and so convincingly transforms and transcends it. What may at first seem an apt shrinkage and a loss of those wider spaces and forces (the Indias, the sun) which vitally energised and opened the other poems of mutual love, is in fact a deft movement between dimensions. Like saints, the lovers exchange the perishable space of this world for the flawless reaches of eternity. Not only that, but for all future time on earth, they stand as an ideal of perfect mutual harmony. At one level, the poem triumphs over space by distilling into it a vibrant personal force. Such power might well seem to risk exploding in these dangerously constricted limits. But at another level Donne defuses this perilous energy, at once retaining the richly-compressed private spaces of literature, and sweeping out into the vastness of future time. And it is perhaps the poem's remarkable combination of two forms of psychic space which has been least appreciated. One of the most distinctive things about human life is its ability to substantially defy the usually very tight limits in which it is lived. Compacted within the lobes of the brain, and animated by the murmur of blood and chemicals, are expanses which can send us forgetfully tumbling out of ourselves, and memories which can overpower us with almost physical force. All this was sufficiently compelling to make John Milton (also writing in harsh and constricted circumstances) lament, with apparently genuine feeling, the potential loss of 'those thoughts that wander through eternity'.[208] As Donne himself put it, 'our thoughts are born giants: that reach from east to west, from earth to Heaven, that ... span the sun and firmament at once ... reach all, comprehend all'.[209]

These three poems do seem to effectively confer on women a certain privilege. In the end it is very difficult to say how much. But what power they are afforded is, again, the power to grant stability. In 'A Valediction: Forbidding Mourning' Donne's mistress (or, possibly, wife) is the stable central point of a pair of compasses.[210] If we might be tempted to see her position as tellingly inert and restricted, we should note that Donne elsewhere compares that mathematical 'point' which 'cannot be divided, cannot be moved' with 'the centre ... God himself ... indivisible' and 'immovable'.[211] Where friendship was Donne's 'second religion', love at times seems to be his third. Both, at certain moments, offer him a privileged space in which he can defy 'so momentary a thing as time' and balance himself nimbly on a degraded world as it looks up at him in awe. Again, we perhaps need to recognise that the power of these poems does not belong to women alone, but to love, that 'neutral' thing. We must also bear in mind that we can never quite know how much that love was itself a peculiar creation of Donne's restless and oppressed mind. What we can say is that he felt its worth all the more strongly as he sought to carve himself out a stable and sufficient space not simply on a tiny scrap of land, but in a certain sense from nothing and nowhere (he did not have a recognised social position fit for his abilities and graces).

These poems of defiant intimacy imply a kind of personal psychic economy. That is, Donne can draw closer to a woman in whom he has invested immense resources just *because* the social forces ranged against him now offer another means of self-defining opposition. To put this a little differently: we can claim that even if Donne had not suffered the disaster of his marriage, his emotional ties would have still been marked by the kind of fierce rigour which permeated his mental and spiritual being. We could then partly reconcile the undoubted misogyny of many poems with these more balanced visions of love. For all of Donne's lovers, whether abused or elevated, imply an insistent determination to settle only for the most remarkable, most unmistakably personalised and all-pervading union, felt in heart, brain and guts. This fiercely personal emotion necessarily makes it hard to be sure how much Donne is writing about love, and how much about himself. What we can say is that, in keeping with the religious overtones of Donne's most positive amorous poems, such passion is finally rooted in the immortal Christian soul. It is this strange and elusive entity which we must try to recover in the following two chapters.

Chapter Four

Belief and Sin

> Amorous soul, ambitious soul, covetous soul,
> voluptuous soul, what wouldest thou have in heaven?[212]

I

It is a cold Thursday morning in the Renaissance and you are about to die. Although you are young and healthy, and slept soundly all night, you know as you stand transfixed at your bedroom window that you will be dead very soon. Why? Because the sky is dark, yet also weirdly glowing, filled with a massive whispering rush of wings and the muscular bodies of angels. The graveyard to the right of your house is a chaotic jumble of ruptured turf, fallen gravestones, and of naked men, women and children whose new bodies all look immaculately sound and undamaged.[213] The Day of Judgement has come. Presently the world will burn, and time will cease. Needless to say, at such a moment there is no question of running to one's family and friends, telling them tearfully how much one has loved them. Rather, as automatically as someone ducking gunfire, you fall to your knees and pray, rapidly and ceaselessly, soon drenched in sweat on this cold surprising morning.

We now know that this never happened, either in Donne's lifetime or the centuries to follow. But, as Hamlet rightly noted, the readiness is all. And so, evidently, thought Donne. In a letter from Mitcham to his friend Thomas Lucy, he remarked that 'I would every day provide for my soul's last convoy, though I know not when I shall die ...'. Indeed, he then adds, 'and perchance I shall never die'.[214] 'Perchance I shall *never* die'. What can this mean? At the broadest level, it refers to Christian beliefs concerning the close of worldly time. As we have just seen, all human bodies would finally be resurrected at the end of the world. The damned would have bodies to experience fully the unimaginable agonies of eternal punishment, and the blessed would have a kind of indestructible, exalted flesh during their eternity in heaven. (In the former case, the Medieval theologian Thomas Aquinas had taken pains to prove that amputees would recover all their limbs in order to combust satisfactorily forever.) It is impossible to overstate the importance, to Donne, of this emphatically physical resurrection. Although, in typically theological style, the new body is at once 'the same and not the same' as the old, it is repeatedly clear that such corporeality is central to Donne's idea of heaven. His favourite theological authority, St Augustine, had indeed speculated on the physical details of the resurrection with tellingly scientific rigour:

> Will aborted fetuses rise? Will Siamese twins be two people or one in the resurrection? Will we all be the same sex in heaven? ... Will we have to eat? Will deformities and mutilations appear in heaven? Will nail and hair clippings all return to the body to which they originally belonged? Will men have beards in their resurrected bodies?[215]

But the resurrection, like death itself, could not be predicted. It might happen the next day, the next minute, or several centuries after one's flesh had crumbled from the bones, and one's dust soaked back into the soil.

Not only was this resurrection emphatically corporeal, but the whole process of it (the practical mechanics, we might say) was meticulously defined by theologians. Some bodies would have disintegrated within their graves, and be reconstituted from this altered but still limited organic material. Others would have not only decayed but been dispersed as dust, swept away by the wind, dissolved in the sea - perhaps even eaten by animals. This required a different kind of resurrection, but was of course no obstacle to the omnipotent God. When Donne speculated that 'perchance I shall never die', he was evidently referring to another (seemingly paradoxical) kind of resurrection: namely, that of those who were still *alive* on the Day of Judgment. He might, he imagines, in fact be among those yet on earth when this epic finale of all history is staged. As indicated, the sublime artistic achievements of Renaissance Christianity are well rivalled by that imagined apocalypse. The entire cosmos would burn. Angels would call across the universe, 'Surgite mortui!' ('Arise, ye dead!'), and the dead, though they could 'hear not thunder, nor feel ... an earth-quake', would quite literally hear these angelic reverberations and come thronging in a sudden wild swarm back through the turf:

> At the round earth's imagined corners, blow
> Your trumpets, angels, and arise, arise
> From death, you numberless infinities
> Of souls, and to your scattered bodies go
>
> (*Holy Sonnet* 7)[216]

Strictly, Donne and all other remaining humans would actually die at this point. But to be fair this seems to have been more a kind of token marker of the change from one world to the next. As he explains, 'we who are then alive ... will have a present dissolution of body and soul, and that is truly a death, and a present redintegration [*sic*] of the same body and the same soul, and that is truly a resurrection'. However, 'we shall die, and be alive again, before another could consider that we were dead'.[217] This kind of point is echoed a few decades later, when Sir Thomas Browne observes that 'some graves will be opened before they be quite closed'.[218]

The Renaissance heaven, then, was as solid and precise as the religion which would ideally lead one to it. We will learn more of it, and of the psychology underlying Donne's wish to 'never die', in chapter seven. What, though, of Christianity as experienced on earth? This too seems to have been a surprisingly robust entity. If we compare Renaissance Christianity with that of the Victorian era (a time when religion was far less secure, yet still dominated the lives of millions), we find that the former was much tougher, and better able to comprehend a range of practices and expressions than a faith whose chief qualities seem to have been prohibition and repression. In 'The Flea' we saw Donne punning on the Christian trinity ('sacrilege, three sins in killing three'), and in elegy 19 he explains how we know female 'angels from an evil sprite' because 'those set our hairs, but these our flesh upright' (ll. 23-4).[219] Although he was probably embarrassed about this in later life, these and other religious jokes are perfectly consistent with fervent piety. Indeed, jokes as a rule tend to encode certain basic cultural assumptions. Accordingly, Donne's seemingly irreverent witticisms are a sign of how pervasive, adaptable and readily understandable religious thinking was – the living cultural vocabulary, we might say, of his times. Moreover, the religious language of formal devotion itself has a vein of sensuality which later centuries would have found unacceptable. 'Christ Jesus', Donne tells us, 'lies between the breasts of his Church, and gives suck on both sides.' Similarly, 'we are bound to suck at those breasts which God puts out to us'.[220] Though no doubt also influenced by a similar nostalgia to T.S. Eliot, W.B. Yeats seemed to catch something of this robust and inclusive faith when he said that Donne's 'pedantry and obscenity' were 'the rock and the loam of his Eden' – the signs of a surer, weightier piety which convinced Yeats that 'one who is but a man like us all has seen God'.[221]

And we have, of course, already stumbled upon the strange elasticity of Renaissance Christianity, during our brief view of St Paul's church in chapter one. For most Victorians the rough secular traffic jostling under those sacred walls would have been blasphemy beyond imagining. Elizabethans or Jacobeans might have answered that the church was only the body of faith; the word of God, by contrast, was its essential soul. This impression is borne out by the immense popularity of sermons in Renaissance England. Thus Donne refers to how many will eagerly 'thrust to fore-noon's, and afternoon's sermons'.[222] Perhaps most memorably, in 1623 the crowd which thrust to Lincoln's Inn chapel to hear Donne himself preach was so great that auditors risked being crushed to death, and at least two or three seem to have fainted.[223] We might say, then, that the Victorians and later generations had inherited something like the fragile skeleton of Renaissance religious culture. The flesh, nerve, muscle and skin that had given it feeling, power, and the beauty of living surface texture had long ago rotted away, and the nineteenth century was obliged to worship its sad idol with something of the false hush of visitors to a museum. In what follows I will try to flesh out that skeleton. This is a difficult task in a relatively short space, and readers wanting further detail are strongly urged to look at whole books devoted to the subject.[224]

In any modern attempt to recover the general and particular force of Renaissance religious belief and behaviour, a certain distortion is unavoidable. Asserting that these people were essentially made of Christianity, we may still feel that they could have apprehended some other kind of identity. Probably very few could. And yet, much of the devotional writing left to us by Donne is often marked by that peculiar psychology of one who had – albeit in a harshly ironic way – experienced a certain choice and a certain consequent relativism. This chapter looks first at signs of a continuing instability and ambiguity resulting from Donne's chequered religious history. Secondly, it shows how pervasive and influential sin was as a state of mind. Thirdly, it explores the Protestant theology which not only encouraged, but actively enforced, such minutely introspective faith, and suggests that Donne's own sense of sin and spiritual interiority were in many ways emphatically Protestant. Fourthly and finally, it examines some of Donne's most forceful and material images of sin, chiefly in the set of devotional poems known as the *Holy Sonnets*. That collection, I will argue, offers us a complex dramatisation of Donne's dualistic religious allegiance, his persistent insecurity, and his mutable, elusive sense of self.

II

In 1619 Donne sent a copy of *Biathanatos*, his unorthodox defence of suicide, to his friend Sir Robert Ker. Here Donne not only distanced himself from his book of the previous decade, but also intriguingly divided the self of 1619 from that of the years before ordination, explaining that *Biathanatos* was 'a book written by Jack Donne, and not by Dr. Donne'.[225] The convenient split between two unequal halves of a life presented as broadly secular and as emphatically sacred was initially to prove attractive to critics attempting to structure Donne's biography and literary output. As later commentators were to realise, the split was too convenient and too absolute to be true. Donne of course did change, as almost all people do across the span of a lifetime. But in many ways the changes were ones of degree, not of kind. For Donne, the problem was just that the older identity *could not* be fully shut out of the present. What the letter offers us is not so much a simple biographical outline, as a careful and necessary self-reconstruction. Having stepped out of and away from the doubtful skin of Jack Donne, the doctor could, in theory, distance himself from various facets of his life before 1615. This is not to say that Donne was *consciously* reinventing himself. On the contrary, he was probably motivated by a strong and integral need to feel that he was now a genuinely different person.

One particular aspect of his past which we can imagine Donne wishing to banish was Catholicism. But his relation to it in his later lifetime appears to have been both tenacious and ambiguous. 'You know I never fettered nor immured the word Religion', he tells Goodyer (in a frustratingly undated letter), 'not straitening it friarly ... nor immuring it in a Rome, or a Wittenberg, or a Geneva.' These different churches, he explains, 'are all virtual beams of one sun, and wheresoever they find clay hearts, they harden them and moulder them into dust; and they entender and mollify waxen ... Religion is Christianity, which being too spiritual to be seen by us, doth therefore take an apparent body of good life and works.'[226] It is almost certainly significant that the explicit and coded admissions of these lines are made only to Goodyer, Donne's closest and presumably most trustworthy friend. The opening phrase implies that the different doctrinal laws of Catholicism, and Lutheran or Calvinist Protestantism ('Rome ... Wittenberg ... Geneva') in fact constrain and limit religion – perhaps indeed obscure the beams of the ultimate 'sun' which over-rules all these earthly variants. The claim would have been startling to the fervent Protestants who heard Dr Donne, week after week and year after year, insisting that Protestantism was the only acceptable form of Christianity.[227] But its implications are finally sincere. Donne's own experience of religious divisions had indeed been a restrictive and harsh one. The image of imprisonment and oppression ('fettered') is, then, consistent with the secretive and outlawed religion in which he was first raised. Secondly, the belief that all these various forms of Christianity can do equal good is an implicit validation of a personal character fundamentally constituted by its Roman Catholic upbringing, and later forced to deny it. And finally, the transcendent 'religion ... too spiritual to be seen by us' is not only conveniently distant, authoritative and secure, but remarkably akin to the rarefied, extra-mundane worlds of love or friendship blown like fine glass from the mind of Jack Donne.

This inclusive view of Christian faiths is certainly open to attack. We could, for example, view it as a slippery refusal to fully confront and deny Catholicism. And that, we might feel, is inconsistent with that temperamental rigour so influential in Donne's life and work. If we look a little more closely, however, we can see here a different *kind* of rigour. Donne's negotiations are in fact an attempt to preserve a holistic version of himself. Quite simply, youth and Catholicism had come first. Donne was made of them – not entirely or unchangeably, but at a certain ultimate and indestructible level. And so we find the careful religious and personal negotiation between Rome and Wittenberg, Catholicism and Protestantism, recurring in various ways in his letters. Perhaps most tellingly, he observes to a friend that, 'it is sin to do against the conscience, though that err'; returning to this issue when he tells the Marquess of Buckingham that his library has more Spanish books than any others.[228] 'Their authors in divinity', he explains, 'though they do not show us the best way to heaven, yet they think they do. And so, though they say not true, yet they do not lie, because they speak their conscience.'[229] Interestingly, Donne seems here to use a very Protestant ethic (the value of the individual conscience) to defend individual Catholic believers, in spite of their general doctrinal error.

Elsewhere we find him implicitly admiring Catholicism even as he seems to deride it. 'French papistry', he observes in a letter of 1612, 'is but like French velvet – a pretty slack religion, that would soon wear out, and not of the three-piled papistry of Italy and Spain.'[230] On the surface we meet here a predictable contempt for the notoriously luxurious and worldly qualities of those latter two Catholic nations (supposedly the most decadent, and undoubtedly the most powerful in the world). Yet beneath this there is a grudging respect for the solidity and substance of Roman and Spanish faith. Such a feeling would be consistent with Donne's deep-seated attraction toward emotional and spiritual states characterised by density, system and resilience. Whatever faults Italy and Spain may have, they – unlike France, and the frustrated exile of *Biathanatos* – know precisely *who* they are. One cannot easily say the same of the nominally Protestant preacher, born and raised a Catholic, who stated to his friend Sir Robert Ker that, 'My tenets are always for the preservation of the religion I was born in.'[231]

Yet if Donne did not always know absolutely who he was, he seems to have made his momentous entry into the Anglican ministry in good faith. Back in 1607 he had turned down an invitation to this profession. That refusal was made in the dark era of *Biathanatos*, and some months before he had received his wife's long-withheld dowry from George More. Why? We cannot be finally certain, but the answer given by Izaak Walton seems plausible. While Donne felt personally that he had sufficiently banished the sins of his youth, he could not be sure that society felt the same, and that he would not therefore dishonour the church by his association with it.[232] Donne's son (also John) claimed that his father's *Essays in Divinity* were written especially 'as debates betwixt God and himself, whether he were worthy ... to enter into Holy Orders'.[233] This process of externalising his doubts (and, we might say, of 'talking' to God) may well have helped Donne reach his final decision. And perhaps by late 1614, when he finally agreed to enter the Church, he felt that the tainted social memories of his past had faded. Perhaps, equally, he felt that he owed himself, his wife, and his children the relief of a secure – and definite – position after a further seven years in the wilderness. Whatever the case, it hardly seems unreasonable to claim that Donne *consciously* felt sincere about his decision of

1614, while having been actually or partially motivated by the persistent starkness of his personal life.[234]

Donne would have been sharply aware that his religious motivations, decisions and feelings could easily have been sinful in themselves. Our present interest in the link between apostasy and belief is a little different. Did his ambiguous – partly voluntary, partly forced – movement across two violently opposed Churches ultimately cause Donne to regard not just earthly religion, but *all* religion, with an underlying doubt? This does not mean that he did not believe in Christianity. Rather, it means that his piety was shot through with stubborn veins of uncertainty or relativism which continually make themselves felt in the distinctive qualities of his religious writing. To T.S. Eliot, this made Donne 'dangerous' (at least by comparison with his fellow preacher, Lancelot Andrewes).[235] To us, it makes him more sympathetic, richer, and dynamic. Preaching at Whitehall, Donne recounted the tale of a French Protestant who had effectively sold himself to the Roman church for a pension of three hundred crowns a year. The story gives an uneasy echo of Donne's own changes of faith and of fortune. This French convert, being asked, 'Sir, which is the best religion, you must needs know, that hath been of both?' answered, 'Certainly, the religion I left, the reformed religion, must needs be the best religion, for when I changed, I had this religion, the Roman religion, for it, and three hundred crowns a year to boot.' No doubt Donne took his own change of allegiance more seriously. But his use of the tale is personally revealing, nonetheless. For he further adds his fear that such men come to look sceptically on either of the chief Christian faiths, falling into 'a nullity, or indifferency to either religion', rather than 'a true, and established zeal'.[236] Had this happened to Donne? To put it a little differently: was his clearly genuine piety distinctively shaped and animated by his apostasy? While he could hardly be accused of 'nullity', his persistent restlessness and mobile energy could well be seen as the lack of an *established* zeal' – one absolutely definite and fixed spiritual anchorage.

The Protestant Reformation as a whole appears with hindsight to have been ultimately responsible for undermining the absolute authority of Christianity.[237] What was it like, then, to live out that broader crisis in the space of one mind and one lifetime? Having heard that Goodyer's religious faith has been impugned, Donne admits in a letter on the subject that 'this I have feared, because heretofore the inobedient Puritans, and now the over-obedient Papists, attempt you.' He goes on to explain that it is best to keep to one form of religion if possible, even though another form is acceptable for others: 'You shall seldom see a coin, upon which the stamp were removed, though to imprint it better, but it looks awry and squint. And so, for the most part, do minds which have received divers impressions.'[238] Is Donne in fact writing to him*self* as much as to his friend? The following pages should help us to decide.

III

Among the various features of Renaissance Christianity long since diluted or wholly evaporated, sin is one of the most important and central. For Donne and his peers sin was not an occasional accident or a vice of the irrecoverably wicked. It was a way of life: 'we sin constantly, and we sin continually, and we sin confidently, and we find so much pleasure and profit in sin, as that we have made a league, and sworn a friendship with sin.'[239] There is, Donne tells his audience, 'nothing else but sin in us: sin hath not only a place, but a palace, a throne, not only a being, but a dominion, even in our best actions.'[240] If Renaissance religious belief in general often appears to us to have the systematic force and reach of modern science, there appears equally to be a whole science and taxonomy of sin and sinners. Donne identifies one kind of soul which is 'scattered upon the daily practice of any one predominant, and habitual sin', and another 'indifferently scattered upon all'. This latter 'swallows sins in the world, as he would do meats at a feast ... baits at every sin that rises, and pours himself into every sinful mould he meets'.[241] Notice that the second kind of sinner looks remarkably like that contemptible fop of the Satires - someone whose instability and lack of gravity caused him to be exhaled 'like light dew'. Similarly, that man who 'in the compass of a few days ... neighs like a horse in the rage of his lust over all the city', and presently 'groans in a corner of the city, in an hospital' is 'as many men, as he hath vices'.[242] So we already perceive that sin, in keeping with the term 'dissipation', can imply a certain rootless, chameleon dispersal of an identity which ideally should be firmly anchored and centred within the individual. Yet if these sins of the energetic social voluptuary may especially repel one side of Donne, they are by no means the only snare to be feared. Even 'in our age, in our sickness, in any impotency towards a sin, in any satiety of a sin, we turn from our sin, but we turn not to God; we turn to a sinful delight in the memory of our sins'.[243] St Paul, Donne notes, 'calls ... sins the members of our bodies, as though we were elemented and compacted of nothing but sin'.[244] At times the Renaissance Christian appears to be eating and drinking sin, to be stumbling and fighting their way through it, to be breathing and dreaming sin, as if the very air were humming with those legions of invisible demons in which many people still believed.[245]

One vital facet of this habitual and incurable human condition was its influence on the self. In chapter two we examined how Donne's self functioned in certain literary creations. But this is how the self looks to us, peering back through a powerful telescope across oceans of cultural distance. Sin, by contrast, is how the self frequently *felt* to Donne and many contemporaries. 'Self-love', Donne explains, 'cannot be called a distinct sin, but the root of all sin ... To love our selves, to be satisfied in our selves, to find an omni-sufficiency in our selves, is an intrusion, an usurpation upon God.'[246] We can, then, only fully understand the Christian self if we see it as stranded within a complex web of very serious and very meaningful human errors. To us, the sins in question often look bewilderingly minute and subtle. In a relatively early letter which confirms that Donne's notions of sin were far from purely public or superficial, he reflects on the difficulty of telling right from wrong:

> so the devil doth not only suffer but provoke us to some things naturally good, upon condition that we shall omit some other more necessary and more obligatory. And this is his greatest subtlety, because herein we have the deceitful comfort of having done well, and can very

hardly spy our error because it is but an insensible omission and no accusing act.[247]

Even the fervent believer, it would seem, treads a narrow, uncertain path through a kind of psychic minefield, where the most nebulous and slightly nuanced signs mask hidden dangers of colossal magnitude. What is one to do in this terrifying labyrinth, overlooked by a mysterious God who may almost appear to have a warped sense of humour? We find Donne consoling himself that 'if I do not adhere to this enemy [Death], dwell upon a delightful meditation of that sin, if I do not fuel, and foment that sin, by high diet, wanton discourse, other provocation, I shall have reason on my side, and I shall have grace on my side'.[248]

Yet, as the coupling of 'reason' and 'grace' implies, correction and salvation are far from being purely a matter of a good heart, overflowing with rawly emotive zeal for truth and piety. Rather, as T.S. Eliot rightly intuited in his notion of Donne's sensuous intellect, the heart itself must be moulded and cleansed by the painstaking attention of a cautious mind. Indeed, for many Christians at this time, mere mention of the heart could evoke the popular biblical text, Jeremiah 17.19. 'The heart of man', we are told, 'is deceitful and wicked above all things, who can know it?' Accordingly, 'while the body sometimes grows weary of acting some sin', the heart, Donne warns, 'never grows weary of contriving sin'.[249] As his fellow preacher Anthony Maxey put it in 1605, 'there are not more windings, nor more turnings in a maze, or in a labyrinth, than are in the heart of man'.[250] 'So must he that affects this pureness of heart', Donne explains, 'sweep down every cobweb that hangs about it. Scurrile and obscene language; yea, misinterpretable words ... pleasurable conversation, and all such little entanglings, which though he think too weak to hold him, yet they foul him.' The vigilant believer must 'remember, that as a spider builds always where ... there is most access and haunt of flies, so the devil that hath cast these light cobwebs into thy heart, knows that that heart is made of vanities and levities.'

While the weight of sin undoubtedly varies, it can also be gradually built up of small cumulative errors: 'as many lascivious glances as shall make up an adultery, as many covetous wishes as shall make up a robbery, as many angry words as shall make up a murder; and thou shalt hath dropt and crumbled away thy soul, with as much irrecoverableness, as if thou hadst poured it out all at once.'[251] Here we encounter a self whose interior spaces are not so much a private refuge, as an obscure breeding ground for the fertile vermin of sin. We glimpse, too, something of the surprising materiality of the soul, precisely 'crumbled away'. And yet, ironically, the positive aspect of the Christian soul was – like God and heaven – largely invisible during this life. Its outline and character could be gauged most effectively by negative indices, as if the thorns of sin showed up drops of blood when they punctured an otherwise imperceptible entity.

Within this obsessive science of sin, the skill required to analyse human wickedness in microscopically fine detail can hardly be overestimated. Donne's sometime contemporary, Edward Reynolds (like Donne, a preacher to Lincoln's Inn), wished earnestly that 'every man would single out some notable sins of his life, and in this manner anatomise them, and see how many sins one sin containeth, even as one flower many leaves, and one pomegranate many kernels'. The image of the densely packed seeds of the pomegranate in particular, suddenly revealed within what had previously appeared just one compact unit, gives a sense of neurotically obsessive partition and multiplication. Reynolds himself reflects that this 'could not but be a notable means of humbling us for sin'. We, by contrast, may feel that it implies a kind of morbid fascination, tinged with more than a hint of self-absorption.[252] A further reaction on our part might be a certain bewildered irritation. We can, admittedly, perceive recognisable variations of this obsessive self-monitoring and self-control in our own culture. At one extreme anorexia or bulimia show a similar pattern of repetitive and negative personal definition. More commonly, an obsession with physical fitness appears to play an equally central role in many lives. But the crucial difference is that such behaviour is not overtly believed to have serious and widespread ethical implications. In ethical terms, Renaissance ideas of sin often look frustratingly trivial or impractical. Numerous sins appear to have no measurable effect upon anyone save the individual in question.

There are two broad answers to this. First: considering such issues from a relatively detached, agnostic perspective, what we realise is that sin is a remarkably effective way of making sense of the world, and one's own relation to it. It cannot be too heavily stressed that, for Donne and many others like him, a sense of the possibility of a sin was a habitual automatic reflex, continually moulding, colouring and sectioning one's feelings, memories, and sensations, minute after minute and day after day. One felt depressed ('melancholy', to use the popular seventeenth-century term). Why? Because one had somehow temporarily distanced oneself from God. One was sick; one's children died. Why? Because – as everyone knew – humanity was intrinsically sinful. Sin and death were generally the result of original sin in Eden, and particularly of individual sins in one's own life. One should, indeed, be thankful for one's own non-fatal illnesses (what Donne at one point calls 'the advantage of sickness'), which were God's way of correcting and warning the wayward believer.[253] So, if Christianity did not often make the everyday world materially better, it did explain why it was so bad, as well as promising that the next could be far superior.

Secondly, the mysterious ethical stance of the obsessive sinner can also be clarified if we move within the distinctive theological world of Donne and his peers. Was the whole economy of sin and repentance quite so limited and sterile as it appears? To such criticisms Donne would have explained that sin was committed not simply against one's fellow men and women, but – ultimately and fundamentally – against God and Christ. An especially difficult concept for many of us to truly grasp now is not just that Christ had died for sin, but that sinners were perpetually crucifying him again and again by their current strayings from God. The notion can be seen vividly in the context of swearing. To blaspheme, in this period, one merely had to utter the word 'God' or 'Christ' in any manner or situation that was not accepted as religious. So Donne hopes that 'those angels ... when they look down hither' will not see Christ 'scourged again, wounded, torn and mangled again, in thy blaspheming, nor crucified again in thy irreligious conversation'.[254] With still more excruciating physical precision Donne warns the swearer that Christ

> is come into thy mouth, to thy tongue; but he is come thither as a diseased person is taken into a spittle to have his blood drawn, to have his flesh cauterised, to have his bones sawed; Christ Jesus is in thy mouth, but in such execrations, in such blasphemies, as would be earthquakes to us if we were earth.[255]

Here we encounter most forcefully the material power and knotty substance of Renaissance language, and of sacred language in particular. And, again, we encounter the material reality and weight of sins which now have no ethical consequence for many of us.

Yet for Donne and many others sin was a matter of intense personal drama. Vast quantities of rigorously-channelled mental energy were expended in the fear, the identification, and the repentance of sin. The whole process was relentlessly active and precariously unstable. As Michel Foucault has emphasised, people's involvement in seemingly oppressive power relations is in fact often sustained by a degree of reciprocity – the conscious or unconscious sense that one gains at least some limited power in subordinating oneself to the laws of a greater system.[256] If we transfer this theory to the realm of Renaissance belief, we might say that the seemingly sterile habits of religious self-policing cherished by so many afforded a certain psychological empowerment. Without sin, after all, the soul would have nothing to do. In Donne's own words: just as 'salt preserves flesh, so temptations preserve the soul; not the sinning, but the discerning that it is, nay that it was a temptation to sin, preserves the soul'.[257] Sins, then, can be partly positive if one is at least able to recognise them. Looking at the issue in broader, sociological terms, we can further argue that the restless activity of self-inspection and purification gave a cathartic outlet for energies which could not easily be applied to more practical methods of mending human suffering. Even had they wished to, few people could engage in politics in any effective way to relieve poverty, and probably still fewer could make serious progress in medicine or other sciences. Ultimately, though, we need to view the issue of sin not just personally, or socially, but from a theological point of view. So far, we have examined the outer skin of Protestant religious behaviour. If we now cut down to the basic doctrinal skeleton of the reformed faith, we can fully understand just why its adherents were so minutely fascinated with their inner lives.

IV

For many Protestants, the active self-government witnessed in Donne's writings helped to create a religious self which felt at least relatively secure. So Donne can claim that 'some man may be chaster in the stews, than another in the Church; and some man will sin more in his dreams, than another in his discourse'.[258] That belief in particular alerts us to an important point: sin was a question of who one *was*, and how one felt, as much as what one did. We can begin to see, then, that sin was indeed often doing something positive for those who felt they could make headway against its pervasive tidal forces. It was an integral component in the definition of Christian identity. By the late 1590s, Donne's nominal religious identity was that of a Protestant. In the present context, three elements of Protestant theology are especially relevant. First, at the most visible and tangible everyday level, the reformed Church had stripped away or diluted numerous Catholic habits, ceremonies, and artefacts. A nervous believer could no longer have the comfort of telling rosary beads in their fingers, or repeating an exact number of 'Hail Marys' as a reliably mathematical cure for a particular sin.[259] The Catholic theory of the mass insisted that the blessed bread and wine were *literally* Christ's blood and body, and thus had somehow undergone a magical transformation in the presence of the faithful. Protestantism replaced the Catholic idea of 'transubstantiation' with the essentially dilute notion of 'consubstantiation'. This view held that the body and blood were already present, and so reduced the magical or miraculous qualities of the ritual (as well as the power of the priest). We cannot quite say that Jesus had been brutally snatched from the very mouths of the faithful. But it may well have felt to some that they lost a dynamically vibrant, supernaturally immediate version of religious communion.[260] Moreover, the loss of these kinds of mediation was aggravated by the further loss of the human agents who occupied such a rigid and detailed hierarchy within the Roman Church. Although the new religion was far from democratic in its official structure, it had shifted a considerable weight of spiritual responsibility onto the shoulders and into the heart of the lone Protestant individual. A Catholic priest had effectively taken responsibility for one's confession of sin, and as indicated dished out simple penances which to many probably had the efficacy of clinically-tested medicine. We can already guess that by contrast with the tightly-organised economy of sin, hierarchy and repentance used by the Catholics, Protestant piety was a quite lonely affair.

The second issue is that of salvation. The Catholic dead went either to heaven or hell. Even the saved, however, must first be cleansed of their earthly sins before entry into a blissful afterlife. This occurred in the intermediate zone of temporary (though perhaps prolonged) suffering known, according to its function, as purgatory. The transition from purgatory to heaven could be assisted by the continued prayers of the living, with the rich bequeathing money for extra masses in order to buy their way out more quickly still. (Looking at this admirably businesslike conception of eternal salvation and piety one can begin to understand how pseudo-disciplines such as Business Studies and Management have so successfully taken over the role of Theology in universities.) Protestantism had abolished purgatory. But this was not all: English Protestant theology further insisted that all of humanity was absolutely *predestined* either to heaven or to hell. We find Donne musing on the terrifying uncertainty of this situation in Lent 1629:

> Sad and disconsolate, distorted and distracted soul! ... Intricated, intangled conscience! Christ ... never tells thee of a Judgement therefore, because thy name was written in a dark book of Death, never unclasped, never opened unto thee in thy life. He says unto thee lovingly and indulgently, fear not ... but he never says to the wickedest, in the world, live in fear, die in anxiety, in suspicion, and suspension for his displeasure.[261]

A dark book of Death ... Here was one work of literature that even the formidably erudite Donne could not lay open on his desk. The harshness of Predestination has often been remarked on. How could God have damned a considerable section of humanity (not only before they were born, but before Creation itself) without any precise reason? For a twenty-first century agnostic (and probably for many Christians) there is no longer any easy answer to such a question. What we can say is that this seeming harshness was in a sense just the other side of that fiercely rational and logical faith, now long softened, and sunk from head to heart. For God was, after all, omniscient as well as omnipotent. And so, unpalatable as the idea may be, He would have to have known the fates of all human beings. The idea may be harsh, but it is at least intellectually rigorous.

In theory, Predestination rendered all Christian thoughts and actions – regarding oneself, God, or others – wholly powerless to assist salvation. In practice, Protestants (for all their rigour) felt compelled to escape this intolerably deterministic situation. They did so through the kind of minute and unceasing personal vigilance outlined above, believing that they were looking for previously inscribed signs of grace.[262] And it is this which forms the third distinctive habit of Protestant piety. The believer of the reformed religion did not habitually reach out to priests, to images, to statues of the

Virgin Mary or to Christ, but typically moved *inwards*. Let us try for a moment to gain just an impressionistic sense of this change. Massive quantities of energy, of meaning, of responsibility once diffused through the spatial and temporal framework of the Catholic Church – itself riveted together over fifteen centuries – are now distilled and compressed within the panting heart of a single person. For many of these potentially lone Protestant individuals the Church did still take some of the burden. But it is worth remembering that for the Puritans even that limited help was unacceptable. Small wonder, then, that the zealot who we encountered outside St Paul's should have been drawn and trembling. The miracle, indeed, is that he did not explode.

We now have a clearer idea of why Donne could be more concerned about an individual's inner security than their outer circumstances (why one man could be 'chaster in the stews, than another in the church'). So we find him explaining to Goodyer that

> I have over-fraught myself with vice ... I have much to take in, and much to cast out; sometimes I think it easier to discharge myself of vice than vanity, as one may sooner carry the fire out of a room than the smoke; and then I see it was a new vanity to think so.[263]

Notice how Donne at first hopes that his self-policing will allow him to root out the most dangerous and substantial cause of sin, before realising that it is sinful to even imagine that he could really do so. A few years later we find him turning more positively to divine aid: 'if you be come to this love ... of pureness of heart', then you must be certain 'never to shut your eyes at night, til you have swept your conscience, and cast your foulness into that infinite sea of the blood of Christ Jesus ... never to open your eyes in the morning, but that you look out to glorify God in the rising of the sun.' Again, piety appears more a state of mind and heart – an attitude to the world – than of actions. So Donne recommends that one should remember 'especially to look inward, and consider, whether you have not mingled poison with God's physic ... whether you have not mingled licentiousness in that which God gave you for a remedy against fornication'.[264] Is there a hint of oblique egotism here? God, after all, is omnipotent and omniscient. Accordingly, it could be a little arrogant to imagine that one could so easily deflect and damage His intentions.[265]

Very occasionally, Donne does appear to have a stable, peaceful sense of spiritual intimacy, as when he talks of

That soul, that is accustomed to direct her self to God, upon every occasion, that, as a flower at sun-rising, conceives a sense of God, in every beam of his, and spreads and dilates it self towards him, in a thankfulness, in every small blessing that he sheds upon her; that soul, that as a flower in the sun's declining, contracts and gathers in, and shuts up her self, as though she had received a blow, when soever she hears her saviour wounded by an oath, or blasphemy, or execration.

Notice the gendering of this relationship with an unimaginably powerful and masculine God. That opposition is further developed when Donne goes on to imagine the soul as a musical instrument – one which, 'whatsoever string be strucken in her, base or treble, her high or her low estate, is ever tun'd toward God', and so 'prays sometimes when it does not know that it prays'.[266] In this rare instance Donne imagines how one might successfully naturalise pious habits, and so live religiously with less effort and less fear. Yet even this brief moment of rest is partly countered by the hint of tremulous nervous anticipation in the finely-tuned instrument, submitted to a divine and ultimately mysterious hand.

And more commonly, the once Catholic Donne displays a heightened form of Protestant self-doubt. Snatched out of the old collective piety of Catholicism, the Protestant sinner is stranded alone, centre-stage in an at once personal and cosmic drama, where the audience cannot be seen, and might at any moment watch you vanish forever through a trapdoor without the faintest word of warning. At the most basic level this situation prevents the fervent Christian from ever resting, given the necessity of perpetual repentance for original sin, and perpetual gratitude for Christ's sacrificial cancellation of that initial Fall: 'when I have spent myself to the last farthing, my lungs to the last breath, my wit to the last metaphor, my tongue to the last syllable, I have not paid a farthing of my debt to God.'[267] Secondly, one further needs, as a Protestant, to be continually assured of one's special 'election' to heaven; to feel the ultimate saving grace of God's mercy. One had been predestined. But to where? Heaven, surely? And yet ... The maddening uncertainty of this question was sufficient to cripple some Protestants with a nervous fear that would now be treated as mental illness; and in at least one case with a voluntary self-punishment which almost resulted in death.[268] What was the solution to this? As we will see, it is not easy to feel that Donne finally discovered one which fully satisfied his peculiarly demanding nature. But any action, it seems, was some relief, and Donne was nothing if not active, in his piety as in so much else. The devotional poems known as the *Holy Sonnets* stand as Donne's most intriguing dramatisation of religious anxiety. Before looking at them in detail, this final section aims to show just how forceful their pious emotion was, by comparing it with some of Donne's most emphatically materialising images of faith and sin.

V

In one important sense, the sheer release of devotional speech and writing was itself a vital form of escape from Donne's religious fear:

> Grief brought to numbers cannot be so fierce,
> For he tames it, that fetters it in verse.
>
> ('The Triple Fool')

Whether in the private intimacy (and immediacy) of prayer, or in the act and result of writing, the anxious believer was able to externalise, shape and control the terrifying whirl of emotions which otherwise could spiral into chaos within, seeming greater than the sum of their parts by their sheer disorder and negative energy. These acts also afforded that most basic achievement of all language: they were in every sense a form of articulation. As the influential linguist Ferdinand de Saussure long ago implied, a vital function of writing or speech is the slicing up into manageable parts of an otherwise fluid and amorphous mental medium (the sub-linguistic thought sometimes referred to as 'mentalese').[269]

What could be better suited to such aims than the human body? As chapter five will show, this usually holistic entity was itself now being skilfully and newly cut up in ways which freshly impressed its depth and complexity on the popular imagination. So, Donne and his audience will not 'consider sin here … as a stain, such as Original sin may be, nor as a wound, such as every actual sin may be'. The first is insufficiently three-dimensional, one might infer, and the second lacks intricacy. Rather, Donne envisages sin as 'a burden, a complication, a packing up of many sins, in an habitual practice thereof'.[270] We encounter '*peccatum complicatum*, sin wrapped up in sin, a body of sin'; and 'a complicated, a multiplied, a compact sinner, a body, rather a carcass of many, of all sins, all that have fallen within his reach'.[271] By such images Donne insists on a dense, organic intertwining, whereby sin assumes the structural and functional qualities of the body. Both are indeed habitual, dynamic, and complex problems. And both sin and the body are associated with the impiety of 'inwardness', of

214

cultivating an interior ego which threatens to rival or deny the Almighty. Both are intuited as devious, secretive, immeasurable and worryingly autonomous. But this embodied sin can at least be effectively limited and attacked with relative ease. Just as 'the body of man ... is best understood, and best advanced by dissections, and anatomies, when the hand and knife of the surgeon hath passed upon every part of the body, and laid it open', so 'when the hand and sword of God hath pierced our soul, we are brought to a better knowledge of our selves, than any degree of prosperity would have raised us to'.[272] This strategy of externalising, isolating, and thereby disempowering one's enemy takes a number of forms.[273] In 1623 Donne suffered a near-fatal illness. During his feverish confinement he wrote a series of religious reflections, published, after his recovery, in 1624 as *Devotions upon Emergent Occasions*. At one point in this remarkably intimate and urgent work he asks:

> My God, my God, why is not my soul, as sensible as my body? why hath not my soul these apprehensions, these presages, these changes, those antedates, those jealousies, those suspicions of a sin, as well as my body of a sickness? why is there not always a pulse in my soul, to beat at the approach of tentation to sin?[274]

A pulse in the soul - where the body of sin was at times usefully distanced from the speaker, the notion of the pulsing soul (perhaps genuinely betraying the beating of a sinfully agitated heart) collapses all back into one's own body again. Perhaps nothing could so poignantly convey the mingled intimacy of Donne's relation to God, and his underlying anxiety at the elusive, uncertain character of the human soul. To hope to see it might be too much – but to at least *feel* it, and sense its healthy response to the perils of temptation ...

In that kind of image, Donne effectively remakes the body and its owner in more pious form. As we have seen in the case of God's piercing but corrective sword, such spiritual re-creation can be violent. At times, the ultimate cure for sin genuinely seems to be the destruction, not of some purely metaphorical body, but of oneself. Donne's attraction to such divine violence is subtly ambiguous. It is at once thrilling, terrifying, and – at least potentially – reassuring. So Donne reminds us that God's angels alone are agents of titanic power: 'creatures, that hath not so much of a body as flesh is, as froth is, as vapour ... and yet with a touch they shall moulder a rock into less atoms, than the sand it stands upon.'[275] These strange beings have the same mixture of delicacy and unrelenting power found in Renaissance Christianity itself, shimmering the strings of a harp with one hand and pulverising solid matter with the other. It may well be with a lingering Catholic impulse that Donne attempts to throw them, as comforting mediators, between himself and God. But elsewhere the believer appears stranded alone, a solitary Protestant under the unblinking eye of 'that mighty, that weighty ... God, that blasts a state with a breath, that melts a church with a look, that moulders a world with a touch'.[276] This being, if angered, 'needs no trumpets to call to armies' but will merely 'hiss and whisper' in order to 'dissolve and pour out, attenuate and annihilate the very marrow of thy soul'.[277] Something of this ambiguous and mesmerising power touches the body of the speaker when he 'feels that a fever doth not melt him like snow, but pour him out like lead, like iron, like brass melted in a furnace', and indeed 'doth not only melt him, but calcine him, reduce him to atoms, and to ashes, not to water, but to lime'.[278]

Donne's pious images of corporeality and sickness already impress on us a faith notable for its physical force, energy, mass and – at times – violence. But it is in the nineteen devotional poems known as the *Holy Sonnets* that the drama of faith and doubt is most sharply focussed and most forcefully enacted. These pieces are undoubtedly Donne's best religious verses. The brashly memorable openings of his secular poetry are echoed in lines such as

Death be not proud

What if this present were the world's last night?

Batter my heart, three-person'd God ...[279]

Perhaps most importantly, the *Sonnets'* insecurity and imbalance is their ultimate strength and drive. It is essentially this side of Donne's richly nervous psychology that T.S. Eliot responds to when, in a delightfully quaint comparison, he prefers Donne's fellow preacher, Lancelot Andrewes: 'Donne's sermons ... are certainly known to hundreds who have hardly heard of Andrewes; and they are known precisely for the reasons because of which they are inferior to Andrewes.' To put it another way: Andrewes was more spiritually assured than Donne, and therefore more dull. Or, to listen again to Eliot, Donne 'is the more dangerous' and 'Andrewes ... the more medieval, because he is the more pure'.[280] We need not waste time on the contemptible sleight of hand coded in this notion of 'purity'. What is interesting is the tellingly overcharged word 'dangerous'. It seems fair to say that this is hardly a fit description for a man known only to the minutest fragment of the world's population, then or now. But Donne was dangerous for Eliot, if not for others. This was because he absorbed and covertly wrote out the history of a slowly disintegrating religious worldview. More precisely, Donne's irrepressible individuality clashed, for Eliot, with the Dean's religious faith. Already capable of ruffling the smooth waters of Christian orthodoxy in the sermons, such a quality was naturally the more pronounced in explicitly personalised devotional poetry.

One further aspect of Donne's personality probably also disturbed Eliot. As emphasised above, Donne's shift from Catholicism to Protestantism formed his religious psychology in a lasting and fundamental way. At the most basic structural level the *Holy Sonnets* are riven by the ambivalence of Donne's dual allegiance. Louis L. Martz has demonstrated the close parallel between Donne's identifications with Christ, and the deliberately empathetic and sensuous imaginings encouraged in the meditational exercises of the Jesuits.[281] And so, in poems almost certainly written long after his apostasy, Donne chooses an overtly Catholic literary model. We find this in vivid iconic set pieces such as the 'picture of Christ crucified':

> Tears in his eyes quench the amazing light,
> Blood fills his frowns ...
>
> (*HS* 13)

The precise focus on Christ's eyes and the lines of his brow matches the contemplative focal points traditionally offered to Catholic believers in religious pictures or statues. Again, the imagining of 'this present' as 'the world's last night' suggests a deliberate exercise, focussing an intense piety by the rigorous stripping away of all the normal buffers of a safe worldly routine.[282] The speaker suddenly confronts an abyss in which neither time nor space exist, and steels himself for a leap of faith into this black hole of eternity. More ambiguously, the empathetic vein is rendered with impressive boldness by a poem in which the speaker 'becomes' the crucified Saviour:

> Spit in my face ye Jews, and pierce my side,
> Buffet, and scoff, scourge, and crucify me ...
>
> (*HS* 11)

As noted, this personal identification with Christ is legitimate, at least in Catholic terms. But as in Donne's secular poems, the desire to twist the metaphorical screw a few degrees tighter threatens to leave convention unrecognisable. And, as we will see, the potential egotism of these lines is also suspiciously consistent with the more doubtfully self-centred qualities of the *Holy Sonnets*.

On the surface, that opening is clearly a fine example of the desire for self-directed violence. Yet it is arguably outdone by the most famous poem in the collection:

> Batter my heart, three-personed God; for you
> As yet but knock, breathe, shine, and seek to mend;
> That I may rise, and stand, o'erthrow me, and bend
> Your force, to break, blow, burn, and make me new.
> I, like an usurped town, to another due,
> Labour to admit you, but oh, to no end,
> Reason your viceroy in me, me should defend,
> But is captived, and proves weak or untrue,
> Yet dearly I love you, and would be loved fain,
> But am betrothed unto your enemy,
> Divorce me, untie, or break that knot again,
> Take me to you, imprison me, for I
> Except you enthrall me, never shall be free,
> Nor ever chaste, except you ravish me.
>
> (*HS* 14)

Vaunting Donne's love of paradox in the notion of an imprisoned freedom, this sonnet captures the sense of a soul perpetually besieged by sin, and unable to defend itself without divine aid. As with 'the bracelet of bright hair about the bone',

221

the first line literally batters the reader under a deftly alternated run of plosive and aspirant stresses, pursuing this with the desire for God to 'break, blow, burn'.[283] Yet the most startling plea for violence is that of the final couplet. The metaphor of love and marriage culminates in a curious desire to be not just filled with God, but raped.[284]

The gender implications of this remarkable image will be considered in a few moments. Let us look firstly at the general violence of the piece. Why does Donne so actively solicit this? A clue is offered in the first of the *Sonnets*:

> Thou hast made me, and shall thy work decay?
> Repair me now, for now mine end doth haste,
> I run to death, and death meets me as fast ...

Tempted by 'our old subtle foe', the speaker warns that 'not one hour I can myself sustain', unless

> Thy Grace may wing me to prevent his art,
> And thou like adamant draw mine iron heart.

The poet's emphasis on the world, flesh and devil as all naturally weighing him down toward hell suggest that 'wing' should mean 'give wings to': God will assist him in the difficult flight upwards. Yet if anyone could succeed in fusing that sense with the 'necessary violence' of being 'winged' like a shot bird, it would be Donne. And the paradox of a corrective wounding would certainly match not just sonnet 14 but numerous moments in other poems and prose. As John Stachniewski has noted, this poem 'attempts to enact ... the conversion process described by [Donne's contemporary] William Perkins: "he that will believe in Christ must be annihilated, that is he must be bruised and battered to a flat nothing.""[285]

The *Holy Sonnets* present us, then, with an implicit preference for one form of violence over another. It is better to be battered, ravished, buffeted and scourged than to fall without help into the jaws of that 'gluttonous death' who 'will instantly unjoint/My body, and soul'.[286] At the same time, we can rightly suspect that such unrelenting force is an ultimately Protestant creation. All those potentially rogue destructive energies – once staggered and checked through the numerous devotional grids and artefacts of Catholicism – have now cut dangerously loose and plummet, in an unstoppable rush of power, directly from heaven to earth. And yet, we may also begin to feel that the *Holy Sonnets'* demands for violence are in fact to be understood quite literally and seriously. The speaker is not running from this torrent of divinely unleashed energy, but inviting and prostrating himself before it. Indeed, in the necessarily continuous spiritual agitation which wracks the lone Protestant sinner, he is effectively creating this violence, transforming the simmering personal heat of anxious piety into a meaningful absolute power.

The violence of the *Holy Sonnets*, therefore, is not just divine violence, but meaningful and redemptive violence. As Donne explains in a particularly vivid evocation elsewhere, 'as long as God punishes me, he gives me physic ... If God break my bones, it is but to set them straighter, and if he bruise me in a mortar, it is but that I might exhale, and breathe up a sweet savour, in his nostrils.' God may 'handle me how he will, so he cast me not out of his hands; I had rather God frowned upon me, than not look upon me'.[287] Similarly, 'if there be any ... that was never affected with ... the glory of God ... it must be God's work to bruise and beat him, with his rod of affliction'.[288] 'His good way is, to beat us into his right way again, by his medicinal corrections, when we put ourselves out of his right way.'[289] When Donne begs, in his poem 'Good Friday. 1613',

O think me worth thine anger, punish me,
Burn off my rusts, and my deformity,

the message becomes unequivocally clear.[290] The worst fate is to be *not* worth God's anger, not to be subjected to the harsh but ultimately purifying force of redemption. Thus, 'it was a harder and an angrier speech then it seems, when God said to his people, *Why should ye be smitten anymore?*'[291]

What does all this tell us about the peculiar desire to be ravished by God? Looking at a broadly similar range of statements running through Donne's sermons, we find that the nervous Protestant is often feminised in a variety of more or less obvious ways. At times such expressions are no less intimate – though less violent – than the encounter of *Sonnet* 14: 'let that mouth, which breath'd [souls] into us, at first, breathe always upon them, whilst they are in us, and suck them into it self, when they depart from us.'[292] Donne himself takes responsibility for this kind of powerfully masculine formation and reformation of human life when he tells his congregation that 'my vicarage is to speak of his compassion and his tears. Let me chafe the wax, and melt your souls in a bath of his tears now, let him set to the great seal of his effectual passion, in his blood, then.'[293] We first met this image, of a male hand moulding loose matter, in chapter three. There, the dashing cavalier of the elegies was claiming that he himself had created and refined the mistress he was discreetly 'borrowing' without her husband's knowledge. Now we find that both Donne's audience and he himself are keen to feel themselves moulded and heated – as, indeed, Donne was during his fever of 1623, a condition which he saw as God's 'chafing of the wax, that thou mightest seal me to thee'.[294] The pious believer is keen, then, to open himself up, passively and perhaps sensually, to the divine touch or breath of God. Such ambiguous passivity is again present in his wish to fall under the sweeping and piercing gaze of the Almighty. 'All things', Hebrews 4.13 informs us, 'are naked and open to the eyes of God.' 'Canst thou hope', Donne asks his listeners in 1622,

> that that God, that seeth this dark earth through all the vaults and arches of the several spheres of heaven, that seeth thy body through all thy stone walls, and seeth thy soul through that which is darker than all those, thy corrupt flesh, canst thou hope that that God can be blinded with drawing a curtain between thy sin and him? ... when he hath planted legions of angels about thee, canst thou hope that thou hast taken away all intelligence, if thou have corrupted, or silenced, or sent away a servant?[295]

This power of potentially oppressive surveillance, with its distinctively Protestant sense of eyes looking down directly on oneself, may be seen as a transformation of the more overt violence found elsewhere. So, when we are told that 'the eye of God is always open, and always upon thee', the statement wavers uncertainly between reassurance and threat.[296] At other times an all-encompassing beneficence and protection takes over:

> That the eye of God is open upon me, though I wink at his light, and watches over me, though I sleep, that God makes these returns to my soul, and so studies me in every change, this consideration, infuses a sweeter verdure ... upon my soul, than any taste of any one act ... can minister unto me.[297]

Again, in a remarkable image, Donne fuses that sheltering gaze with a gendered relation that implies not only copulation but pregnancy: 'we read ... of some creatures ... which hatch their eggs only by looking upon them; what cannot the eye of God produce and hatch in us?'[298]

Given the resourceful elasticity of both patriarchy and Christianity we should perhaps not be too surprised that all those frequently negative or inferior qualities of women (passivity, mutability, and lack of stability) can be so thoroughly revalidated in the right circumstances. What is arguably more interesting is the way that Donne also slyly validates him*self*. As we have seen, his writing and his various personae are characterised by a restless succession of metamorphoses. Donne was fascinated by change. Indeed, he was made of change. When you had been so absolutely one thing, and then found yourself absolutely its opposite, how could you ever quite believe that there was any final, stable centre at which you could rest? The language of religious redemption takes this potentially negative fluidity and recasts it as a kind of human and divine alchemy, a teleology of purifying, cathartic change toward a blissful final entity, rather than that all too familiar slippage of decay that filled Donne's eyes and nostrils in the streets of London. Wax and metal, the scent of bruised herbs, or gold beaten so fine that it could blow away: in theory all this was part of a process which would ultimately come to rest in the absolutely unchanging heaven of Christian theology.[299] Yet it is hard not to wonder if Donne, as poet and person, came secretly to relish the bewitching mutability of human life – to relish most of all his own godlike powers in the Eden of language, where one thing could so ingeniously become another at the flick of a pen.

And this force itself was of course a form of self-expression and of self-assertion. For all their overt subordination beneath the figures of God and Christ, the *Holy Sonnets* do not quite eliminate the independent human ego. As suggested, the identification with Christ in number 11 is shadowed with the danger of egotism; and that spectre surfaces ironically in the (admittedly self-conscious) query 'But who am I, that dare dispute with thee/O God?' It has been noted, indeed, that even Donne's requests for punishment take the form of imperative commands: 'Batter my heart', 'Repair me now.' We may, then, see an ambiguous emphasis in the phrase 'make *me* new' (*HS*, 14, 1. 4). And if so, we are only responding to the covert logic of Protestantism in general, where the most supposedly angry gaze of the Lord still acts as a creative spotlight, outlining and nourishing the individual who feels its heat upon them. Elsewhere, in Donne's 'A Hymn to God the Father', there is a similar wavering between self-abnegation and egotism, when the speaker repeatedly asks for forgiveness only to insist that 'I have more' sins (and, we might say, thus deserves more attention).[300] These hints are most clearly encapsulated by a startling lapse in one of Donne's sermons. As we have seen, the idea of sickness as a positive, corrective force bestowed on sinners by the Almighty was pervasive and serious, and frequently acknowledged by Donne. Yet on this occasion, he implicitly resents the loss of his personal identity, rather than gratefully accepting the presence of God: 'in poverty I lack but other things; in banishment I lack but other men; but in sickness, I lack my self.'[301]

A modern psychoanalyst would readily see the persistent demand for help with one's corrupt nature as an indirect but powerful form of egotism or attention-seeking. And Donne himself is occasionally able to recognise something similar, as when he tells his audience, 'do not weaken the merit, nor lessen the value of the blood of thy Saviour, as though thy sin were greater than it'.[302] In practice the speaker of the *Holy Sonnets* seems very frequently to forget this caution. But perhaps his most extraordinary version of such covert egotism is his wish to have 'all the joys of all the martyrs, from Abel to him that groans now in the Inquisition ... condensed into one body of joy'. Possessed of this conglomeration of corporeal agony and pious delight, the speaker would experience 'all this joy of all these martyrs', which would 'be such a joy, as would work a liquefaction, a melting of my bowels'.[303] Here, perhaps more strikingly than at any other point, the sensuous force of Donne's religious feeling spontaneously bursts into a solid three-dimensional mass which one might describe as a kind of 'hyper-' or 'meta-body'. And yet at the same time the astonishing desire to personally experience – at once – every single pain suffered by thousands of men and women is no less egotistical than the fierce contempt of the Satires, the self-reliance of the Elegies, or the exalted love of 'The Canonization'.

In the light of that last strange imagining we might well be prompted to re-read the divine violence of the sermons and *Holy Sonnets*. Is Donne in fact *creating* such violence, in order to spiritually reanimate a now colder religious atmosphere? In theory, the believer's fear and his yearning for a forcible divine presence stem from the uncertainty of personal salvation. In reality, it may be that Donne at times felt not simply alone under the eye of God, but utterly alone in a rapidly changing universe. Such feelings, whether conscious or unconscious, are strong enough to produce numerous expressions of emptiness, and an unnerving sense of distance from a Creator whose traditional presence and functions were now increasingly eroded.

Much of the richness of Donne's writing comes from his ability to soak up and transform the liberated energies of a slowly crumbling religious system, like some finely nervous tuning fork, involuntarily catching and reworking the changing harmonies of the Christian universe. What we must not forget is that Donne's individual creativity was all the more powerful just because he refused to *overtly* believe that its divine source was merely a creation of the human mind. The process of cultural change which underlies and shapes much of his literary output seems in his lifetime to have been just rarely glimpsed, in tantalisingly brief, coded forms. Let us in conclusion take two examples which neatly focus the changing relations between religion, language and the self.

In 1605, the first part of Miguel Cervantes' *Don Quixote* was published.[304] This massive novel succeeded in effectively patenting a whole curious state of mind (honoured, in later decades, by the new adjective 'quixotic'). But what did it mean to be 'quixotic' at the time when the book first appeared? The errant knight of this tale is driven by a hopeless yet powerfully creative nostalgia for a world of chivalry and grandeur now faded, if not vanished. He is continually mistaking the ordinary and the particular for the remarkable and the general. The comedy of the novel therefore derives from, and crucially marks, an important shift in the perception of meaning and reality: laughter spurts up in the contrasting friction between Quixote's view of the world, and Cervantes' ironic distance from it. As Foucault puts it, 'Don Quixote's adventures form the boundary: they mark the end of the old interplay between resemblance and signs and contain the beginnings of new relations.'[305] Much of the book's comedy, for Foucault, derives from the (failed) 'attempt to transform reality back into a sign ... a sign that the signs of language really are in conformity with things themselves'.[306] As the sixteenth meets the seventeenth century, 'flocks, serving girls and inns' no longer 'resemble castles, ladies and armies', but 'remain stubbornly within their own ironic identity'.[307]

Just over a decade later, in a sermon of 1616, Donne cites the Catholic saint, Philip Neri – a figure who was reportedly wont to cry, in his religious ecstasies, 'O Lord go farther from me, and let me have a less portion of thee.' Conversely, the Donne of the *Holy Sonnets* betrays an attempt to work himself up into a kind of 'typological ecstasy', so as to turn reality back into a sign.[308] If his own personal static of religious uncertainty can be transmuted into the sense of an absolute divine power, then particular reality is united with a general significance. Precisely after his citation of Neri, he wonders, by contrast, 'who would be loath to sink, by being over-freighted with God, or loath to over-set, by having so much of that wind, the breath of the Spirit of God?'[309] Neri or his followers, of course, might well view the Protestants of Jacobean England as drained of spirituality, needing to draw their God closer, rather than asking Him to 'go farther from me'. Where the Catholic mystic was too full, Donne is in fact too empty.[310] That religious emotion which spontaneously overflowed from various Catholic mystics and saints is effortfully, persistently created and recreated by Donne. The at times startling violence of his God is in part the reflection of an older, tougher form of Christianity than later ages would create, as the God of fear gave way to the God of love. Yet such violence can also be seen as the distilled and projected poison of individual fear, producing a deity which in some ways looks like a phobic object, overcharged with personal neuroses. We will find in our conclusion that this God retained sufficient weight and force to significantly shape Donne's attitude to death. Chapters five and six, however, show that in some very serious ways it was indeed becoming increasingly difficult to make reality conform to the accepted signs of religious thought.

Chapter Five

New Philosophy

> As new philosophy arrests the sun,
> And bids the passive earth about it run,
> So we have dulled our mind, it hath no ends;
> Only the body's busy, and pretends;
> As dead low earth eclipses and controls
> The quick high moon, so doth the body, souls
>
> (Verse Letter)

I

By a neat historical coincidence, two of the founding texts of modern Western science were published in the year 1543. One was Nicolaus Copernicus' *De Revolutionibus Orbium Coelestium* ('On the Revolutions of the Heavenly Bodies'). The other was Andreas Vesalius' *De Fabrica Humani Corporis* ('On the Fabric of the Human Body'). We will look briefly at the former in a few moments. Our chief concern in this chapter, however, is with the little world of man, rather than the grander one of the cosmos. Vesalius' book offered a radical new approach to human anatomy. Poised somewhere between art and technology, between religion and science, its extraordinary anatomical illustrations still dazzle and stun the eye centuries later, effortlessly bewitching the viewer after decades of photography, cinema, and computer-aided representation.[311] With his depictions rapidly plagiarised and reproduced all across Europe, Vesalius had effectively invented the new image of the interior body. And, while the illustrations were clearly works of painstaking skill, they were in fact remarkable purely by being *visual* representations (skilled or otherwise), rather than unverified textual assertions. In past decades and centuries, anatomy books had been largely or entirely unillustrated works. By contrast, Vesalius' book aimed to *show*, rather than merely say. In our time, that attitude is a seemingly axiomatic principle of the scientific method. But in Vesalius' era, his attempt to demonstrate past errors by re-examination of present and actual bodies was a surprisingly controversial, if not outrightly bizarre, notion.

In 1540 Vesalius carried out a public dissection in Bologna. Despite his later eminence, at this point he was in the lowly position of manual assistant to his conservative tutor, Matthaeus Curtius. In a manner typical of the pre-scientific attitude to knowledge, Curtius read about the body from Classical textbooks, while Vesalius then attempted to illustrate these often flawed statements on a freshly-killed criminal corpse. In the present case, we are fortunate to have a surviving eyewitness account of the long series of lectures and demonstrations, penned by a visiting German student, Baldasar

Heseler. Here are Vesalius and Curtius, arguing about the causes of pleurisy. The former has just suggested that the classical Greek anatomist, Claudius Galen (131-c.200AD), was in error on this point:

> Curtius answered ... No ... Domine, we must not leave Galen, because he always well understood everything, and, consequently, we also follow him. Do you know how to interpret Hippocrates better than Galen did? Vesalius answered, I do not say so, but I show you here in these bodies the vein without pair ... always here – he knocked with his hands against the middle of the chest – occurs inflammation and pleurisy, not at the two upper ribs ... Curtius replied: I am no *anatomista*, but there can be other veins nourishing the ribs and muscles besides these. Where, please, Vesalius said, show them to me. Curtius said, do you want to deny the ducts of Nature? Oh! Vesalius said ... I, again, talk about what is visible.[312]

By challenging an essentially static conception of ancient anatomical theory, Vesalius effectively opposes a scientific viewpoint to a religious one. Thanks to Heseler, then, we are offered a front-row seat at one of the more notorious clashes between religion and science. Or ... are we? We need to bear in mind that the very notion of a contest between science and religion is a relatively modern invention.

In the sixteenth century, science as it would later be known was still struggling to invent itself. The study of medicine, of astronomy, botany and chemistry all fell under the general category of Natural Philosophy, and this itself was subordinate to Theology.

To us, nothing seems to expose the bizarre privileging of text over observation better than Curtius's 'do you know how to interpret Hippocrates better than Galen did?' The real substance and structure of the body has here been doubly shifted from our sight and our grasp. It is not simply a textual creation, but one ancient medical text interpreting another. Wrenchingly counter-intuitive as this may appear, it was nevertheless the integral foundation of élite medical teaching and treatment in almost all European universities and cities well into the sixteenth century. To understand how this apparently fruitless and unworkable attitude survived so long we need to appreciate just how powerful textual authority was. The ultimate and essential truth about the entire cosmos, past, present and future, was written in two books, the old and the new testaments of the Christian bible. A substantial number of Christians probably knew these works by heart. Moreover, those two books themselves sat in their unquestionable glory at the top of a colossal pyramid of related but subordinate texts. Shelf after shelf, mile after mile down a precisely mapped intellectual dead end, stretched the innumerable, venerably learned commentaries upon the Bible. Astonishing amounts of ingenuity and painstaking labour were devoted simply to interpreting two books.

What we can begin to grasp, then, is that intellectual endeavour was largely a matter of preserving and interpreting what had been written very long ago, whether in the Bible, in the ancient medical books of Hippocrates and Galen, the comprehensive philosophy of Aristotle, or the delightfully erroneous encyclopaeadias of general knowledge provided by the 'Natural History' of the Roman scholar, Pliny the Elder. The very notion of learning something fundamentally, radically new about the world did not exist for most educated people. In a period in which, as Foucault puts it, 'nature and the word' could 'intertwine with one another, forming, for those who can read it, one vast single text', by far the dominant attitude to the world was that of 'commentary' – a mode which 'halts before the precipice of the original text' and '*sacralises* language'.[313] By contrast, a few unusual men such as Francis Bacon favoured 'criticism', a stance which 'speaking of language in terms of representations and truth, judges it and profanes it'.[314] This latter attitude, though, was embryonic, marginal and relatively powerless. It is probably correct to say that, in Vesalius' period, one could not even be understood if one attempted to speak outright in the language of criticism. So, in response to what Curtius no doubt saw as an axiomatic rebuttal ('do you know ... ?') Vesalius is arguably strategic in swerving away from speech altogether: '"I do not say so, but I show you here in these bodies the vein without pair ... always here" – he knocked with his hands against the middle of the chest...' – "occurs inflammation and pleurisy, not at the two upper ribs."' With hindsight, this encounter beautifully encapsulates the clash of two of the most influential worldviews in Western history. Curtius may as well be sat alone in the silence of a great library. Vesalius, as he swings down his fists on the corpse before them, slices not just through chill winter air, but through the settled weight and dust of ancient and inaccurate medical textbooks. The immediate result is a necessary incomprehension. The two men are not simply arguing, but refusing to agree on the space in which they could even begin to genuinely argue. 'I', Vesalius insists, 'talk about what is visible.' Curtius does not deny this visibility, but he is unable to recognise the importance which his rival (and nominal servant) accords to it.

We know that Vesalius did indeed laugh last and longest. In his text he denounced men such as Curtius, 'like jackdaws aloft in their high chair, with egregious arrogance croaking things they have never investigated but merely committed to memory from the books of others'.[315] By contrast, Vesalius' work offered an eloquent fulfilment of the implicit manifesto of 1540 – the *Fabrica* was remembered essentially for what it *showed*, rather than for what it said. Yet in at least three ways we can see how Vesalius himself still partly belonged to that now discredited world of Curtius and all his influential peers. First, he created the basis of a scientific future by trying to define a purer, truer version of the Classical past. While he came openly to disagree with Galen on many points, he had begun in the spirit of commentary, reverently scraping accumulated dirt from the works of Hippocrates and Galen (these were after all Greek texts, which could be rightly or wrongly interpreted in a linguistic sense). Secondly, for some time he was hindered by Galenic and Christian beliefs which – as we shall see in detail presently – occasionally made him behave a little like Curtius himself. For what especially fascinated Heseler throughout this series of demonstrations was nothing less than the anatomical location and processing unit of the human soul. The continuing power of this entity was so great that, like some strange magical forcefield vibrating out of the human body, it effectively distorted the normally steady arm and eye of Vesalius, and the perceptions of the students around

241

him. A third point is perhaps the most subtle and most persuasive. While the illustrations of *De Fabrica* were the work of one or more professional artists (Titian being considered a plausible candidate), Vesalius himself influenced their design and execution to a strong degree. And, if we compare these depictions with the anatomy figures of the far more developed and assertive science of the eighteenth century, what we realise is that, at the crucially extra-rational level of the visual, Vesalian anatomy effectively fused religion and science. Later images are colder, flatter, lacking the vibrancy, confidence, and irreplaceable first thrill of discovery which so potently animate the figures of *De Fabrica*. The painstaking technical achievements of Vesalius' pictures, with their skillful use of perspective and shading, and remarkable mimesis of organic substance, should not be forgotten. But the wonder which galvanises them is essentially religious. There is a certain reverence in these images which corresponds to that habit of 'commentary' identified by Foucault.

This chapter considers Donne's attitude to emergent science from the viewpoint of anatomy. The following section briefly contextualises anatomical innovations by outlining similar intellectual shifts in the area of astronomy. The third goes on to argue that Donne was both attracted to anatomy for its powers of embodying and defining the mysterious, and secretly afraid that such rigorous analysis would too relentlessly hollow out the spiritual density of the human body. A fourth section tightens the focus of that claim by showing how dissection had problematised not only existing material ideas, but also a whole long-established understanding of the human soul. Finally, the chapter uses these claims as a way of reading one of Donne's most famous poems. Is 'The Ecstasy' merely a poem about the unification of typically rarefied lovers, or is it, more broadly, also a covert attempt to *re*-unify a body and soul progressively severed by the insistent probing of the dissector's scalpel?

II

As we will see, there are specific reasons why changing attitudes to the human body alone were able seriously to disturb Donne and some of his shrewder contemporaries. But such changes were in fact taking place in a context of more general intellectual turbulence.[316] The cosmos itself, the whole vast starry envelope of space encompassing the earth and the other planets, had been radically reconceived in various ways by the time that Donne, in 1611, wrote these famous lines:

And new philosophy calls all in doubt,

The element of fire is quite put out;

The sun is lost, and th'earth, and no man's wit

Can well direct him where to look for it.

And freely men confess that this world's spent

When in the planets, and the firmament

They seek so many new ...

(Anatomy of the World)

As noted above, Copernicus had originally published his *De Revolutionibus* in 1543. But his own version of the 'heliocentric hypothesis' – with its consequent displacement of the once central earth – had been cautiously expressed. It was in Donne's lifetime that this and other innovations gained their most disturbing momentum. Galileo now asserted Copernicus' dangerous opinion with sufficient force to attract the violent threats of the Catholic Church. Over in Germany, Johannes Kepler, equipped with newly powerful telescopes, showed that planets revolved in ellipses, not perfect circles, and discovered new stars in a cosmos supposedly mapped entirely and for all time. Similarly, new astronomical instruments and associated mathematics were able to show that the spatial extent of the universe was vastly greater than once believed.

As the most fundamental boundaries and structure of the known world slid and shifted discordantly around him, Donne's reaction was typically ambivalent. On several occasions he attempts to mock the presumption of the new astronomers.[317] But on others his ever eager and open mind cannot resist a more balanced engagement with recent discoveries.[318] He in fact owned one of Kepler's books, and had clearly read another; and there is also convincing (though surprisingly unremarked) evidence that the two men indeed met.[319] A sense that humanity must reconfront its approach to knowledge on all sides is well summed up in a sermon of 1626:

> What one thing do we know perfectly? ... Young men mend not their sight by using old men's spectacles; and yet we look upon nature, but with Aristotle's spectacles, and upon the body of man, but with Galen's, and upon the frame of the world, but with Ptolemy's spectacles.[320]

The underlying basis of Donne's involuntary fascination is captured when he admits that, in the firmament there are 'scattered more eyes than any ciphers can esteem or express. For, how weak a stomach to digest knowledge, or how strong and misgoverned faith against common sense hath he, that is content to rest' in the old, Aristotelian 'number of 1022 stars?'[321]

Looking closely at Donne's contempt for those with so 'weak a stomach to digest knowledge' we can view this compulsive attraction to change in two broad ways. As noted above and in chapter one, Foucault saw Donne's period as one beginning to reconceive its most basic attitudes to knowledge. The older, dominant stance was one which forcefully centralised all phenomena in toward the irresistible gravity of the Creator. Another influential thinker, Mikhail Bakhtin, broadly echoes this viewpoint through his ideas of the relations between politics and language. For Bakhtin, social and political structures soak right down through the most precise habits of written language. A dominant and essentially tyrannical system produces an equally limited form of expression, flattening out genuine diversity by its obsessive central emphasis. Much of Donne's religious discourse would fit Bakhtin's description of 'monoglossia'. Such 'unitary language', Bakhtin argues, reflects 'the theoretical expression of the historical processes of linguistic unification and centralization, an expression of the centripetal forces of language'.[322] Donne wishes to 'digest knowledge' into one coherent intellectual stance. Bakhtin would see, in that metaphor of absorption and homogenisation, the centripetal habits of those who could only admit variety as a tamed and subordinate element in a totalising, essentially tyrannical and monolithic system. Yet knowing what we do of Donne we can also say that his hungry desire to devour the world, to bend it to his stubborn will, was a distinctively *personal* habit. More precisely, it was peculiar to his demandingly intellectual faith, seeking to encompass all known elements, while still (unlike the most rigid Christians) admitting the genuine material reality of those elements (whether these were the new stars, the new body, or new world of the American continents). As we will see, however, even Donne's intellectual stomach was not strong enough to chew up all the novelties appearing around him, as religion slowly, painfully began to give way to something like science.

III

Anatomy came late to Britain. Medicine at this time was controlled by the Royal College of Physicians, an élite, monopolising body with roughly the same attitude as Vesalius' opponent, Curtius. The College was frequently trying to prevent unlicensed practitioners from working in London, and one of its tests for such people was whether or not they could read Latin. This leaning toward the literary and theoretical was compounded by the fact that most of those thereby prevented or discouraged from practising were far more empirically-minded than the physicians themselves. So, while anatomies had been performed since 1540, they had been exclusively the work of the Barber-Surgeons Company, an entity which was unquestionably subjugated, in accordance with its dedication to crude manual labour. But even in Donne's childhood this situation was beginning to change. In 1581 the physicians proposed their own public dissection, thereby giving anatomy new prominence and prestige. In the early years of this new demonstration (known as the Lumleian) there appears to have been continuing resistance from many physicians, who were fined for not attending or performing dissections. But in 1615 William Harvey – a sometime Royal Physician, and soon to outline the controversial new theory of the circulation of the blood – was appointed Lumleian Lecturer. Harvey's zeal for dissection, experiment, and pathological observation was so great that he not only vivisected many animals, but even performed post-mortem autopsies on his own father and sister. It was also in 1615 that Helkiah Crooke, a Fellow of the Royal College, published *Microcosmographia*, a massive folio which – while once again plagiarising Vesalius' illustrations – was arguably still more impressive in actual appearance than *De Fabrica* itself. This monumental volume of over a thousand pages was hardly available to many. But the shrewdly opportunist Crooke produced a much cheaper epitome, *Somatographia Anthropine, or a Description of the Body of Man*, in 1616. Importantly, this new book was largely pictorial, containing explanatory labels, but very little continuous text. For many, then, what dominated the imagination after 1616 was the image, as much as the idea, of anatomy.

As we saw in chapter two, Donne used anatomy rhetorically in his poem 'The Damp'. It also features in 'Love's Exchange', and 'The Legacy'. Helen Gardner argued that all these poems were written in the 1590s.[323] If so, Donne here showed a typically sharp eye for the new and the strange. Until the late 1570s Britain in general seemed barely to have heard of anatomy. In following decades, it seized on it with that peculiar zeal that only the first wave of cultural novelty can sustain. In 1576 there appeared John Woolton's *A New Anatomy of Whole Man*, and Thomas Rogers' *The Anatomy of the Mind*, with at least a further 115 'literary anatomies' appearing in print or manuscript by mid-seventeenth century. These were not strictly medical books, but ones which transposed various of the intellectual and methodical habits newly championed by dissection. Like Crooke, authors in this new quasi-genre were often opportunistic, reissuing older works as 'anatomies' without any alteration save to their title. Yet at the same time literary anatomies made implicit and explicit claims to the compellingly virtuosic skills of medical dissectors. Piercing unrelentingly through the body of a given subject in all its depth, breadth, intricacy and minute detail, writers now promised an at once totalising, exact and rigorously unsentimental exposure of their chosen topics. Perhaps most of all, these works implicitly conceded the supposed *objectivity* of the new dissection. But precision and exhaustiveness were not the only qualities which attracted writers to this burgeoning rhetorical treasury. Knowledge now became increasingly spatialised. As if in stunned tribute to the dazzling Vesalian illusion of interior cavities and volume, the depth of the body threw open new depths of thought. All in all, Jonathan Sawday - whose study *The Body Emblazoned* first comprehensively charted the rise and roles of Renaissance anatomy - seems justified in referring to a pervasive 'culture of dissection' in Donne's period.[324]

What attracted Donne to anatomy? At one level, he had certain basic advantages. His stepfather, John Syminges, was a Fellow and sometime President of the Royal College of Physicians. They were soon living in a house close to St Bartholomew's hospital, and the founding papers for the Lumleian were in fact signed in the family home in 1582 (as we have seen, Donne was old enough to attend Oxford just two years later). Again, medicine and the new public dissections were informal but popular facets of the broad gentlemanly education of young law students. Perhaps more integrally, Donne's insatiable curiosity extended up to astronomy and down to the minutest composition and behaviour of material bodies comprised of atomic particles. This side of Donne is persistently evident in the writings of a man too often identified as purely, abstractly cerebral:

> Know'st thou but how the stone doth enter in
> The bladder's cave, and never break the skin?
> Know'st thou how blood, which to the heart doth flow,
> Doth from one ventricle to the other go?
>
> *(Progress of the Soul)*

Throughout his poems and prose Donne shows a striking capability for concrete and vivid physical nuance. A sweating body glistening with the febrile shimmer of mercury; a kitchen wench saves thirty years' of candle scrapings to buy wedding clothes.[325] We learn how 'torches which must ready be,/Men light and put out' to ignite them the more quickly; how 'water gives a crookedness, and false dimensions to things that it shows; as we see by an oar when we row a boat'; and how pearls are formed, growing 'bigger and bigger by a continual

251

succession and devolution of dew and other glutinous moisture that falls upon them, and there condenses and hardens'.[326] This kind of attentiveness is broadly that of the scientist, and is indeed similar to the vivid evocations of substance, colour and texture which animate William Harvey's lecture notes on anatomy.[327]

Throughout his life Donne shows respect for dissection as a physical state-of the-art: 'we understand the frame of man's body', he claims, 'better by seeing him cut up, than by seeing him do any exercise alive; one dissection, one anatomy teaches more of that, than the marching, or drilling of a whole army of living men.'[328] A similar respect is implied by his opinion that, 'you may as well call him an anatomist, that knows how to pare a nail, or cut a corn'.[329] But as we will see, his attitude was finally far more complex and uneasy than one of general admiration. Much of the wide cultural fascination with anatomy seems to have stemmed from the intrinsic novelty and ambiguity of the freshly perceived human interior. There is a certain universal edge of the uncanny about this region, at once wholly familiar and strangely alien to most of us. As Gunter von Hagens' remarkable exhibition, *Bodyworlds*, clearly showed, our response to the inside of the body broadly echoes our response to great art. In either case, it is very hard to adequately paraphrase our reaction in plain words. For Donne's contemporaries the novel rediscovery of this uncanny realm was made all the more breathtaking by new standards of artistic execution and perspective. Small wonder, then, that their response seems at times to have rivalled the mingled terror and wonder of their simultaneous encounter with the outer new world of America. What should be emphasised most of all is that anatomy held the special fascination of ambiguity. For some years no one could definitively fix its accepted nature or meanings, in either medical or rhetorical terms. It was intriguing and culturally valuable for its very fluidity and instability. At times writers are clearly throwing the word 'anatomy' into a passage with the vague but shrewd opportunism of one hurling a rhetorical firework, boldly flourishing a hand at the general dazzle of the phenomenon without worrying about its integral legitimacy in that particular context.

Donne's own response to anatomy was fundamentally ambiguous in a very serious way – one which both reflected and developed the more curious incidents witnessed by Heseler back in that Bologna winter of 1540. We have already found Donne drawn to anatomical depth, solidity and darkness in his numerous assaults on the body of sin and earthly corruption. In those cases, one attraction of the human interior was its ability to effectively fill a gap, to give form and substance to something immensely significant but unnervingly intangible. But Donne also found various secular uses for anatomy – or, at least, nominally secular ones. Take, for example, 'A Valediction: Of my Name in the Window'. On the surface, this is a typically agile, carelessly dazzling love poem. Before he leaves her, the poet cuts his name into his mistress' window with a diamond. In a familiar motif of amorous entanglement, the lovers are interwoven, as the mistress sees both the name, and her own reflection, in the glass. Also familiar are the swift transformations the name undergoes: it becomes the spare but essential inner framework of bones, a skeleton signifying the temporary death of parting; it is granted the magical or cabbalistic virtues of a word which can utilise the power of the stars at a given conjunction. Animated with these stellar influences, the name is therefore essentially alive. Characteristically, Donne also throws its living vibrancy more directly at the reader's eye. The 'trembling name' briefly shimmers in the frame of the jolted window, jealously watching the woman as she stares out at another man. Again, the name's mystic power and life are such that it will sign itself over the subscription of some rival's letter, or steal into the mistress' imagination as she attempts to address her own epistle to this new favourite. Finally, with that deceptive offhandedness so common to many of the Songs and Sonnets, Donne decides that all the preceding has been merely the idle talk of a dying man, figuratively breathing his last in the act of parting.

But if we pierce and fold back the outer skin of this piece, we find that its inner core harbours more durable and fundamental contents. Near its centre is embedded a conceit of resurrection. The poet imagines the name as his 'ruinous anatomy' (tellingly, the latter word was at this time the more common term for 'skeleton'). So,

> ... as all my souls be
> Emparadised in you, (in whom alone
> I understand, and grow and see,)
> The rafters of my body, bone
> Being still with you, the muscle, sinew, and vein,
> Which tile this house, will come again
>
> Till my return repair
> And recompact my scattered body so

One general effect of this is to remind us how easily present to the imagination was the whole seemingly fantastic process of resurrection which we met in the previous chapter. Why, though, is it here at all? There is a good chance that the poem was written in the 1590s (possibly when Donne was actually about to sail on one of his military voyages). If so, then the new public anatomies instigated in the 1580s would have been fresh in the minds and imaginations of Londoners. In theory, the poem uses 'anatomy' simply to mean 'skeleton'. Historical context, however, indicates that matters are not so simple. The skeleton appears to have been a compelling, almost oddly novel entity at this point, and one which was indissociable from the whole arresting *process* of painstaking physical division and reduction conducted by the anatomists.[330]

What role does this newly anatomical skeleton play in Donne's poem? Recall that, for Renaissance Christians, the entire human organism – whatever its state of dissolution or incoherence – must be 'recompacted' at the resurrection. Donne seems, then, to be paying a certain uneasy tribute to dissection. On one hand, it forces upon viewers the extraordinary complexity of the body which God must recreate. On the other, it presents a spectacle of the most devastating material annihilation – one which, in its combined rapidity, and its unrelenting precision and exhaustiveness, was perhaps more startling than the effects of war, disease or time. Accordingly, with habitual rigour, Donne here effectively tests God's powers against the most challenging obstacle available. Indeed, as David A. Hedric Hirsch has persuasively argued, Donne may well be cutting down – etymologically and figuratively – not just through flesh and tissue, but to those most basic 'atoms' of matter recently rediscovered by Renaissance physics, and present in the word 'anatomy' itself.[331] Elsewhere, passages in his sermons similarly indicate that – notwithstanding the theoretical power of an omnipotent God – the whole process of resurrection intrigued and troubled him.

But if one layer of the poem disrupts Christian theology, another asserts an element of resurrection and afterlife which was especially important to Donne. That is: as Hirsch has further demonstrated, both atoms and the 'anatomy' of the bones effectively offered Donne a certain final, irreducible substratum of matter, a kind of guarantee of material permanence. There would, as Donne often insists, be bodies in heaven. Moreover, one would also be *oneself* in heaven. And so we now begin to grasp a crucial link between those two bare outlines of the human individual, the signature and the skeleton. Each of these is the defiantly personal core, reduced yet essential, of the self. We find Donne engaging in an act of self-dissection which aptly combines intellectual rigour (is there something else? can we go further?) with the immediate sensuous wonder of all that neatly coiled and compacted organic structure, reflected from the anatomist's scalpel into the stunned eyes of the assembled London audience. We might, then, now reread the assertion 'So shall all times find *me* the same', inflecting that stubborn monosyllable with an ambiguous emphasis that in fact stretches beyond earth and into heaven. It is also worth adding that the resurrection conceit, playfully according godlike status to the mistress who has 'emparadised' the poet's tripartite soul, gives us an especially convincing example of Donne's recurrent need for anchoring points of stability. The fact that such sites can shift so fluidly from one's lover to one's God only confirms that they are products of Donne's personal psychology as much as entities in their own right.

Donne's 'Valediction', then, roots down to the atomistic nucleus of the soul that finally underwrites Christian identity. In 'The Funeral', anatomy and the soul are again peculiarly spliced – but now in a way that disperses selfhood through an elaborate web of organic substance. The speaker asks

> Who ever comes to shroud me do not harm
>> Nor question much
> That subtle wreath of hair, which crowns my arm

For it is, he claims, 'my outward soul', standing in for that now fled to heaven. How can this be? The poet explains that

... if the sinewy thread my brain lets fall

    Through every part,

Can tie those parts, and make me one of all;

Those hairs which upward grew, and strength and art

    Have from a better brain,

Can better do it

Understood to unite body and soul by their pervasive transmission of vaporous spirits from the brain, the nerves are here elided into the strands of hair coiled about the skeletal wrist. The idea that the nerves thus effectively catalysed the soul throughout the body had long been established. What was still very new and arresting when Donne wrote was the *image* of this nervous web, as captured in *De Fabrica*. For many readers this must have lain like a veil over the poem as they read. And Donne himself succinctly pays tribute to it when he pitches us down into the breathtaking new space of this body, jolting the very word 'fall' over the open gap of the line-break, and watching it magically ramify into the delicate filigree spreading down from head to foot.

In this poem both the woman and the human soul are at once central and absent. The hair stands in for one, the nerves for the other. We are confronted, therefore, with a familiarly restless shift of meaning and emphasis. The poem seems briefly to be about love. It then also becomes a piece about the nature and function of the human soul. In each case we meet the old tendency to grasp and focus on some single crux of stability and permanence. And yet, the most conspicuous vehicle for that role here is not the absent woman or absent soul, but the defiantly present Vesalian body. Once alerted to the visual subtext of the poem, what catches our attention most (as it would that of Donne's peers) is that astonishingly fine dispersal of anatomical substance, something which potently fuses art and life, in that no real body could ever quite look that way, and no painter simply conjure it from their unaided imagination. The immortal soul is edged out between the extreme and scattering brightness of hair, on the one hand, and those integral fibres plunged within the darkness of the body, on the other.

The lines from 'The Funeral' are, moreover, not the only ones which appear to depend on Vesalian representation. As noted, Donne's own literary anatomy of 1611 was commissioned by Sir Robert Drury for his recently dead daughter, Elizabeth. Donne wrote a second commemorative piece in 1612 (after which, we may imagine, Jonson had stern words with him one evening and prevented a third). This 'second anniversary', subtitled *Of the Progress of the Soul*, essentially celebrates the release of Elizabeth's soul from its passing earthly status to full heavenly glory. Describing the flight of this unleashed soul through what seems to be real space, Donne imagines how, 'ere she can consider how she went', Elizabeth

> At once is at, and through the firmament.
> And as these stars were but so many beads
> Strung on one string, speed undistinguish'd leads
> Her through those spheres, as through the beads,
> a string,
> Whose quick succession makes it still one thing:
> As doth the pith, which, lest our bodies slack,
> Strings fast the little bones of neck, and back;
> So by the soul doth death string heaven and earth.

In its own right this stanza is remarkable for its evocation of a blur of speed which to us seems very much like a jet trail. More precisely, it is striking how Donne so unexpectedly dives from the vast reaches of space into the 'pith' of the spinal marrow. Why this comparison in particular? There seem to be two plausible answers. One is that he again betrays an involuntary fascination with images continually recurring to his mind, and which – as I have argued – were attractive in part just for their rhetorical malleability. Secondly, he is also specifically intrigued with what superior anatomical knowledge implies about the function of that partly physiological entity, the human soul. For this pith was thought, like the nerves, to unify body and soul by transmitting spirits from the brain.[332] Even here, where he might more loosely have talked about the spine – and been equally well understood – Donne notably forces his way into the deepest inner core of the organism, as if intent on having the conductive charge of the soul vibrate its pulse through his fingers. Moreover, the image not only evokes the complexity and tension of the new body ('strings fast'), but further anatomises the spine into the whole interlocking ladder of 'little bones' which form it. Again, therefore, the arguably pious yearning for a more intimate contact with spiritual essence produces a certain irony. Donne might actually be said to throw across the gap between heaven and earth not the soul, but the body. The question of how successfully he really manages to string heaven and earth is one to which we will return at the close of this chapter. What might already be wondered here is if Donne typically relies not on any finally assured cosmic power, but on his own creative ingenuity, and on a personal energy aptly caught in that hot white streak of bewildering velocity, piercing all the spheres of the firmament.

If Donne's anatomical imagery is noteworthy in a eulogy for a dead girl, it becomes quite remarkable when applied to the Almighty himself. One of the strangest features of Renaissance anatomy was the convention of self-dissection. While anatomy figures all tended to be oddly alive, some compounded that paradoxical status by proudly wrenching apart their own bodies to reveal the spaces within, or flourishing the knife which had flayed them in one hand, and their skin held out like a cloak in the other. Sinners in particular were fond of transferring this habit to the realm of pious self-inspection, claiming that they had unsparingly rifled the most furtive corners of both body and soul. But no one ever seems to have twisted the scalpel quite as Donne did on Easter 1628. His sermon text being I Cor. 13.12 ('For now we see through a glass darkly, but then face to face'), he emphasises how our worldly knowledge of God is limited and partial. On earth He is dimly perceived through 'the book of creatures', through the Church, and by 'the light of faith'.[333] Only in heaven will humanity move beyond this mere 'infancy' and 'cradle of knowledge'. And there, Donne imagines, God will reveal himself as actively and dramatically as the self-dissecting *écorchés* of the textbooks: 'our medium, our way to see him is *patefactio sui*, God's laying himself open, his manifestation, his revelation, his evisceration, and embowelling of himself to us, there.'[334] The figure of God '[dis]embowelling' himself would have been an extremely unlikely possibility prior to Vesalius or

Harvey. The suspicion that anatomy was frequently irresistible – despite its potentially taboo and transgressive qualities – for its power to cut down to the darkest core of truth or wonder, is amply verified here. Donne leaps out into the most bewilderingly abstract and unknown spaces, only to find his hands swiftly plunged back into the reassuring gristle and pith of the viscera. The formless mystery of an absolute divine essence becomes so elusively tantalising that it collapses into a knowable, warm organic substance which can be seized within the human fist.

The way in which Donne pitches the robust and intricate substance of the body into these frustratingly abstract zones leads us to a number of cognate habits in the same period. The very first literary anatomies were of the soul and of the mind. In following years there were a further six anatomies of the soul, spirit or conscience, with Robert Burton's famous dissection of melancholy similarly aiming to embody what was otherwise elusive and unmanageable.[335] The broad pattern is clear enough. Works such as these involuntarily admit the unrivalled power of anatomy to open up, divide and demystify the most abstract or secret entities. Reviewing this situation with hindsight, we find an ironic embrace, by Christianity, of an emergent cultural attitude which in following decades would increasingly undermine the traditional religious worldview. The method of anatomy, even used in a loose rhetorical way, was sufficiently attractive for various religious purposes to seem a welcome gift. Only later would it become apparent that it had in fact been a kind of Trojan horse.

But glimpses of the future tensions between religion and science were already available in Donne's lifetime. In 1623, for example, we find him reconsidering the old analogies between the 'little world of man' and greater world of Nature. It is now, he decides, 'too little to call Man a little world'. Unpacked, unravelled and heaped up, the 'veins ... sinews ... muscles' and 'bones' of the body would be 'rivers ... mines ... hills' and 'quarries' of such magnitude that 'the air would be too little for this orb of Man to move in, the firmament would be but enough for this star.' Man, Donne now concludes 'hath ... many pieces, of which the whole world hath no representation'.[336] Again, in a sermon of 1627 he reflects on the Christian obligation to accept the authority of the entire Bible as one absolute Truth. Accordingly, he warns that: 'for matter of belief, he that believes not all ... he takes Jesus in pieces, and after the Jews have crucified him, he dissects him, and makes him an anatomy. We must therefore teach all.'[337] At one level, the startling violence of a dissected Christ reflects the peculiar material density of sacred language. The Saviour elsewhere

265

mangled and torn in a blasphemer's mouth is here pierced and ruthlessly partitioned by virtue of an irreverently analytic (or 'critical') attitude to Scripture. But that precise objection also implies another, more fundamental one. What Donne is ultimately attacking – consciously or otherwise – is anatomy's aggressively demystifying power. Scripture, he insists, is intrinsically mysterious, and intrinsically holistic. It must be accepted and swallowed whole in one single act of faith.

For Donne of all people, however, such a stance itself contains a further difficulty. His faith, as numerous examples make abundantly clear, is an insistently rational one. Yet in the effectual opposition between the rational enquiry of the anatomists, and a comprehensive faith in the Bible, Donne sets up a faint but significant tension, splitting Christian belief from the curious intellect. The two cannot now be so easily digested and homogenised in one stomach. We might indeed say that, where anatomy could at times be used to fill a gap, here it in fact seems to create one in its effectual division of reason and faith.[338] My final section argues that anatomy was now also threatening to traumatically sever a long-established Christian integration of the body and the soul.

IV

To fully understand the peculiarly tense relationship between anatomy and religion, we need first to return, both to the events of Bologna in 1540, and to the longstanding theological and medical ideas which converged within that candlelit anatomy theatre.[339] We have seen Vesalius clash with his tutor, Curtius. But other frictions were no less troublesome to him. During the dissection of the human head his student audience was agitated into a state of nearly riotous disorder.[340] Why? The answer shows us just how deeply anatomy was still mired in the Christian (and effectively Medieval) world. They expected to see anatomical proof of the immortal human soul. And so, apparently, did Heseler. Squinting at the always uncanny textures of the interior body as they wavered still more strangely under the light of tall candles, he watched Vesalius dissect the nerves running from the eyes. Interestingly, he stood close enough to observe that these were 'large, white and concave'. It was just at this point, however, that Vesalius 'became very confused, upset and bewildered, owing to the noise and disorder that the students then made'.[341] Perhaps only briefly glimpsing the brain's most sacred structure in a consequently hurried dissection, Heseler was fortunate to have another chance some days later. In a presumably now calmer atmosphere, and in daylight, the young German watched keenly as Vesalius 'at last ... showed us the *rete mirabile* ... situated higher up in the middle of the cranium near where the arteries ascend, and forming the plexus in which the *spiritus animales* are produced out of the *spiritus vitales* transferred there'.[342] This plexus, Heseler goes on to explain, was 'a reddish, fine, netlike web of arteries lying above the bones, which I afterwards touched with my own hands'.[343]

The '*rete mirabile*', or 'wonderful net' was so called because, as Crooke explains, 'this net compasseth the glandule ... and is not like a simple net, but as if you should lay many fishers' nets one above another'. It was 'admirable' because 'the replications of one are tied to the replications of another so that you cannot separate the nets asunder', these being 'all of them so wrought into one another as if it were a body of net meshed together not into breadth only but into thickness also'.[344] The net was also conceptually, as well as aesthetically 'admirable'. For in this frail interweaving of human organic fibres the fluids of the body somehow blurred into the vapours of the immortal soul – refined, as Heseler notes, from vital into animal spirits.[345] This remarkable structure thus spanned the zone between spirit and matter in two related ways. Physiologically, it acted like some kind of organic alchemical apparatus, formed of closely interwoven and narrow convolutions which *looked* sufficient to transform matter into spirit, once this spirit had been – in Crooke's words – 'boiled and laboured' up into the brain.[346] Secondly, as the faintly mesmerised evocation of this 'moebius strip' entanglement implies, one could not fail to detect here the miraculous artifice of God. The wonderful net was not only a physiological zone of transition but – more subtly – a psychological one. Rapturously lost in the contemplation of this organic labyrinth, the viewer experienced a wonder sufficient to carry them, as well as the rarefied spirits of blood, across that intriguing space. Small wonder that Heseler should want not only to see, but to deliberately *touch* this chimaerical organ.

But there was one quite considerable problem. The net had been discovered by that eminent medical authority, Galen, during his dissections of cattle and apes. Ironically, Galen chose for this sacred task (about which he himself probably had different ideas to later Christians) a structure which was particularly large and impressive in certain animals, but which in humans is so small that, as Crooke admits, 'a good eye can scarcely discern it'.[347] Because Galen had apparently *not* dissected humans, Christian medical theory inherited this peculiar theological timebomb, ready to explode in the faces of those finally perceptive enough to look for what had so often been merely talked about or vaguely gestured at. As I suggested above, even Vesalius himself initially struggled to reconcile the reality of the interior body with the established notions of theology. So, in 1540 we find him performing a kind of scientific conjuring trick. As Heseler relates, 'before he cut and demonstrated the three ventricles of the brain, he showed them to us on the head of a sheep which he had brought so that we should better see them in man'.[348] What exactly was going on here? Vesalius seems to have been caught in a difficult crisis of theological and medical transition. In a striking symbol of perception conditioned by expectation, he effectively slides the *rete* of the sheep's head in between his viewers and the human brain, hoping it will act as a kind of curious magnifying glass. After all, what else could a sheep's head be doing in this context? Animals do not have an immortal soul.[349]

It is perhaps unsurprising that the most cherished possession of Christian theology was not abandoned without a fight. In later decades anatomists continued to argue about whether the *rete* actually existed (the French anatomist Casper Bauhin insisted it did) or if there were other plausible substitutes, such as the surrounding veins observed by Heseler, or one of the ventricles of the brain. In Donne's lifetime we find equivocation and confusion still persisting. Even Harvey seemed either undecided, or afraid of admitting a definite opinion. In his lecture notes he simply recorded ongoing medical debate without taking sides.[350] But tellingly, toward the end of his long life, in 1651, he was to openly and violently denounce the whole notion of numinous 'spirits' as a chimaerical fallacy: blood alone, he insisted, did all that spirits were supposed to.[351]

What was Donne's attitude to this situation? We can already guess that he was not one to be satisfied with sophistical or purely abstract answers to the problem of body-soul unity. Medieval theologians, for example, had broadly recognised certain potential difficulties of the 'embodied', physiological soul. If it did indeed pervade the body, then what happened if a limb, hand or even finger was lost? One typically Scholastic and paradoxical approach to this kind of delicate issue was that the soul was essentially 'everywhere and nowhere' in the human body (rather, indeed, like God in his universe). And we find Donne referring to the belief that, while 'our souls are truly said to be in every part of our bodies', yet 'if any part of the body be cut off, no part of the soul perishes, but is sucked into that soul that remains'.[352]

Elsewhere Donne displays the kind of precisely-focused empirical curiosity which Medieval thinkers often lacked. For example: the soul would surely leave a body once its head was severed. And, given the soul's physiological functions, the body should at once fall motionless. Why, then, can it sometimes be seen (evidently in public executions, which Donne himself seems to have witnessed at least once) to not only rake the air with its hands, and shift its feet, but even to roll the eyes and tongue of a head now lying in a basket on the ground, or clutched in an executioner's fist? So Donne mused in 1612.[353] And though he found a nominal answer to that conundrum, it seems that he was indeed seriously dissatisfied with existing theological dogma on the soul. In a letter to his friend Sir Thomas Lucy he states that, 'as ... princes travailed with long and wasteful war descend to such conditions of peace as they are soon after ashamed to have embraced; so philosophers, and so all sects of Christians, after long disputations and controversies, have allowed many things for positive and dogmatical truths which are not worthy of that dignity'. Giving some examples from the area of medicine, he then adds: 'I think it falls out thus also in the matter of the soul.'[354] These lines carry a remarkably unorthodox implication. To a perceptive thinker, theology was as much a contingent and imperfect thing of this world as the roughly political solutions of national leaders. Donne then proceeds to recount the problems associated with the 'infusion' of the soul. There must, he believes, be a moment when it actually enters or activates in the human embryo. Unhappy with existing theory on this vital subject, he concludes that 'there is yet therefore no opinion in philosophy nor divinity so well established as constrains us to believe both that the soul is immortal, and that every particular man hath such a soul'. Although 'out of the great mercy of our God we do constantly believe' as much, he is 'ashamed that we do not also know it by searching further'.

These words neatly capture the genuine faith which was so persistently offset by insatiable mental curiosity. It is not enough to simply, blindly believe. Note that Donne twice uses the word 'ashamed' (and once, similarly, 'dignity'). The inadequacy of dominant notions on the subject is not simply a matter for anxiety, but an issue of personal pride or intellectual integrity. He wishes, he implies, to be infallibly 'constrained' into belief. More broadly, the general topic of Donne's letter – the relation between gestation, biology, and theology – reappeared just a decade after his death in a notoriously heretical denial of the soul's immortality. In his tract *Man's Mortality*, the Christian heretic Richard Overton unrepentantly forced the soul into the realm of proto-scientific experiment. If the soul really *is* an entity, he asked, and must be actually released from a dying body, then what kind of immortality would a man have if he and his soul were suffocated in a sealed vessel? Where would the soul go?[355]

In a sermon of 1622, Donne implies that his discontent with current ideas of body-soul unity had in fact prompted him to take a predictable and decisive step. Denouncing the boundless capacity of human appetite, the preacher asserts that,

> we know the receipt of all the receptacles of blood, how much blood the body can have; so we do of all the other conduits and cisterns of the body; but this infinite hive of honey, this insatiable whirlpool of the covetous mind, no anatomy, no dissection hath discovered to us. When I look into the larders, and cellars, and vaults, into the vessels of our body for drink, for blood, for urine, they are pottles, and gallons; when I look into the furnaces of our spirits, the ventricles of the heart and of the brain, they are not thimbles; for spiritual things, the things of the next world, we have no room; for temporal things, the things of this world, we have no bounds.[356]

Three points can be gleaned from this passage. First, Donne appears to have attended at least one anatomy. Just after the phrases 'no anatomy, no dissection' he plainly says 'when I *look* ...'. Secondly, he seems to have been looking closely at those sites of body-soul processing, the 'furnaces' of spirits. We then have, thirdly, a parable of human imperfection. The vessels of the spirit are 'not thimbles'; those of the flesh are 'larders and cellars', 'pottles and gallons'. Yet beneath this surface layer of meaning we also find a further level. Donne's metaphoric complaint is an all but literal statement of the topical problem facing theology: the newly-investigated body does indeed 'have no room' for the soul. If anyone should want to actually see, and be impressed by, that remarkable organic bridge between spirit and matter it would be the writer who so continually delighted in smudging the boundary between life and death, between this world and the next. But, as if in some neat myth of the early meetings between science and religion, that fabulous texture of veins and arteries had dissolved beneath the pressure of the eye that sought it, corroded and melted by the too coarse air rushing into its sacred space. Once again, language must fill the gap. So Donne conjures the 'insatiable whirlpool of the covetous mind', a richly suggestive image which gives a surface impression of intense activity, masking supposedly hidden depths. And, at the same time, where we might expect some unchanging, inviolable entity, we seem to have *only* motion and energy, the slippery vortex of fluid change which so fascinated Donne in his elegy 'O let me not serve'.

Instead of that rigorous intellectual 'constraint' Donne had sought in his letter, we appear once more to be offered something notably similar to 'blind faith' in this powerful but impressionistic image.[357] The desire to encompass all within the charmed circle of a toughly devouring piety has failed, and a key element of faith has been abstracted and dematerialised. Let us now look at how that ongoing crisis is obliquely addressed in one of Donne's most famous poems.

V

'The Ecstasy' has often been considered one of Donne's most successful lyrics. The word 'ecstasy' in this context derives from the supposed 'out of body' experiences of Catholic mystics – believers so exalted by their unworldly piety that they were known to levitate or even fly. In the simplest terms, then, the poem is an evocation of rarefied love, and one remarkably like that blurred space of the *rete*, in which matter and spirit were temporarily all but indistinguishable. Similarly, the love presented by Donne is neither merely spiritual nor merely physical:

> This ecstasy doth unperplex
> (We said) and tell us what we love,
> We see by this, it was not sex,
> We see, we saw not what did move

For Ezra Pound, this depiction of a personal experience suffused by the numinous was entirely persuasive. The poem, to him, was 'platonism believed. The decadence of pretty speeches and trying to find something to say temporarily checked.'[358] Perhaps Pound was influenced by a similar nostalgia to that of his friend, T.S. Eliot. But if such praise were ever deserved, 'The Ecstasy' probably is the place for it. As far as it succeeds, it does so in a way quite different from many of Donne's more famous poems. Its effect is that of a steady, measured, persistent amplification and cementing of essentially one argument. 'Here is a unity beyond ordinary imagining. This is what it is like, and these are its effects and its foundations.'

In the opening stanza of the poem, a general sensuality is derived from the transposition of the human body into the natural world:

> Where, like a pillow on a bed,
> A pregnant bank swelled up, to rest
>
> The violet's reclining head,
> Sat we two, one anothers best

We then pass to the physical body proper:

Our hands were firmly cemented

With a fast balm, which thence did spring,

Our eye-beams twisted, and did thread

Our eyes, upon one double string

One reason for the kind of success felt by Pound is that a surprising amount is packed up in these few lines. Both 'cemented' and 'firmly' have a tactile quality which is mutually reinforcing; while the 'fast balm' further solidifies the interlocking hands by a fusion effective for its assonance as much as for its implicit viscosity. The active and heavily stressed word 'spring' provides a sharp additional dynamism. For us, the use of 'balm' could seem to in fact rarefy what otherwise might be reduced to 'sweat'. But it is important to remember that, for Donne, 'balm' or 'balsamum' was an integral part of human physiology.[359]

The entwining of the lovers' 'twisted' eye-beams points, equally, to a peculiarly materialistic Renaissance theory of vision, connoting an entanglement quite as physical as modern notions of pheremonal attraction. In the early seventeenth century there seems to have been no firm agreement as to whether vision involved 'intramission or extramission' (eyes receiving light rays or emitting them). In this case, Donne appears to favour the latter view. Not only is this a notably proactive one, but importantly, as A.C. Crombie notes, it held that 'the soul effected vision by means of a specific "visual pneuma" sent from the brain along the optic nerve to the eye'.[360] Within two lines Donne compresses, moreover, not only a general theory of optics, but a neoplatonic interchange whose technical details are more fully expounded by the arch-neoplatonist, Marsilio Ficino:

> Lycias he stares on Phaedrus' face, and Phaedrus fastens the balls of his eyes upon Lycias, and with those sparkling rays sends out his spirits. The beams of Phaedrus' eyes are easily mingled with the beams of Lycias', and spirits are joined to spirits. This vapour begot in Phaedrus' heart, enters into Lycias' bowels: and that which is a greater wonder, Phaedrus' blood is in Lycias' heart.[361]

In that famous example of Greek love, the process of almost cannibalistic osmosis is such that 'Lycias, whose blood and body contain with every passing day more and more of Phaedrus' likeness', will 'in time appear like Phaedrus "in some colours, or features, or feelings, or gestures"'.[362] Such an idea now strikes us as remarkably quaint. Yet Donne's contemporary, Francis Bacon, one of the most intellectually advanced men of his age, still believed that various classical philosophers had enjoyed long life because they conversed with young men, 'their spirits ... being recreated by such company'.[363]

In Donne's poem, the 'double string' of his image augments this active, Ficinian exchange, suggesting a kind of perpetual circulation of spirits within a closed loop. John Carey misleadingly glosses this as 'a loop of string, with four pierced eyes on it'.[364] For what Donne evidently had most firmly in mind, and what fits with the integral argument of the poem, is the 'eye-strings' of the human optic nerves. Not only does Donne elsewhere imagine a man pulling 'at an oar, till his eye-strings, and sinews, and muscles broke', but the fusion of the two lovers' bodies and souls depends on an exchange of visual spirits which are *physiologically* transmitted from the brain and soul, out through the eyes.[365] To appreciate how definitely material and chemical this was, we need only note the period's widespread educated belief in 'specular contagion' – the notion that plague, for example, could be passed on by sight alone.[366]

Finally, at the crux of the poem, we meet the essentially religious underpinning supposed
to guarantee the personal union of the two lovers:

On man heavens' influence works not so,

But that it first imprints the air,

So soul into the soul may flow,

Though it to body first repair.

As our blood labours to beget

Spirits, as like souls as it can,

Because such fingers need to knit

That subtile knot, which makes us man:

So must pure lovers' souls descend

T'affections, and to faculties,

That sense may reach and apprehend,

Else a great Prince in prison lies.

'Imprints' has a tactile quality which may faintly surprise us. Air capable of receiving this imprint becomes strikingly grainy and smudged – perhaps also unexpectedly dense. And we are right to pause here. What we are sensing is an at once widespread, habitual, yet now radically alien belief in the persistent and substantial influence of the planets and stars upon human life. This was no vague astrology of loose psychological interpretation. People died of these influences. They caused diseases: hence 'in-fluenza' ('in-flowings'), and hence Donne's awareness that one must follow a special diet, and take other standard precautions, each year during the rise of the dog star.[367]

Having thus asserted the lovers' special unity with reference to the cosmic links between micro-and macrocosm (the influences of the heavens, the link of body and soul) Donne is able to justly command

To our bodies turn we then, that so
Weak men on love revealed may look ...

Or – is he? Throughout 'The Ecstasy', Donne repeatedly deals with the question of boundaries: between one person and another; between impersonal physical entities; between heaven and earth; and between soul and body. As with the flight of Elizabeth Drury's unleashed soul, he essentially straddles these boundaries by means of material substances: the 'new concoction' received by a hypothetical observer; a hybrid flower derived from the transplanted violet; a hybrid metal ('allay'); and the air which, though less tangible and delimited, is still chemically dense and active, 'imprinted' by heavenly in-flowings.[368] Is there in fact a hint of over-assertion in these repeated material images, and the supple thread of corporeality which they weave through the poem? Have the lovers ever quite escaped their bodies at all?

Two eminent readers thought not. Herbert Grierson, Donne's first serious editor, felt that Donne had 'not entirely succeeded in what he here attempts. There hangs about the poem just a suspicion of the conventional and unreal Platonism of the seventeenth century.' Consequently, 'in attempting to state and vindicate the relation of soul and body he falls perhaps inevitably into the appearance ... of the dualism which he is trying to transcend. He places them over against each other as separate entities and the lower bulks unduly.'[369] The novelist and critic C.S. Lewis was still more emphatic. Lewis thought 'The Ecstasy' a 'nasty' poem, and insisted that 'love does not prove itself pure by talking about purity' nor 'keep on drawing distinctions between spirit and flesh to the detriment of the latter and then explaining that the flesh is after all to be used'.[370] It is no accident that Lewis's surprisingly unacademic term 'nasty' so neatly echoes Eliot, who thought Donne 'dangerous'. Both men were – or became – committed Christians. Lewis's response is in fact a suitably angry reaction to what Grierson more evenly detects – that the poem ultimately exposes the destabilised, failing spirituality of Donne's era and imagination.

The poem presents an interweaving of spirits threaded on the 'double string' of the optic nerves. We met these nerves

283

in 'The Funeral' in a similar context of body-soul physiology. And indeed, back in Bologna in 1540, it was the nerves running to the eyes which Vesalius was dissecting when the simmering excitement of the Italian students suddenly exploded into the tumult of 'noise and disorder' that so disturbed him.[371] A further vital clue is bound up in the 'subtle knot' of the poem's pivotal stanzas. The 'spirits' which 'knit' this are notably echoed in Crooke's description of the *rete mirabile* itself, 'so called from the wonderful knittings of the twigs of arteries proceeding from ... the basis of the brain'.[372] Was Donne by this stage still able to confidently say what or where the subtle knot was? We have seen him, in the convenient privacy of a personal letter, admitting that theology disappointed him on the question of the soul, and of body-soul relations in particular. In the previous chapter we have also seen him opposed to the Catholic saint, Philip Neri, and wishing that the spirit of God might swell his veins and arteries with a more intensely forceful pressure. We seem to find, then, that 'The Ecstasy' is not a simple love poem, much as it ostensibly resembles those other amorous encounters, with their delicious melting of world and self into the minute and boundless liquid of a lover's eyes. Rather, 'The Ecstasy' uses love to respiritualise a human body whose innermost core has been radically dislocated and problematised by the anatomists' scalpels. We do not quite have to say that

Donne thought the organic aspect of the soul to have been destroyed. But the very debate over it had dangerously relativised and undermined something once securely fixed and known, along with other established religious certainties such as the structure of the heavens and position of the planet earth. The spiritual process implied in Donne's poem stands uncertainly poised between the positive wonder of a physicalised, re-vivified soul (one whose bodily mediation is now explored in the anatomy theatre), and the ultimate price to be paid for subjecting the spiritual to so close an empirical scrutiny. On one side we have the pious upsurge of curiosity which burst out among Heseler's fellow students, and which impelled him to minutely inspect and touch what he believed to be the organic juncture of body and soul. On the other, we have the undeniably reduced, if not vanished, *rete mirabile*, and Donne's own anatomically-inspired complaint: for 'the things of the next world, we have no room.'

Yet, as I have already argued, it would be naive to imagine that the erosion and loss of the Christian soul could occur quickly or straightforwardly. Moreover, while the anatomical status of the soul offers many fascinating insights, there are other ways of approaching the peculiar transition which we find illustrated in Heseler's notes and Donne's poem. If we think again of that eagerly gulping whirlpool of the covetous mind, we might begin to wonder whether or not the undoubted loss of a central Christian possession was also effectively a gain for the human individual. At least in the short term, as the peculiar energies of the soul not only broke loose, but temporarily allied themselves to the organic power of the Vesalian body, perhaps certain Christians were able to harness this destabilised force for their own opportunistic purposes. And so we might ask: does 'The Ecstasy' have to quite succeed or fail in the various ways which Pound, Grierson and Lewis imply? We have nothing left of the Christian soul, as experienced by the Renaissance, save those pieces of art and writing in which its peculiar energies were condensed and suspended, like some now extinct creature caught on the wing and trapped in amber. Perhaps 'The Ecstasy' is such a poem. Let us ask a slightly unusual question. What did it *feel* like to have a soul? To be a little more precise: what did it feel like to have a soul for which one was prepared to die, and which was present – for the sufficiently pious – in every sudden rush of blood, every surge of brain chemistry, catalysed by an especially fervent moment of prayer or repentance? We saw Donne attacking those pitiful 'thimbles' of the spirits. Did he in fact believe that these might actually grow *larger* in a more exalted Christian?[373] When he claims that 'an idle soul, is a monster in a man ...' and that, 'that soul that does not think, not consider, cannot be said to actuate (which is the proper operation of the soul) but to evaporate; not to work in the body, but to breathe, and smoke through the body', he certainly appears to indicate a porous boundary between moral force and physical vitality.[374] Again, in 1624 he tells us that 'if the body be lame in any limb, the soul must be lame in her operation, in that limb too'.[375] What did the physiology of the soul feel like? This is the kind of issue that – while so fragile and unstable as to have long ago evaporated from the dry pages of historical documents – must have continually and intensely dominated the lives of the pious. (Why else should you worry about losing the soul in your amputated finger?) What was it like for Heseler, that cold January day, to lay trembling fingers on the filigree of veins and arteries which he imagined at that moment to be pulsing in his own skull, agitating raw bodily matter into something like the breath of God? The Renaissance soul was as peculiarly pervasive, organic, sensuous and precise as Renaissance Christianity, seeping down through all the layers and details of social structure and personal life. What did it feel like to have that kind of soul? To Donne it seems at times to have felt remarkably like the emotions of sexual love experienced in his youth:

Through the ragged apparel of the afflictions of this life, through the scars, and wounds, and paleness, and morphews of sin, and corruption, we can look upon the soul it self, and there see that incorruptible beauty, that white and red, which the innocency and the blood of Christ hath given it, and we are mad for love of this soul, and ready to do any act of danger, in the ways of persecution, any act of diminution of our selves in the way of humiliation, to stand at her door, and pray, and beg, that she would be reconciled to God.[376]

Let us say, then, that it felt not just fundamental – but that it felt, indeed, like oneself, and one could no more let it go than one could abandon or deny one's own thoughts and memories. And so, if 'The Ecstasy' is not quite a straightforward poem about the full force and delight of what it was to have an immortal soul, perhaps it tells us what it felt like to begin losing it. And perhaps, if it succeeds in some way, it does so because one tried all the harder to evoke and to securely delimit what became ever more precious as it slipped through one's fingers. We are not dealing, here, with a crisis of faith that in any way resembles the final death agonies of Christianity in the late-nineteenth and early-twentieth centuries. We do not have to say that Donne emphatically disbelieved either the religion he grew up with, or the one he later grew into. The issues are at once more complex and more interesting than that. Let us rather imagine that, in his repeated desire to 'flesh out' and resolidify his spirituality with the various materials of the body, Donne ironically resembles the frustrated figure of Vesalius in 1540: 'I do not say so, but I show you here ... in these bodies ...'

Chapter Six

The New World

I

A few years after the French Revolution began in 1789, the radical writer Thomas Paine published a famous dissection of the internal and historical inconsistencies of the Christian Bible.[377] Nowhere is Paine more gleeful than in his assault on scriptural geography:

> The most extraordinary of all things called miracles ... is that of the devil flying away with Jesus Christ, and carrying him to the top of a high mountain ... and showing him and promising to him *all the kingdoms of the world.* How happened it that he did not discover America; or is it only with *kingdoms* that his sooty highness has any interest?[378]

Although posed many decades after Donne's death, Paine's unusually direct question serves to focus our attention on a fundamental problem for Renaissance Christians, at a time when they were still slowly and dazedly absorbing the uncharted and bewildering wonders of the American continents. What was it like, as you sailed by a new route to a familiar land, long detailed on ancient maps, to one day find yourself looking at the gently swaying palms of a country that soon appeared to have no ships, no books and no machinery?

For Columbus, who first achieved this ambiguous feat, it was in one sense quite unremarkable. He had been seeking India. So, in a strangely stubborn denial of his monumental discovery, he continued to insist that this *was* India.[379] And in an oblique but important sense that kind of denial persisted among Europeans in the decades down to and through Donne's own lifetime. Numerous attempts, explicit and implicit, were made to align America with what was already known and accepted about the world and its peoples. Donne and his contemporaries attempted to see what they already knew. But under sufficient pressure, even the most longstanding and durable conceptual framework will begin to buckle. Many Christians could not have seen or heard of the Americas without being agitated by a shower of vital questions. Once it became clear roughly where and what these new continents were, the alien winds of the Carribean, Guiana and Peru began to stir pages in the libraries of Rome, Wittenberg, London and Madrid. As these ancient dry leaves fluttered under that strange new influence, they showed no trace of a land-mass swarming with bizarre flora, fauna, and unimaginable reserves of gold. Least of all could they explain its human inhabitants. It is the unstable and difficult relationship between these two responses – the tendency to make the strange familiar, and the final difficulty of denying its genuinely uncanny qualities – which this chapter traces through scattered clues in Donne's poems and sermons. What at one moment seemed an exhilarating expansion of mental and physical horizons was at the next the source of fear, confusion, and even anger.

We will see presently how Donne responded to the conundrum of the New World. But what precisely was it that he and his peers had to adjust to? The Renaissance response to America once again plunges us back into a religious mindset quite startling in its unrepentant simplicity and rigidity. The world had been made at one stroke, in less than seven days. Some time after the fall of Adam and Eve in Eden, their descendants had again been punished by God for their sins. From the supposedly global flood of the Old Testament, only Noah and his family, along with their shipful of animals, were saved. Like all the rest of humanity in Donne's time, the Americans (and their fauna) were ultimately descended from those sole survivors of Noah's ark. Two immediate problems thus arose. The Americans – and especially the North Americans – now seemed to have only the most rudimentary technology. As the mathematician and friend of Sir Walter Ralegh, Thomas Hariot, noted in the 1580s, the Virginians were ingenious and well-organised within their own limits.[380] But their world did seem to be physically very limited indeed. They had neither ocean-going ships, nor world maps. They had almost certainly not left America in recent times. How, then, had they arrived there from the Old World, from the time and land of Noah which must have been their ultimate origin?

The question was serious enough to prompt a number of quite detailed theories. Perhaps there had at one point been a slender land bridge between east and west, for example.[381] Perhaps – and here we meet one of the more startling revisions of scripture prompted by America – there had indeed been a *second* divine Creation, producing all those distinctive new creatures not found in the Old World.[382] Even had a satisfactory answer been available here, a further question was no less baffling. How had the descendants of Noah, who must at some point have had knowledge of Christianity, been degraded to such a primitive condition? Degrees of 'savagery' varied, of course, from peaceful communities of small-scale agriculture and hunting, to the fabulously mythic ferocity of the cannibals. Yet none of these groups looked recognisably marked by the traces of Christianity. Perhaps their passage across from the Old

World had been so long ago that historical and geographical distance from Christian civilisation had combined to obliterate all evidence of scriptural knowledge and Old World civilisation among them. Others saw the Americans' primitive religious rites as Satanic parodies of true piety. Again, to some they were so clearly unregenerate as to have been descended from that mythically wicked branch of Noah's family, the 'cursed race of Cham'.[383] One theory even held them to be the ancestors of the Bible's wandering Jews.[384]

Along with this range of responses, there must also have been a broad spectrum of more basic, less precisely rational reactions. To put it simply, America must have been more real to some Europeans than to others. Christians of an especially theoretical, abstracting cast of mind could conceivably have begun to absorb the Americas at a purely conceptual level. But Donne, typically, seems to have been struck throughout his lifetime by the living, particular presence of these new lands, as well as by their status within the conceptual frameworks of Christian truth. To some – if only in dreams, or at the lowest, weakest hour of night – the Americas must have offered one all but unthinkable, unspeakable possibility: namely, that the Christian God had no more heard of them, than they of him.

The peoples of South America soon knew his name all too well. It is now difficult to separate the facts of Spanish occupation from fiction. Yet, viewed as part of the broad, dark world history of racial and religious hostility and incomprehension, the legendary slaughters credited to the Spanish look all too plausible. As early as 1493, Pope Alexander VI had drawn a line on a map, granting new territories on the west of it to Spain, and those on the east to Portugal.[385] As the breath of God filled the countless sails of these two powerful nations in voyage after voyage, they must have been reassured to know that they were allowed (initially by Queen Isabella of Spain, and later by the Pope) to actively enslave or subdue either the cannibals of the Americas, or any infidels who resisted conversion to the gentle faith of Jesus.[386]

If surviving accounts of the Spanish conquests are true, then their armies murdered and tortured millions of the native population of the Caribbean and of Central and South America. We read countless tales of unarmed Indians betrayed after agreeing to surrender, roasted alive on grills, strung up over slow fires in rows of thirteen (in memory of Christ and his apostles), fed to dogs, their children brained on rocks before their eyes. In a verse letter Donne talks of how the virtuous at court are as helpless as 'Indian 'gainst Spanish hosts' of soldiers.[387] And he was certainly a nominal Protestant by the time he wrote, in *Biathanatos*, of the '20000 children' supposed to have been 'sacrificed yearly' in the island of Hispaniola alone, since the Spanish first reached the Indies.[388] We know that the Protestants who avidly read, repeated and reproduced the tales of Spanish atrocities had their own special reasons for demonising the activities of their Christian enemies. And one commentator, William S. Maltby, has prosecuted this propagandist argument to an especially strong degree in his book, *The Black Legend*.[389] Yet at one quite basic level it is striking how ready some critics have been to complacently reduce the reported holocaust of the New World to the purely textual matter of representation. This is convenient because such armchair theorising avoids the need to actually consider if these things happened. Without finally concluding that they did, it remains important to remember that they could have done – and that, in other broadly similar contexts, they have done. History is not just written. Albeit in a space often less easily graspable than the pages of books, it is really lived, by real people. At a second level we also know – as Protestants were keen to point out – that the original stories of Spanish atrocities derived not from their Christian antagonists in Britain and Germany, but from a Spanish eyewitness, the Jesuit, Bartolomé de las Casas (1474-1566), who first published his *Brief Relation of the Destruction of the West Indies* in Seville in 1552.

The religious implications of Spanish primacy in the New World will be pursued in detail shortly. What we also need to recognise before grappling with Donne's various responses to the Americas is that the Spanish and Portuguese were plying their legions of ships across the Atlantic for one very urgent and concrete reason in particular. We have heard Donne referring to the east and west 'Indias of spice and mine'. And the mines of the 'West Indies' were no idle myth. South America, in the Renaissance, was a land fabulously, almost inconceivably rich in gold. As Robert Silverberg notes, the depository at Seville received 993,000 *pesos de oro* from the New World between 1516 and 1520, with the figure rising to 1,038,000 *pesos* from 1526-30, after a brief slump in the early 1520s.[390] Historians have gone so far as to claim that the Spanish economy was fundamentally shaped – indeed distorted – by the staggering quantities of gold plundered from the New World – reserves of raw wealth so great that for decades at least they discouraged Spain from developing a productive internal economy of its own. As if by some dark alchemy, Spanish ships sailed out with the base metal of swords, guns and bullets, transforming it in storms of fire and blood into the glittering cargos that ballasted their returning holds. With Spain already the most powerful nation in Europe, the consequences of its monopoly of New World gold (and territory) were serious for Britain. Possessed almost with an insidious will and mind of its own, 'Indian gold' (warns Sir Walter Ralegh in 1595) 'endangereth and disturbeth all the nations of Europe ... purchaseth intelligence', and 'creepeth into councils ...'. Should the King of Spain take Guiana, Ralegh further adds, 'he will become unresistable'.[391] As Donne himself notes, by the early seventeenth century this monarch was said to have 'in Europe almost three hundred thousand miles, and in the new world seven millions'.[392] So Ralegh, in 1595, made what he assumed to be a tantalisingly close bid for some of this vast mineral treasure, during a voyage down the Orinoco river into Guiana. Cautious as one must be with his first-person account in some places, the narrative related in *The Discovery of the Large, Rich, and Beautiful Empire of Guiana* (1596) remains a compelling and unique tale of Renaissance contact with the New World, an intriguing form of early travel writing which creates its own uncertain space between fact and fiction. So compelling and real was the lure of South American gold that in 1616, Ralegh (though then imprisoned for many years following court intrigues against him), was specially released by James I so that he could make one last try for those yet untapped fathoms of gold that glittered somewhere under the plain Guianan rocks. In the event, he failed – and now still more disastrously than he had twenty years' before. In those early, heady days of the 1590s, however, things were very different. Let us try to gain some sense of how they looked to an energetic young law student, catching the reflected gleam of the Americas, in all their danger and wonder, through the immediate dazzle and opportunity of Elizabethan London.

II

> Come, Madam, come, all rest my powers defy,
> Until I labour, I in labour lie.
> The foe oft-times having the foe in sight,
> Is tired with standing though they never fight.
> Off with that girdle, like heaven's zone glistering,
> But a far fairer world encompassing.
> Unpin that spangled breastplate which you wear,
> That th'eyes of busy fools may be stopped there.
> Unlace yourself, for that harmonious chime
> Tells me from you, that now 'tis your bed time.

Here in Donne's Elegy 19, 'To his Mistress Going to Bed', we are in some ways returned to familiar territory – the stalking-ground of the gracious and opportunistic youthful persona, moving in a bright rustle of silk and suavity among the enticing female treasures poorly guarded by dull parents and undeserving husbands. But this poem, after its general conceit of amorous warfare, develops its vaunted sexual conquest in a way specifically indebted to the shimmering wonder of the New World. At its simplest level it is a kind of extended strip-tease, detailed through the at once graceful and imperative commands of the watching male. In a neat parable of Renaissance gender relations the poem itself accumulates a variety of ingenious conceits, verbally dressing up the scene as the woman is stripped ever more bare of the clothing that conspicuously defines her. And tellingly, this dualism is further compounded by the way that her clothes, rather than herself, speak more clearly than she does, with the 'harmonious chime' of the watch (worn over the ties of the stomacher) being more welcome to the poet than any words.[393] Ventriloquised through characteristic male notions of the period, she also speaks an ambiguous yet eloquent language of nature:

Your gown going off, such beauteous state reveals,
As when from flowery meads th'hill's shadow steals.

For the writer who in a letter quite precisely noted how 'shadows upon clay will be dirty, and in a garden green and flowery', we can infer that this image might have been visualised with a similar immediacy when it was written.[394] That sense of a real, sensuously felt and apprehended concrete presence is important. And its associated charge of excitement suddenly spills out of the pen when – now bedded with his half-naked mistress – the speaker exults,

> Licence my roving hands, and let them go
> Before, behind, between, above, below.
> O my America, my new found land,
> My kingdom, safeliest when with one man manned,
> My mine of precious stones, my empery,
> How blessed am I in this discovering thee!

Again, all this is in one sense carefully staged. We can gauge as much from the sly puns – on the royal licences granted to colonial companies, and on 'discover' as 'uncover'. Yet that familiar level of detached control also seems to coexist with a genuine fascination in the presence of the unknown.

That second, more unstable and open level of the poem is subtly conveyed even through the neatly iambic wanderings of the roving hands. Those five restless words ('Before, behind, between, above, below') are in one way typically aggressive – something like a kind of verbal octopus, or the boarding of a rival ship by approaching confusingly from all sides at once. Yet they also signal a powerful underlying *need* to securely encompass a territory which must be touched to be quite believed, and whose imaginative presence is in fact far more mobile and unnerving than the hands vainly seeking to grasp it. Here if anywhere the desire to absolutely set one's defining seal is far more a symptomatic hope than a viable reality. Behind that brief, very familiar figure of the vagina as a 'mine of precious stones' there lay the whole ongoing saga of the Spanish conquest of South America. When Donne elsewhere referred to 'Guiana's rarities', or still more specifically to the evident failure of Ralegh's 1590s' voyage ('Guiana's harvest is nipped in the spring,/I fear') he must have had some knowledge of precisely what was at stake in such ventures.[395] Let us take just two examples. In late 1532, during the early phase of the European frenzy for gold, the Spaniard Francisco Pizarro took hostage Atahuallpa, the King of Peru. Atahuallpa first offered to cover the floor of his cell (around twenty five by seventeen feet) in gold by way of ransom. The Spanish, we are told, were so stunned that they did not quickly reply. Mistaking the silence of rapturous greed for disappointment, the King now promised he would fill the entire room – or, as was presently agreed, fill it to a marked line some nine feet up the wall. And so he did. For months sweating llamas sagged under the various weights of bullion that was to slowly rise in gleaming layers in this soon legendary room of gold. In one of the many acts of European betrayal committed in the Americas, Atahuallpa himself was finally killed regardless.[396]

Some sixty odd years later, Ralegh remained convinced that there was a still more fabulous store of wealth than the painfully gathered accumulation of that bright room. In Guiana, he was sure, there was an entire city of gold. In Manoa, or El Dorado ('the golden one'), the most routine objects were made of this abundant native metal. Indeed, it was so plentiful that the region's King was coated from head to foot with gold dust in an annual ceremony.[397] It was for this that Ralegh and his men braved the floods and alligators of the Orinoco, the superior might of the Spanish, the terrible poisons of South American tribes, and all the mundane sordid hardships of Renaissance voyages by river and sea. It was for this that the notoriously extravagant James I temporarily released Ralegh in 1616. Ralegh heard tales of it (he thought) from native inhabitants. He had maps drawn. And why should this highly educated, inquisitive and learned adventurer doubt his ultimate prize? He was also ready, after all, to credit tales of the 'ewaipanoma' or 'men whose heads grew beneath their shoulders', and of the Amazons, that mythical race of female warriors detailed in classical histories, and now understood to maintain their defiantly matriarchal communities just a few miles from where Ralegh stood, listening to the tales of Spanish or Guianan informants.[398]

In some ways Ralegh's golden city was a place of the mind. It may well have become especially so during his years caged in the Tower of London, where he was often engaged in alchemical experiments.[399] Yet we have to understand that it was not only that. The Renaissance capacity for wonder was undoubtedly greater than the dreams of the average European today. (Indeed, it probably lies closer to that fierce optimism of those modern descendants who have since come to dominate North America.) These *terrae incognitae* in which the British now began to tread were in some ways more like outer space than like the definitely known, mapped, and exploited countries of the world. What was so distinctively intoxicating about them, though, was that they were a little like the moon in 1969: distant and astonishing, and yet – if you could make yourself believe it – you were actually *there*. The New World, then, was both strange and true, incredible but finally undeniable. It was something which male Europeans now possessed, yet which they also found persistently elusive, unnerving, or bewildering. Little wonder, then, that the New World was implicitly and explicitly gendered. America was female. 'Guiana', as Ralegh explains, 'is a country that hath yet her maidenhead, never sackt, turned, nor wrought.'[400]

Just what did this mean? We have already caught a glimpse of what it meant to Donne, both here and in chapter three. This was a realm of underused, untamed and uncivilised matter. With such a notion already in place, one can see how it was potently intensified by tales of South America in particular. Ralegh's remark was no idle throwaway comment. What, after all, was the most glaringly dominant quality of this region? It was fertile. We hear of grassy plains 'twenty miles in length', of 'flowers and trees of that variety as were sufficient to make ten volumes of herbals ... birds of all colours, some carnation, some crimson, orange tawny, purple, green, watchet, and of all other sorts both simple and mixed'.[401] Just beyond the titanic natural power of the waterfalls of Caroli the landscape sweeps away in almost paradisal vistas:

> I never saw a more beautiful country, nor more lively prospects, hills so raised here and there over the vallies, the river winding into diverse branches, the plains adjoining without bush or stubble, all fair green grass ... the deer crossing in every path, the birds towards the evening singing on every tree with a thousand several tunes, cranes and herons of white, crimson, and carnation perching on the river's side, the air fresh with a gentle easterly wind, and every stone that we stooped to pick up, promised either gold or silver by his complexion.[402]

And beneath all this, as if its subterranean energy was barely checked by the rock and soil which contained such vital pressure, the magical fecundity of gold (actually imagined, at this time, to 'grow' like an organism) secretly swelled and ripened in the dark womb of the earth.[403] Indeed, as we see above, to Ralegh and his men it sometimes appeared to all but pave the ground they walked on.

The speaker of Donne's elegy, then, has good reason to be excited. And, while this is undoubtedly one of his more secular poems, we must remember that gold also had a numinous, quasi-religious significance now hard to appreciate. Columbus in particular was supposed to have been captivated by its perceived spiritual dimension. And in 1625, Donne, after referring to 'the western hemisphere, the land of gold, and treasure', describes God himself as 'the land of gold, centrical gold, visceral gold, gremial gold, gold in the matrice and womb of gold, that is, essential goodness'.[404] As we have seen in chapter three, he would keep returning to the special mutability of gold. From that heavy mass compacted under the ground it could be hammered out to such a fineness that it would blow away. We seem here to meet an implicit teleology – a sense of matter rarefied into a higher spiritual state and yet still – crucially – in some way recognisably itself.[405] We will encounter a particularly important version of that spiritual transformation in our concluding chapter. What we need to recognise here is that, for all the familiar mood of brash sexual opportunism, Donne's elegy also contains a certain core of something like religious wonder. We do not need to read the piece as a poem about the female capacity for generation to believe that the still mysterious issue of gestation partly underlies that simulated yet real tremor of awe, poised momentarily at the mouth of the unknown. At a general level we know, after all, that raw fecundity was one of the basic defining characteristics of women. Similarly, strangeness and otherness were in part just what inspired sexual attraction. We might therefore ask: is America heightening the strangeness of women, or is a woman being used to heighten America's strangeness? Perhaps both – but what we can also claim is that the amorous exploration of this poem is not unlike the safely limited re-creations of social power found in Donne's other Elegies. The woman offers a useful way of cautiously flirting with the wonder of a country whose fully alien presence might elsewhere threaten to uncontrollably flood the baffled imagination. This little kingdom can be safely and easily manned, and managed.

And yet, a woman would not be sufficient to spark that gleam of fascination with the unknown if she was not herself genuinely unknowable in many ways. In a certain necessary psychological sense women had to be unknowable – to be different – in order that men could fully know themselves. So, in keeping with Woolf's shrewd image of the distorting mirror of gender relations, men continually constructed and reconstructed a female otherness that helped define their own identities.[406] One especially powerful example of this was indeed the whole longstanding mystification of childbirth. This, as commentators have emphasised, was the only area in which women had such massive and legitimate professional dominance, and from which men were correspondingly excluded. At the start of chapter three we saw Donne writing a letter while his wife laboured to release her child in a separate room of the house. And in Elegy 19, it is to that curiously enclosed female domain that he finally turns. With the mistress now retaining only her underclothes, he first toys with the notion of women as 'mystic books', before – tellingly – abandoning the textual realm for the empirical:

> ... Then since I may know,
> As liberally, as to a midwife, show
> Thyself: cast all, yea this white linen hence ...

That faint dramatic flourish, as we drop to the desired revelation of the third quoted line, gives an ambiguous edge to 'Thyself' – as if, framed by the line-break and the colon, it is indeed the fundamental essence of the female in general, rather than the simple body of one woman, which is aimed at. Having taken such trouble to reach this final goal, Donne now swerves away from it, nervously surrendering it into the professional female hands of the midwives. The gender relations of this elegy are clearly negative from our point of view. But from a Renaissance viewpoint the thrill of discovery seems, rather, to sway precariously between excitement and fear.

We can more fully appreciate that latter quality all the better if we look at a partly similar poem which ultimately offers an essentially fearful, reductive attitude to the open strangeness of female lands. Elegy 18, 'Love's Progress', is broadly structured into three sections. It debates, first, the right way to love, which itself hinges on the true nature of women:

> Whoever loves, if he do not propose
> The right true end of love, he's one that goes
> To sea for nothing but to make him sick.
> And love's a bear-whelp born, if we o'er-lick
> Our love, and force it new strange shapes to take,
> We err, and of a lump a monster make.

This puzzling conceit can be divided into two related parts. Its particular side involves yet one more strange Renaissance belief: namely, that bear cubs were born as shapeless lumps, then licked into their final form by their mothers (hence 'lick you into shape'). Additionally, the conceptual moral drawn from that example concerns the finally limited nature of different creatures. This nature is ultimately so definite and rigid that – in this case – a mistakenly elevated idea of women will only distort them, rather than managing in any way to improve them or oneself. And the exact nature of women?

> I, when I value gold, may think upon
> The ductileness, the application,
> The wholesomeness, the ingenuity,
> From rust, from soil, from fire ever free,
>
> But if I love it, 'tis because 'tis made
> By our new nature, use, the soul of trade.

So we have, secondly, an assertion of women's essential nature (they are to be used or traded) which itself determines how one should love them. In keeping with this insistently reductive and degrading attitude, Donne decides that 'Cupid' is not to be found among the spheres. Rather,

> He's an infernal god and underground
> With Pluto dwells, where gold and fire abound.
> Men to such gods, their sacrificing coals
> Did not in altars lay, but pits and holes.

The broad picture is fairly clear. The 'pits and holes' of ancient religious rites imply the vagina as the proper object of male worship. Note, though, some of the more subtle implications: not only are women associated with a realm of dark subterranean matter, but that region itself, while looking at first tellingly like hell, is not even allowed to actually belong to Christianity at all, being rather the pagan domain of Pluto.[407] Such imagery accords with the more local and pressing sense that the Indians of the New World were themselves somehow outside the scope of accepted Christian theories.

And the remainder of the poem hints further at the uncontained, unknowable qualities of both women and America. The third section is effectively a kind of empirical confirmation of how one should correctly love women. Should they be approached via their heads (thus, implicitly, as intellectual creatures) or from their feet (as essentially animal creatures)? Perhaps unsurprisingly, Donne opts for the latter. Deciding that one must love 'the centric part' as the defining essence of woman, he warns that

> in attaining this desired place
> How much they stray, that set out at the face!
> The hair a forest is of ambushes,
> Of springes, snares, fetters and manacles;
> The brow becalms us when 'tis smooth and plain,
> And when 'tis wrinkled, shipwrecks us again

The voyage runs on, past the 'swelling lips' where one temporarily anchors, to 'a creek where chosen pearls do swell', inhabited by 'the remora, her cleaving tongue'. Finally, 'sailing towards her India', the speaker halts at her 'fair Atlantic navel', having realised that one may now

> upon another forest set
> Where many shipwreck, and no further get.

What is going on behind this seemingly playful screen of ingenious witticisms? We find, first of all, that the female body is at once alluring and perilous.[408] We should not forget what a fundamentally Christian attitude this itself is. But what notably overlays it here is the specific reason why it is so perilous to travel from the *face* to the 'India' of the 'centric part'.[409] The implicit subtext of the poem is that to deal with the face or head is to effectively recognise women's humanity, rationality, and equality. Like America itself, women can be controlled and reassuringly 'known' only if they are safely contained within an emphatically reductive notion of their 'essence'. Once their human reality is more fully admitted, matters become more difficult. And it was of course precisely because such conceptual frameworks were really artificial and imposed that they must frequently be reimposed or reconstructed. Moreover, Donne has already admitted that even the 'centric part' has a certain ambiguous power that exceeds male control:

> Nor is the soul more worthy, or more fit
> For love than this, as infinite as it.

Here, while the vagina becomes a kind of mock-soul, it is also claimed to be 'as infinite' as the Christian spirit itself. At one level the parallel is broadly apt, given that the vagina is the defining essence of women, corresponding to the definitively rational soul of men. At a more buried and perhaps more important level, the phrasing of those lines offers a suitably uncertain tribute to that female space partly apprehended, partly

313

created by men, and marked by the concrete power of gestation, and the more elusive power of the unknown. The vagina, we are told, is as 'infinite' as the soul. Why? Presumably because it connotes the womb, the source of that vicarious immortality conferred by children. Again, it is unbounded insofar as its workings have not yet been convincingly mapped and detailed - even by that new anatomical science which now increasingly exposed the inadequacies of existing medical theory.

Donne's conclusion is only one more covert admission of bewilderment and anxiety:

Rich Nature hath in women wisely made

Two purses, and their mouths aversely laid;

They then, which to the lower tribute owe,

That way which that exchequer looks, must go.

He which doth not, his error is as great,

As who by clyster gave the stomach meat.

A clyster was an enema. One would not trouble to be as resourcefully nasty as that last line, with its abrasive physical grotesquerie, if one did not suffer a correspondingly strong need to degrade and deflate those unnerving spaces of the female largely contrived and maintained by men themselves. That harsh negative energy projects the speaker's own sense of women as unstable psychic entities. They are imaginative presences which in fact cannot be defined, and will not stay still. At once definite and 'infinite' (swallowing one even as one possesses it), the vagina is an essence that cannot be grasped and fixed. Even in Elegy 19 Donne had admitted as much, when his final imagining of the ultimate goal saw him swerving away at the last second, nervously deferring the truth and ownership of his prize to that specially enclosed and independent community of the midwives.

Here, then, are two related versions of Donne's America, partly similar, partly contrasting. Excitement rises, seemingly genuine, fresh, fascinated, only to turn sour, throwing the speaker back on overly assertive strategies of control, the familiar violence of fear and incomprehension. And it is striking how precise the contrasts are. In the first case we encounter the poised, ambiguous thrill of discovery, the poet able to hold onto a seemingly positive wonder as long as there is some distance between him and the object of his admiration. Once closer contact is made, as in 'Love's Progress', with its shift from watching to acting, more fierce defensive strategies are required. As if psychologically overwhelmed by the near presence of a mythical fecundity turned bad (the cannibals, Amazons, and fabulously effective poisons of South America, rather than its hills of gold and Edenic plains) the speaker is all the more in need of those old theories which maintain a threatened male and Christian identity.[410] What we can detect is that America is a mobile, unstable presence for Donne in at least two interesting ways. Not only does his response to it oscillate between excitement and fear, but in its more positive sense alone the excitement and wonder are themselves fluid and amorphous, fitting different psychological moulds at different times. In now looking, secondly, at Donne's nominally more mature, formally religious attitudes to America we need to be aware that under the seemingly changed surface, a similarly powerful, similarly restless, psychic pressure is still at work.

III

In 'A Valediction: of Weeping' Donne creates a tearful moment of parting. Echoing the self-enclosed amorous worlds of 'The Sun Rising' or 'The Good Morrow', he transforms a teardrop into a minute crystallisation of the entire earth:

> On a round ball
> A workman that hath copies by, can lay
> An Europe, Afric, and an Asia,
> And quickly make that, which was nothing, all ...

316

Similarly, one of the speaker's teardrops, printed with the reflected image of the mistress, can 'a globe, yea world by that impression grow'. Around a hundred years after Columbus set foot in America, Donne's version of the world fails to include it. Why? One answer is that Donne is here following the pre-Columbian division of the then-known world, which in its most basic form simply cut a circle in three unequal parts. Asia took the upper half, and Europe and Africa split the lower one between them. For some time, however, maps had been including the new continents of the Americas. Or, to be a little more precise, different versions (particularly of the northern landmass) had been slowly fattening out upon the new charts of the expanded globe. In that quite definite visual sense North America was still growing, as a more accurate idea of its real dimensions became clear. And in another, more subtle but quite real sense it was also growing into full actuality in the minds of many European Christians. The second reason why Donne omits America from his globe, then, can be seen to involve a certain curious – and characteristic – integrity. It will be included only when it has been more thoroughly absorbed – when, we might say, it has been mentally colonised as well as physically discovered.

How could this process of absorption take place? In a verse letter to the Countess of Bedford Donne reveals that he unconsciously felt it to be a fraught and difficult one. Two mutual friends having recently died, he imagines their souls as stars:

> We've added to the world Virginia, and sent
> Two new stars lately to the firmament.

As we will find, this seemingly curious first line appears roughly to mean that Virginia has been 'added' to the civilised, legitimate world of Christianity. We will also find that such a notion is no more purely whimsical than the variously-phrased doubts as to women's human and spiritual status. Yet even in this letter we can see that Virginia has *not* yet been satisfactorily added or absorbed into the comprehensible sphere of Christendom. On one hand, it sits hard by a reference to the 'new stars' whose discovery had so seriously disrupted the known cosmos in Donne's lifetime. Typically, Donne attempts to sweep these within the devouring centripetal control of his imagination (that 'insatiable whirlpool of the covetous mind') by personalising them into the two dead friends. And secondly, that couplet itself only appears after Donne has emphatically lamented the most radical cosmic shift of his era:

As new philosophy arrests the sun,

And bids the passive earth about it run,

So we have dulled our mind, it hath no ends;

Only the body's busy, and pretends ...

We have already seen how the body was threatening to overwhelm the soul. In this context we can also say that matter in general had run ahead of theory. The newly-perceived world (both earth and heavens) has forcibly, undeniably burst through the old conceptual crust which previously contained it. The solution is for the mind to busy itself ever more urgently, remapping and relocating the changed body of the world within the safe magic circle of Christian history.

Donne seems to have at least begun that task in another verse letter, this time to the Countess of Huntingdon.[411] In what is thought to be the remaining part of a now incomplete letter, rather than its actual opening, he talks of

That unripe side of earth, that heavy clime

That gives us man up now, like Adam's time

Before he ate ...

The 'unripe' new world of the Americas is, he imagines, 'from paradise so great a distance' that 'the news could not arrived be/Of Adam's tasting the forbidden tree' (ll. 1-3, 6-8.).[412] Donne has made a fundamental step in 'adding' America to the world in those first lines. No longer wholly absent from his mental map, it has now been located within an implicit Christian teleology. Its unripeness is a kind of positive blankness, an inchoate stage of human and spiritual life, but one which has been vitally included within a knowable, prewritten narrative of Christian history and spiritual progress. And, if we recall Donne's notion of women as fertile land, we can further see how his revalidation of the New World matches the more widespread gendering of the Americas. In an engraving made around 1580 by Theodore Galle we find Columbus, armoured and upright, waking the sleeping, nearly naked personification of a female America from a hammock. Behind her, some distance back, but – as one commentator has emphasised – in the centre of the picture, two female cannibals roast human limbs on a spit.[413] While America is effectively split, here, into good and bad versions, both of these categories are again female.

IV

In his poems Donne frequently draws on that common sense of the New World as both female and malleable, passive and 'unripe'. Elsewhere, we find him more explicit as to how Christians should apply their energetic powers to the issue of the New World. In theory, he and his fellow Protestants had a tightly coherent and systematic vision of what America was, and what it must become. Three related arguments were available to them. The most negative, from our point of view, was the Aristotelian doctrine of 'natural slavery'. Insisting on the same kind of rigid, unchangeable hierarchy of natural types found in Donne's Elegy 18, this held certain intrinsically inferior, primitive peoples to be the natural slaves of their more developed, civilised masters.[414] While broadly consistent with many Christian attitudes expressed by Protestants, this notion was problematic because it was so notoriously associated with the alleged atrocities of Spanish conquest in the New World. At the start of this chapter we briefly met the rare Spanish champion and chronicler of the native Americans, Bartolomé de las Casas. In his mid-century debate on Indian rights, las Casas was obliged to argue against just such theories, propounded by his opponent, Juan de Sepúlveda (1490-1573).[415] A second approach, less tainted than the idea of 'natural slavery', was that captured under the Latin phrase 'res nullius'. Roughly translating as 'things void', the concept derived from legal philosophy. It is paraphrased by Donne when he talks of the 'Law of Nature and of Nations' – something which supposedly declares any country rightfully open to colonisation 'if the inhabitants do not in some measure fill the land', to 'bring forth *her* increase for the use of men'.[416] We can already begin to see an underlying continuity between this view and Donne's images of formless, uncreated and purposeless matter. The parallel is further cemented if we note the claim of the poet George Chapman, that Ralegh and the British should enter Guiana not merely for selfish or national causes, but in order to

> Bear and bring forth anew in all perfection,
> What heretofore savage corruption held
> In barbarous chaos ...[417]

Again, this kind of argument probably alienates and startles us. It calls to mind most obviously the long-discredited 'white man's burden' of the Victorian empire, with its repellent mixture of brutality and Christian self-righteousness. It may be, however, that Renaissance Christians more genuinely believed in their version of this seemingly hypocritical theory. That is, Donne and his peers *needed* to believe it more urgently, reeling as they still were from the early shock of a whole sprawling continent with essentially no right to exist. The Victorians, whose exploitation was especially rampant in Africa, had long known that this 'dark continent' existed, and used the notion of European 'responsibility' more narrowly, to legitimise activities chiefly driven by material aims. We can also viably argue that the Renaissance belief was stronger and more integral because the earlier period believed more forcefully and precisely in the Christian soul. For it was this that provided the third and perhaps the most important attitude to America. As the Indians failed to adequately fill and organise their native land, so too their souls failed – as yet – to thoroughly animate and realise the matter of their bodies.[418] Both were a kind of partially-formed, partially-exploited substance still existing only *in potentia*. The third stance, then, was that of evangelism. While the echo of the ambiguous, inferior female soul is clear enough, what evangelism in theory seems to offer is a real chance for spiritual and human equality. The men of the New World, at least, could be nurtured from their 'unripe' state into one of enlightened, pious rationality.

These three positions (broadly divisible into the philosophical, legal, and religious) formed the more abstract European stance toward America. What were the precise circumstances in which Donne and his contemporaries sought to apply them? As far as Donne's lifetime is concerned, we have four broad phases. The first was the more opportunistic, sporadic ventures into the New World (and against the Spanish) of the 1580s and 1590s. It was these which formed the context for Donne's two colonial elegies. Secondly, there is the first stirring of a sustained, relatively systematic approach to the New found land, marked by the formation of the Virginia Company in 1607. In July of that year one of Donne's letters talked playfully of the colony which would result.[419] And, as noted, he attempted to become secretary to the new company a few months later, in February 1609. Though he failed, he seems to have remained on friendly terms with his successful rival, William Strachey; and in April 1609 he may have attended an important evangelical sermon on Virginia by one William Symonds. We know he was certainly interested in Symonds' views, as he in fact owned a copy of the published text.[420] Again, if the verse letter alluding to Virginia and the 'new stars' did indeed refer to the recently deceased Lady Markham and Cecilia Bulstrode, it was probably written in later 1609.[421] In following years the Virginia project floundered. Stanley Johnson has shown that Donne knew many of those closely involved with it, and so could have been well-informed of its changing fortunes.[422] For some time these looked very bleak. Disease, poor harvests and lack of investment threatened the still relatively small number of colonists in Virginia, with the late teens of the new century being an especially low point of the venture. But from around 1621 prospects began to improve. It is this period which forms a third stage in Britain's colonial and evangelical ambitions. In 1624, however, the Company was finally dissolved. After a brief time of optimistic buoyancy, then, we meet a fourth phase in which Virginia, and America in general, again seem to slip notably from the British grasp and imagination. As we will see, Donne's own attitudes roughly adhere to this four-fold division.

His first loose involvement with the Virginia Company in 1609 seems to have already been genuinely evangelical as well as pragmatic. But we know little about his feelings in that period. From 1621 things are very different. Now that the colonists themselves were more secure, they began to seriously address a long-cherished scheme of converting the native inhabitants (with whom they lived, at this point, in peaceful co-existence). Tellingly, the first aim was to work especially on the Indian children. For this purpose a 'College' would be established. It seems to have been these aims which appealed to Donne. He alludes to them as early as December 1621. On 22 May 1622 he was made an honorary member of the Virginia Company, and shortly afterwards was invited to deliver a sermon to its members, which he did on 13 November.[423] In following months he attended six meetings of the Company, and there are at least six geographic, cartographic or evangelical references in his sermons – beyond that to the Company itself – from December 1621 to spring 1623.[424]

Three references occur prior to the Virginia sermon. Although it would be rash to view them too rigidly as part of a developing narrative of Donne's evangelical attitudes, chronology is especially important in this period. First, then, we find him speaking at some length on Christmas Day, 1621. In a typical opening Donne asserts that 'it is but a slack opinion, it is not belief, that is not grounded upon reason'. He then imagines coming to 'a heathen man, a mere natural man, uncatechised, uninstructed in the rudiments of the Christian religion', and presenting him

> first with this necessity; thou shall burn in fire and brimstone eternally, except thou believe a trinity of persons, in an unity of one God, except thou believe the incarnation of the second person of the trinity, the Son of God, except thou believe that a virgin had a son, and the same son that God had, and that God was man too, and being the immortal God, yet died ...

The heathen's most likely response would, Donne admits, simply be 'not to believe Hell it self, and then nothing could bind him to believe the rest'.[425] But this initial failure is, Donne implies, based on insufficiently detailed and extensive rational evidence. Suppose on the other hand that this heathen were shown the Bible itself: 'these Scriptures', he insists,

> have so orderly, so sweet, and so powerful a working upon the reason, and the understanding, as if any third man, who were utterly discharged of all preconceptions and anticipations in matter of religion ... altogether neutral, disinterested ... nothing towards a Turk, and as little toward a Christian, should hear a Christian plead for his bible, and a Turk for his alcoran, and should weigh the evidence of both ... he would be drawn to ... our Bible ... to prefer it before any other ... he would believe it, and he would know *why* he did so.[426]

Here the positive blankness occasionally associated with the New World Indian is most fully utilised. It is not just that Donne asserts the evangelical power of the Bible. Rather, from a sideways angle we can see him curiously *using* the Indian as a kind of experimental testing ground for faith. The latter has a special value for his ability to 'genuinely', infallibly prove the truth of Christianity – a kind of theological litmus paper irresistibly coloured gold by contact with the Christian bible. We can see how this would fit the proposed College for Indian conversion (and the extra blankness and 'neutrality' of Indian children in particular). Even here, though, with the heathen at first plainly resisting the incredible tenets of Scripture, there is a certain dangerous edge of relativism – something which might have prompted some Christians to freshly, sceptically readdress their own creeds in a time of general instability.

A few weeks later, Donne's positive enthusiasm for conversion is again evident. In his Easter Monday sermon of 1622 he outlines the potentially global Christian community now within sight:

> A man is thy neighbour, by his humanity, not by his divinity; by his nature, not by his religion: a Virginian is thy neighbour, as well as a Londoner; and all men are in every good man's diocese, and parish ... Thou seest a man worship an image, and thou laughest him to scorn; assist him, direct him if thou canst, but scorn him not ... thou knowest not God's purpose ... his way may be to convert that man by thee ... God can work in all metals, and transmute all metals: he can make ... a superstitious Christian, a sincere Christian; a papist, a protestant ...[427]

Again, America is admitted into a narrative of progressive development – here indicated by the period's belief that gold was the natural end state of metals, and one which could in theory be accelerated by those alchemists who attempted to 'transmute' lead through their secret arts. At one level, then, this is an obvious manifesto for evangelism. But if we also link it to Donne's distinctive personal sense of America as a stubbornly real imaginative presence, we can further view it as a tacit admission that he himself *needed* such a reminder of his kinship least of all. America, for him, had indeed invaded London, insofar as he carried its troubling implications with him, an underground stream of questions and details continually spurting up through the once sure conceptual footing of Christian theory.

And in September 1622 we find him again wavering back to an implicitly negative view of the New World. Characteristically, that opinion slips out when he is nominally concerned with another subject – America is ostensibly just part of an illustration. James I had recently issued a set of controversial 'Directions for Preachers', instructions designed to curb supposedly wayward ministers in their style or content. Preaching in support of these, Donne likens his text (Judges

5.20) to 'the two hemispheres of the world, laid open in a flat, in a plain map'.

> All those parts of the world, which the ancients have used to consider, are in one of those hemispheres; all Europe ... all Asia, and Afric too: So that when we have seen that hemisphere, done with that, we might seem to have seen all, done with all the world; but yet the other hemisphere, that of America, is as big as it; though, but by occasion of new, and late discoveries, we had had nothing to say of America. So the first part of our text, will be as that first hemisphere ... but by the new discoveries of some humours of men, and rumours of men, we shall have occasion to say somewhat of a second part too.[428]

Superficially, these 'humours and rumours' belong to the subversive preachers who had displeased James. But in the present context a further implication is all too apparent: America itself is as subversive, novel, as illegitimate and disruptive of established hierarchies, as certain ministers are to the King. Does Donne indeed unconsciously resent being so surprised by this upstart land, not many years after that

Valediction in which he had in fact seemed 'to have seen all' and 'done with all the world' so easily?

These hints of unease had deep and general roots. But Donne may also have been prompted by a particular topical issue - one which had suddenly made Virginia far more dangerous and subversive than a few preachers failing to honour the usual cosy relations of Church and State. For on 22 March 1622 the Virginian Indians suddenly turned against their mysterious new guests, massacring a total of 347 colonists. The news reached England by July, a few weeks before Donne spoke on behalf of James' Directions. But if Donne's negative coding of the new hemisphere was partly influenced by this disaster, his response was relatively mild. Needless to say, few at this time were likely to try and view the event from the Indians' perspective. In a published poem, Donne's own longstanding friend, Christopher Brooke, not only wrenched the familiar imbalance between spirit and matter with especial force – referring to the Virginians as 'souls drowned in flesh and blood' – but argued for an immediate genocide.[429] Donne's sermon of November 1622 needed, then, to address more than just the general conundrum with which America confronted the Christian thinker.[430]

His most obvious response to the challenge set him was a characteristic one. Without going so far as to overtly describe the massacre as a judgment inflicted by God, Donne is emphatic that only a religiously-centred attempt will succeed in the New World:

> if you could once bring a catechism to be as good ware among them as a bugle, as a knife, as a hatchet ... if you would be as ready to hearken at the return of a ship, how many Indians were converted to Christ Jesus, as what trees, or drugs, or dyes that ship had brought, then you were in your right way, and not till then.[431]

Donne's own evidently genuine belief in his personal sicknesses as judgments or formative corrections shows us that his similar attitude to the troubles of Virginia was probably sincere.[432] And so he goes on – with that familiar ability to all but seamlessly elide earth into heaven, or human life into the meaningful events of Scripture – to parallel the recent slaughter with the allegedly global cataclysm of the Old Testament: 'though a flood, a flood of blood have broken in upon them, be not discouraged'.[433] A back row auditor could have lost this one swift reference under a cough as easily as a hasty reader could miss it now. Brief as it is, however, it is in fact part of the sermon's central and intriguing solution to the issues of Virginia and of America as a whole. For what is remarkable about the parallel is not that it simply absorbs the disaster and the colony into a Christian narrative, but that it positively transforms them into a new and powerful opportunity for the chosen Protestants of England.

While the piece has been wrongly identified as the first English evangelical or missionary sermon, it is undoubtedly a very special and very creative (as well as an early) use of evangelical psychology. Typically, Donne approaches the issue of New World preaching and conversion by first addressing a delicate biblical problem which less rigorous and totalising believers might have quietly overlooked. It had stated in the Bible that Christ's apostles were to preach not only in the Middle East, but 'in all the world', 'to all nations'. [434] Had they literally done so? 'Did the apostles in person' Donne asks, 'preach the Gospel, over all the world?' Despite the weighty opinions of the Church fathers 'that the Apostles did actually, and personally preach the Gospel in all nations, in their life', Donne has to concede that their attitude would have differed had they lived after Columbus:

> had they dream'd of this world which hath been discover'd since, into which, we dispute with perplexity, and intricacy enough, how any men came at first, or how any beasts, especially such beasts as men were not

333

likely to carry, they would never have doubted to have admitted a figure in that, *The Gospel was preached to all the world.*[435]

Taken alone, Donne's shift from literal to figurative might not seem a colossal disruption to accepted readings of the Bible. We need to bear in mind, however, that he makes this concession in a period when sceptical observers could indeed have seen the once absolute truths of the Christian Bible to have been seriously dislocated and relativised. Myth, we might say, was turning into history. The empirical world was taking its long overdue revenge on those attractive but finally distorting ideas which had oppressed it for so many centuries. And Donne in particular wanted the empirical and the conceptual realms to be adequately united – to believe with the kind of unshakable integrity which we find in both love poems and religious lyrics.

The reference to animals in the above lines gives us a vital clue to Donne's distinctive apprehension of America. For he had evidently been reading José de Acosta's *Natural and Moral History of the Indies* (1590). A Jesuit and a New World veteran, Acosta engaged with the Americas in all their living detail and reality. And among various difficult questions which he – like Donne – refused to brush aside was the basic issue of human and animal life in the Indies. As noted, native peoples seemed to lack the seafaring capabilities to have made such a voyage from the Old World. Most animals certainly could not have swum such distances. Even allowing for the use of ships, who, Acosta demands, 'would take the pains to carry foxes to Peru, especially of that kind which they call anas, which is the filthiest that I have seen? Who would likewise say, that they have carried tigers and lions? Truly it were a thing worthy the laughing at, to think so.'[436] This kind of issue was for Acosta indissociably linked to his personal experience. On his first voyage to the Indies he had sailed towards that central region of the globe which Aristotle had labelled the 'burning zone' – an area thought so intensely hot that humans might not easily survive it. Having moved into the shade by way of some precaution, what did Acosta find? He was cold.[437] Hastening back into the sun to warm himself, he shivered the ancient fables of the classical world from his shoulders into the bright tropic air.

Donne himself had not been to the Indies. But what vitally links him with Acosta (who he cites in several other places) is his desire to admit America on its own terms. The world which had been so securely and precisely laid out, still and acquiescent in the books of the Christian intellectual tradition, was now a world in process. Its new limits and character had yet to be reset and redefined. Hence Donne's admission that 'we debate with some perplexity': the debate, implicitly, is still happening.[438] It is hard to overstate the importance of this uneasy psychological movement now animating the world in the minds of men such as Acosta and Donne. So the latter, in 1629 asks,

> Who ever amongst our fathers, thought of any way to ... China, than by the promontory of good hope? Yet another way opened it self to Magellan, a strait ... and who knows yet, whether there may not be a north-east, and a north-west way thither, besides?[439]

Such conjectures betray the sense of a world cut loose from its once stable moorings, uncertainly adrift until it can find some new and hospitable shore where it might reorient and fix itself.

And yet Donne does indeed seem to make such a voyage – or, perhaps, to narrate a voyage previously made in the fraught silence of his study – through his Virginia sermon. Let us imagine that the kind of psychic disorientation America inspired naturally produced an uncertain, restless charge of energy in Donne's mind. This energy took a variety of forms at different times – now positive, now negative, occasionally somewhere between. What must be appreciated is that Donne, in 1622, chose not to flee from that energy or to smother it, but to devour and transform it into a compelling vision of the Christian future. So the 'unripe' New World becomes part of a slow but meaningful organic narrative, a gradual evolution toward religious fulfillment and completion:

> Beloved, use Godly means, and give God his leisure. You cannot beget a son, and tell the mother, I will have this son born within five months; nor, when he is born, say, you will have him past danger of wardship within five days ...

Similarly, 'great creatures lie long in the womb; lions are littered perfect, but bear-whelps lick'd unto their shape'.[440] Unlike the woman of Elegy 18, then, America here is not simply an inferior entity that would become a 'monster' if 'o'er-licked' but a lump whose positive blankness can be successfully formed and imprinted by the judicious vigour of English Protestants. In the same breath, Donne's figures of shaping also call up the need for patient 'hammering' and 'filing'. At first glance an edge of the violence urged by Christopher Brooke seems to have intruded. But tellingly it is not the Indians, or even America more generally, which must be hammered and filed. Rather, it is 'the actions of private men, and private purses' (the English) which 'require more hammering, and more filing to their perfection'.[441]

The detail is telling because the sermon is as much about the energetic creation of Protestant individuals as it is about the reformation of America. Perhaps more importantly, it is about the assertion of a quite dynamic, urgent version of reality itself:

> Those of our profession that go, you, who send them who go, do all an apostolical function ... Before the end of the world come, before this mortality shall put on immortality, before the [human] creature shall be delivered of the bondage of corruption under which it groans ... before all things shall be subdued to Christ, his kingdom perfected, and the last enemy Death destroyed, the Gospel must be preached to those men to whom ye send; to all men. Further and hasten you this blessed, this joyful, this glorious consummation of all, and happy reunion of all bodies to their souls, by preaching the gospel to these men. Preach to them doctrinally, preach to them practically; enamour them with your justice ... but inflame them with your godliness, and your religion.[442]

Thus the younger among them, Donne hopes, may live to see their friends and children comfortably settled in Virginia. But, more importantly: 'you shall have made this island [of Britain] which is but as the suburbs of the old world, a bridge, a gallery to the new; to join all to that world that shall never grow old, the kingdom of heaven.'[443]

Just what does this mean? Here we need again to effortfully jolt ourselves back into the sweep and detail of a now profoundly alien set of beliefs. When Donne spoke, a substantial number of Christians quite eagerly and actively expected the end of ordinary life on earth to be brought about by the Second Coming of Jesus Christ himself. Protestant England in particular was marked by varying degrees of a mentality known as Millenarianism or Apocalypticism. In order to absorb and make sense of the traumatic cultural revolution which the Reformation produced, many Protestants read the events following Henry VIII's break from Rome with a fiercely heightened sense of their spiritual significance. They saw these as signalling not only an absolutely new stage of Christian history, but the very *last* stage, before God finally closed up the transient sufferings of world history, and opened the long-awaited glory of the true and real world, the eternal bliss of heaven. Interpretations of this matter varied in detail. What is most relevant at present is the special value accorded by

Protestants to personal bravery, industry and suffering in the context of God's chosen nation. So the numerous martyrs of Mary's time were vital to Protestant identity and history, as a harshly material affirmation of true faith. Moreover, they were also part of a tendency to see the reformed religion not as an innovation, but as a purified version of the earliest Christian church – a time known for its persecution and martyrdom.

And it is this kind of attitude which broadly underpins Donne's ingenious sleight of hand, whereby the potentially unnerving reinterpretation of Scripture becomes a potent opportunity for Protestant missionaries to now complete the work of the first apostles. Was Donne himself a Millenarian? In the sermon he explicitly denies it. And it is important not to recklessly collapse precise divisions of belief which in his lifetime could be a matter of life and death. Yet Donne did own a copy of William Symonds' 1609 sermon. Not only is that work evidently millenarian in its evangelism, but its author had published an explicitly apocalyptic work, *Pisgah Evangelica*, five years earlier. What we can safely claim is that Donne's stance matches the intense spiritual energy and excitement common to Millenarian believers. Donne's most obvious point of divergence from Millenarianism is the issue of precise dating. Millenarian thinkers attempted to map hints from Revelations onto the more radical and violent events of world history, thereby claiming more or less exact dates for the last dramatic finale of the Christian epic narrative.[444] Donne, by contrast, is emphatic that 'God binds not himself to times'.[445] But if we look again at the precise phrasing of that climactic passage, we find a seemingly curious exhortation: '*Further and hasten you* this blessed, this joyful, this glorious consummation of all' (italics mine). This evidently means just what the earlier remarks about the need for universal evangelism had already implied. The last phase of Christian history cannot occur until the gospel has been 'preached to all men'. Yet at the same time it can indeed be 'hastened' if Protestant evangelists are sufficiently vigorous and effective in their preaching (note that 'preaching' need not definitely imply conversion – to simply preach, and at least *offer* a nominal chance of salvation, was clearly a less daunting task than to convert all the people of the Americas). What the sermon has effectively done, then, is to retain much of the basic spiritual urgency of Millenarianism, while rechannelling that energy from the obsession with precise times into the religious efforts of Protestant adventurers and preachers. Cosmic drama has become human drama.

This strategy has three distinctive implications. Perhaps most obviously, it makes a notably Protestant shift of power and responsibility. History, instead of being fully prewritten and preset, now becomes challengingly contingent and open-ended, its climax something which the evangelical fervour of preachers can quite literally pull forward by their own strenuous exertions in the pulpits of the Indies. The seeming loss of precise timing therefore becomes a massive gain in individual power and participation. Secondly, we can view it as a suitably dramatic and active way – for Donne especially – of matching and absorbing the strange wonder of the New World. This massive living conundrum, with its bewildering and inexplicable range of organic, animal and human life, is implicitly harnessed and fused with the restless energies of the Protestant individual and his general view of heavenly glory. And, if we look carefully at the relationship between these two points – broadly questions of time and of space respectively – we can also infer a third intriguing consequence of Donne's evangelism. He seems in fact to have transferred the highly charged religious *time* of Christian fulfillment into the vibrant and fascinating *space* of the Americas.[446] And in doing so he is not simply creating a metaphor – at least not in the way metaphor is now understood. We can only guess at what it felt like to blur that novel space of the Indies into the future epoch it seemed to signal. For some especially zealous Protestants, it might have felt as if time was now indeed a kind of fourth dimension, somehow spliced into the spatial ones previously known – as if America had not simply cracked open the solidity of the Christian Bible, but also opened a door between this world and the next. It is tempting to say that the Last Judgement, the resurrection and the afterlife were all as potently wondrous, distant, and exotic, yet definite and material as America itself. But we could also wonder if at times America was in fact more unreal than that Christian heaven so persistently recreated in speech, thought and ritual, hour after hour amidst the rats, the beggars, and the stench of London.

We can certainly say that America remained for Donne an intoxicatingly rich and open site for the experience of spiritual wonder. As late as January 1626 he argues that

> If you crush heaven into a map, you may find two hemispheres too, two half heavens; half will be joy, and half will be glory; for in these two, the joy of heaven, and the glory of heaven, is all heaven often represented unto us. And as of those two hemispheres of the world, the first hath been known long before, but the other, (that of America, which is the richer in treasure) God reserved for later discoveries. So though he reserve that hemisphere of heaven, which is the glory thereof, to the resurrection, yet the other hemisphere, the joy of heaven, God opens to our discovery … in this world.[447]

This passage requires a similar untangling to certain of Donne's more challenging poems. While we quickly realise that the final 'glory of heaven' corresponds to America, it takes a further moment to appreciate the full privilege America therefore has shed upon it. For although Donne ostensibly matches the earthly 'joy of heaven' (presumably anticipation or sense of it) to the older hemisphere (Europe, Africa and Asia) he effectively admits that the alien wonder and fecundity ('treasure') of America is a more potent source of spiritual inspiration. Just as the bear-whelp of Elegy 18 was recovered for spiritual purposes in the Virginia sermon, so the 'mine of precious stones' which Donne encountered so intimately and concretely in Elegy 19 is here spiritualised into a glowing signal of God's purpose and power.

We can say, then, that the force of Donne's evangelical hopes is attested by the similar wonder and urgency he still demonstrates several months after the Virginia Company itself has been abandoned. And we find the same kind of optimism and ambition driving his piety elsewhere in the post-massacre period, when in 1623 he makes a tellingly spiritual revision of his globe conceit: 'in a flat map, there goes no more, to make west east, though they be distant in an extremity, but to paste that flat map upon a round body, and then west and east are all one.' Equally, 'in a flat soul, in a dejected conscience, in a troubled spirit, there goes no more to the making of that trouble, peace, than to apply that trouble to the body of the merits, to the body of the gospel of Christ Jesus, and conform thee to him, and thy west is east'.[448] Part of this image depends on the well-known symbolism by which Christ himself was associated with the east. Yet in the present context it is also hard not to suspect that we here encounter another covert attempt to spiritually unite the Old World and the New. At the same time, that attempt is different from some of Donne's more fervent efforts in this area. We now see him beginning to abandon both Old and New Worlds as he prepares himself for the next. With the east symbolising rebirth and resurrection, the passage is essentially about closing and protecting the personal circle of one's *own* destiny through reliance on Christ.

We will return to that issue in the final chapter. What we can say in conclusion here is that, on the evidence we have, Donne does indeed seem increasingly to have surrendered both his evangelical confidence and his devouring magnetic grip on a world which again pulls free of his spiritual orbit. This does not make the remarkable achievement of the Virginia sermon any less real. In our own time a person's youth is still real, though their age might seem to blot it out and partly forget it, or the hard face of authority attempt to stare it down as some trivial illusion. But Donne's views did change. In his Easter sermon of 1627 he states plainly that 'the infidel hath no pretence upon the next world, none at all'. He then makes clear that he is thinking of the 'infidels' of America when he further considers that there may be 'an inherent right in the Christians, to plant Christianity in any part of the dominions of the infidels, and consequently, to despoil them even of their possession, if they oppose such plantations ... and such propagations of the Christian religion'.[449] Although this nominally implies attempts at conversion, its emphasis is far more that of intolerant Aristotelian force than of positive spiritual responsibility.

And that sense of a waning evangelical energy, and of a once positive blankness now perceived as more wilfully independent, is neatly captured on Easter 1630. Here Donne tells of 'a West Indian King' who

> having been well wrought upon for his conversion to the Christian religion, and having digested the former articles, when he came to that, *He was crucified, dead, and buried,* had no longer patience, but said, If your God be dead and buried, leave me to my old god, the sun, for the sun will not die.[450]

In a very similar context, in 1621, Donne had boldly confronted just that kind of incredulity with the magical persuasive force ('so sweet, and so powerful …') of Christian Scripture. By now, its force appears to have folded back into a less ambitious personal faith. In 1629, musing on Genesis 1.1 ('In the beginning God created heaven and earth') he gives a faint hint of his older, restlessly consuming faith when he talks of 'that earth, which no man in his person, is ever said to have compassed, till our age'. Does he still wish to personally encompass it him*self*, at least as a coherent spiritual entity? If so, he now appears far more daunted by the scale of such a task. For he goes on to evoke

> that earth which is too much for man yet, (for, as yet, a very great part of the earth is unpeopled) that earth, which, if we will cast it all but into a map, costs many months labour to grave it, nay, if we will cast but a piece of an acre of it, into a garden, costs many years labour to fashion, and furnish it …[451]

Here even the painstaking labours of the garden give a subtle reminder of that forming, organising and exploiting of raw matter which Donne earlier saw as such an inviting challenge. But what is of course most striking is the wearying industry of

347

mapping. Once it had been but the work of a moment to make 'nothing, all'. Where the brisk mental conjurer of the Valediction caught and tamed all the world through the force of personal feeling, bounding it in the minute but living gleam of a teardrop, the aged Dean of St Paul's now indeed finds the world 'too much for man', in more senses than one.

Chapter Seven

Conclusion: 'Glorious Annihilation'

> For certainly the desire of martyrdom, though the body perish,
>   is a self-preservation ... For heaven which we gain so, is
>   certainly good; life, but probably and possibly.[452]

I

> 'Tis the year's midnight, and it is the day's,
>
> Lucy's, who scarce seven hours herself unmasks

So Donne opens one of his greatest poems, 'A Nocturnal upon St Lucy's Day'. Like a slow dead march, following lines evoke not merely this dwindled light, but the withered vitality of the entire world. Yet it is the poet himself, buried within layer upon layer of surrounding darkness, who most absolutely encapsulates this fabulous nullity. Though the sun is all but extinguished, and the world's essential sap exhausted, 'all these seem to laugh,/Compared with me, who am their epitaph'. Ordinary humanity, therefore, can only look on from a distance at this prodigious emotional state:

Study me then, you who shall lovers be
At the next world, that is, at the next spring:
For I am every dead thing,
In whom love wrought new alchemy.
For his art did express
A quintessence even from nothingness,
From dull privations, and lean emptiness
He ruined me, and I am re-begot
Of absence, darkness, death; things which are not.

The speaker of the 'Nocturnal', his voice a shrunken pulse of light seen distantly through winter trees at dusk, is 'the grave/Of all, that's nothing'; 'Of the first nothing, the elixir grown', lower than an animal, a plant, even a stone. And so the poem concludes not by reaching any kind of progressive resolution, but by circling back in on itself, in an echoing reprise that confirms its author's absolute isolation, sealed off in a black hole of despair:

But I am none; nor will my sun renew.
You lovers, for whose sake, the lesser sun
At this time to the Goat is run
To fetch new lust, and give it you,
Enjoy your summer all;

Since she enjoys her long night's festival,

Let me prepare towards her, and let me call

This hour her vigil, and her eve, since this

Both the year's, and the day's deep midnight is.

Donne has long been noted for his personal fascination with the next world, and the uncertain passage into it. Throughout his writings he frequently seems to have not one, but two feet firmly in the grave, and indeed to be digging himself further into it with creative zeal. In what are probably some of his earliest poems he imagines himself as a ghost leaning over his past lover's bed; as the subject of a post-mortem autopsy and a self-dissection; as a corpse about to be shrouded; or as a skeleton rudely exposed to the fresh glare of long forgotten daylight.[453] That last case is especially typical of the unwritten laws of Donne's necropolis. As the gravedigger spies 'a bracelet of bright hair about the bone' we meet the peculiar energy of death which so nervously animates these writings, twisting the leaves around a churchyard in those curiously agitated gusts before a storm. Death and life are not only juxtaposed but deftly struck one against the other. Caught in flight, the resulting spark is flicked down on the page, where its uneasy heat still glows today, in the swift burst of plosive syllables encircling that skeletal wrist. If ever there was an unquiet grave, it was Donne's.

In one way the 'Nocturnal' is very different from these relatively playful forays into the world of the dead. Where he had so often conjured himself deliberately into its shadows, he now seems rather to speak from a position firmly within them. The poem has a certain undeniable, deadly weight, measured and never forced, quietly magnetic in its ability to speak the unspeakable, to move without progress, drawing the reader and itself into ever tighter spirals of darkness and solitude. And yet, the piece is also remarkably typical in its oblique egotism. Not only does the poet cast his personal shadow across and deep into the entire world, but he seems to have paradoxically laid claim to every last grain of sorrow or nullity with such authority that no one else can ever find any for their own grief. Absorbing the alchemically distilled essence of all death in this almost Christ-like act of sacrifice, the speaker seems at once self-denying, and breathtakingly arrogant. Secondly, the 'Nocturnal' is again characteristic in that – for all its persuasive emotional gravity – it still manages to convey a certain undeniable potency: one indeed all the more forceful in its contracted density, like the unimaginably compressed mass and energy of some collapsed star. Certainly, this is no 'ordinary nothing'.

That strange energy of death, here drawn down into a remarkable singularity, takes a number of forms in Donne's sermons. It is worth pausing a moment more over the 'Nocturnal', however, to consider just what gave it such distinctive force. The piece seems indeed to carry death with it as unmistakably as that aura of the bereaved which we sometimes unconsciously sense emanating from a person in the most ordinary context. In the closing lines Donne talks of how 'she enjoys her long night's festival'. Superficially this refers to the 'festival' of St Lucy. But it would be typical of Donne to also include a punning reference to a dead woman, now sleeping in the long night before the resurrection. The woman in question has been identified as either his wife, or as Lucy, Countess of Bedford. If we take the first option, it is interesting to note that the piece then becomes a kind of remarkable inverted love poem, a tragically powerful valediction that by definition can only be addressed to someone no longer able to hear it. We cannot, of course, be absolutely certain that the poem was for either Ann Donne or for Lucy. Yet it is, on the one hand, hard to believe that it is not a genuine memorial; and, on the other, that Donne would write something this forceful for his patron, and nothing comparable for his wife.[454]

Moreover, if we assume only that the piece marks an actual, not imagined, bereavement, then we have in fact already admitted that here as elsewhere, Donne is again 'the first poet in the world'. We have seen that Donne was avant-garde in both his evocation of intimate romantic love, and his prizing of male friendship, in a period marked by seemingly very cool or pragmatic personal relations. If we now extend this surprising lack of personal warmth into the area of death we find that attitudes to bereavement appear from our perspective to verge on the callous. Most famously, the French thinker Montaigne captured the period's peculiar resignation or indifference in the face of habitual mortality, noting that he had 'lost two or three children'.[455] As if by an instinctive defence mechanism, affection or love was cut off when it reached a certain pressure, lest the sudden death of its object should prove too hopelessly damaging. And so we find Donne himself wondering, as his own children lie sick around him at Mitcham, if 'God shall ease us with burials'; comforting a female friend by making an apparently tasteless joke about her recently dead son; and warning his own mother against 'any inordinate and dangerous sorrow' for her dead daughter (incidentally, Donne's own sister by blood).[456] That last case in particular brings us to how the period itself saw these matters, rather than how they now appear from a more detached sociological stance. Sorrow could *be* inordinate and dangerous because it constituted an effective grudging at God's wisdom and ultimate beneficence. For the most powerful aid against routine yet unpredictable mortality was, of course, religion. Where for us the low emotional pressure of Renaissance life seems inextricably linked to the dark undercurrent of death flowing through it, Christianity appears by contrast to have rechannelled psychic energies into a faith conspicuous for its systematic rationality and its toughness. Continually stalked by a figure of death whose chill shadow must have soon grown intolerably oppressive, the Christians of the pre-industrial, pre-scientific world made a bold yet pragmatic decision, turning and facing this spectre with a hard, if not entirely steady gaze of their own, and immobilising it long enough to bind its hands even as they embraced it.

We certainly find evidence for that impression in Donne's sermons. And yet, in the 'Nocturnal' Donne seems to signal a remarkably modern attitude to personal bereavement. Not only that, but in his seemingly unreachable isolation and despair he appears to wholly deny all the Christian attitudes to death so familiar in his era. The event appears not as part of some greater religious scheme, effectively a relief for his wife, part of a natural progression to final bliss, but as the entirely personal crisis of one individual. The phrase 'she enjoys her long night's festival' importantly nuances that impression. Assuming that the subject of the poem was Donne's wife, and that the 'she' is both St Lucy and Ann Donne, we find that the latter is acknowledged as privileged in death, enjoying her release into heaven, even as her husband seeks to adapt to his own personal loss. But this qualification cannot substantially brighten the more general darkness of the poem.[457] Indeed, even if the piece had not been written for Donne's wife, it would remain a quite avant-garde kind of memorial for its time.

In the longer term, however, Donne seems to have shifted his dislocated emotional energies into his religious belief and work. By the time he was ordained in 1615, the chance of a full life seemed to have returned. In one sense, the loss of Ann Donne might have been especially bitter in these circumstances, just when the tide appeared otherwise to have turned so convincingly in Donne's favour. But in the years after that loss his life was far from being a mere epilogue, or steady diminution into melancholy retirement. If we were in any doubt about the force of personal and creative expansion experienced in these last thirteen years, the prose of the sermons offers considerable persuasion. Consider, for example, the strange regret that, 'I have had no looking-glass in my grave, to see how my body looks in the dissolution'.[458] Or take the implicit substitute for that mirror which he offers in 'that brain that produced means to becalm gusts at council tables, storms in parliaments, tempests in popular commotions'. Now dead and mouldering, this now produces 'nothing but swarms of worms, and no proclamation to disperse them'.[459] Indeed, the picture of a skeleton which Donne himself owned in later life could not satisfy his cravings for precise knowledge of the whole *process* of death. 'Painters', he admits, have presented to us with some horror, the skeleton, the frame of the bones of a man's body'. But 'the state of a body in the dissolution of the grave, no pencil can present to us'. When he goes on to insist that 'between that excremental jelly that thy body is made of at first, and that jelly which thy body dissolves to at last ... there is not so noisome, so putrid a thing in nature', he both seems to wish that a painter *could* reproduce such dissolution, and to effectively outdo the most lurid brushwork even as he speaks.[460]

Against these stirrings of the unquiet grave we can set a parallel fondness for death-in-life: 'we have a winding-sheet in our mother's womb, which grows with us from conception, and we come into the world wound up in that winding sheet, for we come to seek a grave ... We celebrate our own funerals with cries, even at our birth.'[461] After this unpromising start, 'all our life is but a going out to the place of execution, to death'. But this, tellingly, should make us all the more vigorous and spiritually alert throughout the journey: 'was there ever any man seen to sleep in the cart, between New-gate [jail], and Tyborne [scaffold]?'[462] Indeed, death is not just within our sight. It is the very substance of our corrupt and sinful bodies:

'thou pursuest the works of the flesh, and hast none, for thy flesh is but dust held together by plasters. Dissolution and putrefaction is gone over thee alive.'[463] From another angle, the period's routine acceptance of morbidity is attested impressively when Donne reflects on how

> we do so little know our selves, as that if my soul could ask one of those worms which my dead body shall produce, will you change with me? that worm would say, no; for you are like to live eternally in torment; for my part, I can live no longer, than the putrid moisture of your body will give me leave, and therefore I will not change.[464]

He is speaking, on that occasion, not at a funeral (or even Easter or Lent) but at a wedding.

What is the result of all this deft spadework in the cities of the dead? It might, after all, seem merely to confirm Donne's withdrawal from life after 1617. At one level, it should be remembered that there is much else besides death in the sermons, and that any preacher was required to concentrate on death to some extent. What is interesting, however, is the precise way that death operates in Donne's writings. Ironically, it affords two forms of oblique self-affirmation. The first derives from the sheer creative drama of Donne's more grimly brilliant evocations. Pausing in the cathartic energy of digging every now and then, he lifts out and rubs clean some rare treasure of necropolis, modestly believing that he has only found, rather than created it:

> take thyself altogether at thy greatest ... all this is but a poor riches ... thou dost but wrap up a snow-ball upon a coal of fire; there is that within thee that melts thee, as fast, as thou growest: thou buildest in marble, and thy soul dwells in those mud-walls, that hath mouldered away, ever since they were made ...[465]

The second, more explicit form of affirmation is of course the assertion of unmistakably Christian identity. Once again, we need to be aware just how thoroughly much of that identity had been eroded even by the nineteenth century, let alone the twentieth. The image of coal burning through snow gives us a certain clue. Again, it is in part another example of the energy of death which pulses beneath Donne's graveyard. But that energy itself was not a purely personal creation. In chapter five we wondered briefly just what it *felt* like to have a soul. That fierce inner nucleus of vibrant heat is in fact an oblique answer. Nominally, it refers to the Original Sin which so inevitably and universally corrupts all human bodies. Yet sin of course presupposes a soul. Effectively, then, this heat also derives from the still more irreducible power of the immortal Christian spirit. Donne's undoubted fascination with death is not simply some vague morbid compulsion. Rather, it is an almost scientific curiosity about the process by which the human soul will be liberated, re-embodied, and taken into the eternal, crystalline purity and bliss of that heaven which, for many Christians, genuinely *was* the real world, and real life.

In chapter four we heard Donne speculating that 'perchance I shall never die'. We also encountered the distinctively solid, sensuous, and precise Christian theology of bodily resurrection on the Day of Judgement. Considering that he may still be alive on earth when this day comes, Donne imagines what we might call 'the resurrection of the living' – those translated into heaven without undergoing any degree of bodily corruption. This imagining has certain special undertones. Given his hope that 'perchance *I* shall never die', it may well be no accident that he talks later of '*we* who are then alive'.[466] He does indeed seem to wish that he will pass almost instantaneously from this world to the next. Why? One answer is this: Donne is never quite able to reconcile himself to the idea of non-existence. Even when imagining his almost instantaneous shift from life to death to resurrection he scruples to admit, perhaps nervously, that this 'requires some succession of time'.[467] What troubles Donne far more than that momentary oblivion, however, is the unknowable space of blank disintegration which *could* potentially intervene between death and heaven. And what haunts him here is not just non-existence, but the precise physical process of 'dissolution'.

'Where', he wonders 'be all the splinters of that bone, which a shot hath shivered and scattered in the air? ... In what wrinkle, in what furrow, in what bowel of the earth, lie all the grains of the ashes of a body burnt a thousand years since? In what corner, in what ventricle of the sea, lies all the jelly of a body drowned in the general flood?'[468] In theory this kind of question is rhetorical, and God's omnipotence is an adequate response to it. Yet it is asked so often, and with such vividly exact detail that one begins to suspect a certain involuntary fascination. Bodily corruption, for Donne, is a zone where 'the worms that we breed are our betters, because they have a life', and where 'the dust of dead Kings is blown into the street, and the dust of the street blown into the river, and the muddy river tumbled into the sea, and the sea remanded into all the veins and channels of the earth ...'.[469] In this bewildering flux of dissolved and scattered atoms one cannot begin to quite imagine the fixed location of oneself or anyone else:

Ask that marble that is worn off of the threshold in the church-porch with continual treading, and with that ... marble, thou mayst find thy father's skin, and body ... The knife, the marble, the skin, the body are ground away, trod away, they are destroyed, who knows the revolutions of dust? Dust upon the King's high-way, and dust upon the King's grave, are both, or neither, dust royal, and may change places; who knows the revolutions of dust?[470]

'Dust royal': perhaps this in particular roused especial wonder or horror in some as they watched their horses stirring the powdered earth of a summer highway. But that was not all. We need, too, to consider the strange possibility that to certain of Donne's peers all dust was holy. Indeed, not only might it *have* once been somebody, but it was also waiting, harbouring a silent invisible pressure of future life.

In theory, the motif of 'death the great leveller' is a recurrent one in the sermons. So, 'as envy supplants, and removes us alive: a shovel removes, and throws us out of our grave, after death. No limbec, no weights can tell you, this is dust royal, this plebeian dust ...'[471] Again, death comes equally to us all, and makes us all equal when it comes. The ashes of an oak in the chimney, are no epitaph of that oak, to tell me how high or how large that was; it tells me not what flocks it sheltered while it stood, nor what men it hurt when it fell. The dust of great persons' graves is speechless too, it says nothing, it distinguishes nothing ... and when a whirl-wind hath blown the dust of the church-yard into the church, and the man sweeps out the dust of the church into the church-yard, who will undertake to sift those dusts again, and to pronounce, this is the plebeian, this is the noble flour ...?

Speechless dust ... is there something more than general poetry in this lament at that dust which 'says nothing'? Does Donne in fact covertly admit his peculiar discomfort with the loss of that powerful self-expression to which we are still paying tribute, some four hundred years later? If he does, we can in fact view his anxiety as part of a more fundamental and quite characteristic unease.

For what produces all these memorable evocations of disintegrated humanity is ultimately the inability to quite accept that one has – at least temporarily – lost one's self. Death's power to level down the social pyramid into one faceless, colourless set of atoms is one thing. Yet the promiscuously sprinkled dust of kings is in reality less shocking than one's *own* fractured substance and personal identity. That integrity, that personal wholeness so persistently chiselled and defended through all the changes of one's life, is now the plaything of winds, birds, tides and indifferent church sextons, whistling idly as they flick the crumbled brains of the great out into the church-yard. It seems to be this quite literal dis-integration that unnerves Donne more than all those images of a body throbbing with worms, or silently rotting. There, at least, is something remotely like oneself. So, when he insists that 'God does not forget the dead; and, as long as God is with them, they are with him', we find another version of that awesome but sustaining gaze encountered in chapter four. And, as in the *Holy Sonnets*, there seems again to be a demand for slightly too much attention, the need to be somehow personally preserved even as 'grains of dust' which no winds nor water can 'carry ... out of His sight'.[472]

Yet this mesmerised sense of one's own helplessly crumbling and severed corpse is only one side of Donne's engagement with death. He is not simply digging himself into the grave, but ultimately digging himself right through it to the vast paradisal realms beyond. For the Renaissance Christian, death was not the slow, one-way entropy of life slowly turning cold, but rather that defiant inner heat of the coal of fire melting its way through the corrupted flesh to freedom. This is not to deny the genuine unease which disintegration clearly provoked in Donne. Typically, his encounters with death offer convincing, all but independent evocations of both fear and hope, faith and doubt. As argued, the peculiarly tough, solid, detailed qualities of Renaissance faith are evident in the all but scientific processes of bodily resurrection. And if Donne is very much of his era there, he is no less so in the way that he pushes on, beyond the temporary chaos of decay, to the triumphant recovery which will succeed it. So, uniting his alternate waverings between change and stability, he transforms the hardships of earthly life into a kind of human alchemy. Just weeks before his death he tells his friend, Mrs Cokain:

> I am not alive, because I have not had enough upon me to kill me, but because it pleases God to pass me through many infirmities before He take me, either to bring me to particular repentances, or by them to give me hope of His particular mercies in heaven. Therefore I have been more affected with coughs in vehemence, more with deafness, more with toothache ... than heretofore. All this mellows me for heaven, and so

ferments me in this world as I shall need no long
concoction in the grave, but hasten to the resurrection.[473]

This is echoed with slight variation in a letter – also to Mrs
Cokain, after her bereavement – where he argues that we may
be 'glad to lay' our children's bodies in the grave, 'where only
they can be mellowed and ripened for glorification'.[474] Some
years earlier, during his near-fatal illness of 1623, he similarly
felt that God had 'called me up, by casting me further down,
and clothed me with thy self'.[475] As he explains to his
congregation, it is 'God's method, and his alone, to preserve by
destroying'. For 'God's first intention even when he destroys is
to preserve, as a physician's first intention, in the most
distasteful physic, is health; even God's demolitions are super-
edifications, his anatomies, his dissections are so many re-
compactings, so many resurrections.'[476] Naturally, then, a
man's sickness is 'but a fomentation to supple and open his
body for the issuing of his soul'.[477] But despite his insistence
that this is 'God's method, and his alone', Donne himself often
takes an active role in this oddly creative self-erosion,
effortfully denying the world in order to get closer to the full
self buried within the dead weight of human flesh. He feels able
to commend the pagan philosopher, Porphyry, because he had
said that 'this enormous fattening and enlarging our bodies by

excessive diet, was but a shovelling of more and more fat earth upon our souls to bury them deeper'.[478] At one level, this is remarkably similar to his derision of that 'dunce' satirised many years earlier as having a soul 'drowned in flesh and blood'.[479] More subtly, it seems to transfer and recreate that nimble, sharply-cut otherness of the elegies or satires into the spiritual realm, offering a kind of metaphysical leanness which reflects the angular features seen in later portraits.[480] If the resultant persona has now become more obviously dependent on God, it is still notably oppositional, and still jealous of its precise self-definition.

The impulse to self-denial therefore appears to be a form of self-affirmation. What is perhaps more surprising is to find that Donne could, in certain circumstances, desire outright self-destruction as a means of effectively recovering his full self. It was evidently in 1607 or 1608 that he wrote his long defence of suicide, *Biathanatos*. And it has also been claimed that this work had a partly personal motivation.[481] Donne himself admits quite unequivocally that 'whensoever any affliction assails me' he feels himself to have 'the keys of my prison in mine own hand', so that 'no remedy presents it self so soon to my heart, as mine own sword'.[482] The notion that the book was Donne's way of writing himself down from a windowsill is plausible. *Biathanatos* can also be seen as personal, however, in more subtle ways. At the broadest level, it is again typical of Donne's persuasive ability to remake the world in his own image. He takes an essentially personal preoccupation and spins it into a web of such grace and authority that even the Oxbridge friends to whom he showed the work, although aware of 'a false thread in it', admitted that this itself was 'not easily found'.[483] But what is most precisely revealing about Donne's view of suicide is the way in which it compares to the sense of personal erosion pervading his Mitcham years.

Throughout the letters written in Donne's period of social exile we find one especially characteristic refrain. Whimsically or grimly, briefly or with elaborate ingenuity, he insists that he is 'nothing'. His fortune, he states, has made him 'rather a sickness and disease of the world than any part of it'.[484] He wittily explains to one friend that although he has no social rank, he is a valuable friend because it is a kind of 'Creation to make a friendship of nothing'.[485] As late as 1612, we find him whimsically imagining that he 'died ten years ago' and is only pleased 'to have kept myself so long above ground without putrefaction'.[486] This habit is far more than merely charming self-effacement. One vital reason for such remarks is that, for the rigidly demarcated society which had shut him out, Donne was indeed a very liminal kind of entity. We have already heard him telling Goodyer that 'to choose is to do, but to be no part of any body is to be nothing'.[487] In a time when success was not only heavily material, but immensely public, Donne lived in private poverty, a beautiful voice and dazzling brain stranded in limbo. *Biathanatos* is his answer to this long and unrelieved death-in-life. Running through a horribly detailed list of famous suicides he opens with that of the Emperor Nero's friend, 'Petronius ... a man of pleasure' (Petronius was notoriously hedonistic). Nero was dangerously unstable and tyrannical, even toward his sometime friends. So, Petronius 'upon the first frown went home, and cut his veins. So present and immediate a step was it to him, from full pleasure to such a death.'[488] It is no accident that Donne begins with this example of all others. Petronius was not just a hedonist but a very charming, clever and elegant one. And yet those personal qualities would not, one feels, have been so admirable to Donne had it not been for his coolly rational and decisive self-termination.

Similarly, for Donne suicide seemed to offer not simply relief, but a new and definite identity, a new self-hood which would ultimately triumph over the horrible nullity of his ambiguous living isolation. He wishes to escape not so much from the 'prison' of his environment, as from his limited and stifling personal identity. So the kind of keenly unsentimental desire for a personal outline glinting with the finest razor edge of wit; or for a love far beyond ordinary human passions, takes a new shape and colour under the heavy shadow of death. Here as elsewhere it finally becomes a case of all or nothing, of being able to know fully what you are, and to convincingly show others. *Biathanatos*, then, is partly a product of Donne's poverty and exile, but not in the narrow, more obvious sense that it offers a desperate escape from simple hardship and social degradation. Rather, what Donne finds most intolerable is the lack of engagement, of activity, and of mental and social space. As he explains to Goodyer, 'when I must shipwreck I would rather do it in a sea where mine impotency might have some excuse; not in a sullen weedy lake, where I could not have so much as exercise for my swimming'.[489] Similarly, he continues to seek advancement with uncertain hope, because he would 'rather wear out than rust'.[490]

From 1615 onwards Donne had at last sufficient scope for exercise. The marginalised personal voice of the Mitcham letters now echoed off the stone and glass of Lincoln's Inn chapel and St. Paul's, not only denouncing auditors for their sins, but – occasionally – for their murmured discussions of the sermon, or failure to remove their hats.[491] There are numerous indications that Donne's life, once progressed some way from his bereavement, was energetic and full. In 1619 he travelled abroad as chaplain with the ambassador Viscount Doncaster.

Come 1623, when he fell seriously ill, he had the King's physicians sent to attend him. In 1625 he preached a sermon over the dead body of James I. With the new King, Charles I, he was on the whole no less popular (and perhaps tellingly, given Donne's vogue with the Cavaliers, Charles especially favoured his poetry).

As noted in chapter four, Donne's personal brush with death left us some of his most memorable and often-quoted prose – the work he wrote during and after the illness of 1623, *Devotions upon Emergent Occasions*. His chief literary legacy from the period, though, is his sermons. Unsurprisingly, much of their style and content is now alien to us. Large sections of them reflect the weight and real presence of a religious attitude increasingly eroded from England in particular in following decades and centuries. But at times they are unmistakably Donne. And, while the pullulating swarm of worms, the whispering desiccation of crumbled flesh, the bewildering reconfigurations of one's jumbled atoms, are especially memorable, that is only one side of Donne's vision of the next world. If Donne had never preached, we would have lacked a special kind of writing – one in which he often retained his gift for dazzling compression, but allied it to a new spaciousness, a controlled architectural construction which offers broader, almost symphonic rhythms to set against the taut miniatures of the poetry. And this expansiveness – a kind of natural progression from the pretty rooms of sonnets into the high austere vaulting of the cathedral – lends itself especially well to Donne's most emphatically positive visions of heaven. The space we encounter, however, is not a general evocation of blissfully still, frozen white arcades lodged above the firmament. Rather, it is a beguilingly personal one. In many ways Donne's heaven is a kind of purified, dazzling mirror of his distinctive and energetic life and self.

So this realm at once reflects the insistent solidity of Renaissance belief, and satisfies Donne's habitual desire for a sensually graspable reality. There is no question of disembodied souls drifting airily about this Christian paradise. 'The Kingdom of heaven hath not all that it must have to a consummate perfection, till it have bodies too.'[492] Not only will the blessed have new physical bodies, but 'in some measure, all the senses shall be in our glorified bodies'.[493] Explicitly refuting the notion of 'airy bodies' as heretical, Donne moreover stresses the superiority of these heavenly creatures:

> The glorified body is become more subtle, more nimble, not encumbered ... for any motion, that it would make ... So hath these glorified bodies *claritatem*, a brightness upon them, from the face of God ... But of all the

endowments of the glorified body, we consider most, *impassibilitatem*, that that body shall suffer nothing ...[494]

We begin now to see the durable reality of that hinted alchemy of diseased and 'mellowed' worldly flesh, broken down, melted away not as a final denial of the body, but a necessary prelude or foundation to some absolute new incorporation. We have seen that heavenly bodies could conceivably have internal organs, genitals, hair and beards.[495] And, in a sense, what could be more defiantly physical than an indestructible body? One could test it, inhabit it, lean on it and experience it with a vibrant confidence that the earthly human carapace would never have sustained.[496] Perhaps indeed it was for this reason that the Christian heaven became, in later decades, 'a crystal-domed sports hall where ... saintly and heavenly bodies, gleaming like the sun and clear like glass ... dart about with supersonic speed between the heavenly spheres'.[497]

Nor is it only the bodies of saved humanity in general that appeal to Donne. In chapter five we noted his characteristic desire to behold – even seize – the most visceral essence of God himself. And this startling moment is in fact just the apex of a formal belief in physical contact with Christ, God, and all the great luminaries of Christian history:

St Augustine ... wish'd to have ... heard St Paul preach, and to have seen Christ in the flesh. We shall have all ... We shall hear St Paul, with the whole quire of heaven, pour out himself in the acclamation, *Salvation to our God* ... and we shall see, and see for ever, Christ in that flesh.[498]

No less characteristic is Donne's desire to fulfil that formidable intellectual adventure first begun in the furtive atmosphere of Hart Hall, Oxford, and the standing wooden coffin of the law study.[499] In keeping with that absolute, direct and complete kind of certainty by which 'we shall see the humanity of Christ with our bodily eyes, then glorified ...', the most tantalising and ambiguous questions of human life will now be unequivocally solved.[500] So, Donne's persistent fascination with the soul in general, and particularly with that delicate zone of transition between matter and spirit, drives him to reflect on the enigma of God's heavenly messengers: 'only the angels themselves know one another ... we shall be like them then ... we shall know what they are ...'. Here on earth, by contrast, 'we know they are spirits in nature, but what the nature of a spirit is, we know not'.[501]

The triumphant mental expansion of Donne's heaven is perhaps nowhere more strangely felt than when he imagines it as absorbing, in a single fantastic reformulation, all these myriad particular arguments and authors he had pored over, in so many languages, by sunlight and candlelight in Oxford, London and Mitcham. For in heaven

> our curiosity shall have this noble satisfaction, we shall know how the angels know, by knowing as they know. We shall not pass from author, to author, as in a grammar school, nor from art to art, as in a university; but, as that general, which knighted his whole army, God shall create us all doctors in a minute ... those reverend manuscripts, written with God's own hand, the Scriptures themselves, shall be taken away, quite away; no more preaching, no more reading of Scriptures, and that great school-mistress, experience, and observation shall be remov'd, no new thing to be done, and in an instant, I shall know more, than they all could reveal unto me.[502]

What we perceive here is that Donne's painstaking engagement with so many abstruse and difficult writings was not any kind of quasi-scholastic way of life, not the melancholy substitute for reality of the compulsive academic, seeking to control a world which they secretly fear; but again a movement through one transient stage, into a more absolute and glorious one. Nothing confirms that more than the startling annihilation of the Bible itself. In the face of this, we realise that the seemingly abstract and hopelessly disconnected theology of the period was in one sense intensely practical, restlessly animated by the desire for a time when one could finally and fully *live* what had previously been only thought upon. Donne envisages something like that 'end of physics' posited by certain scientists, with its bold absorption of all existing knowledge into one central overarching theory.

But these two facets of heaven – corporeality and intellect – would have remained insufficient without one third and final aspect of eternity. Donne would also have friends in heaven. Perhaps, indeed, he would be formally reunited with his wife. Even before he died he had noted to Robert Ker how 'schoolmen dispute whether a married man dying and being by miracle raised again must be remarried'.[503] And that brief aside of a letter is developed with more systematic theological rigour when he succeeds in proving to himself not just the possibility, but the logical *necessity* of heavenly friendship:

> There is nothing to convince a man of error, nothing in nature, nothing in Scriptures, if he believe that he shall know those persons in heaven, whom he knew upon earth; and, if he conceive soberly, that it were a less

degree of blessedness, not to know them, he is bound to believe that he shall know them, for he is bound to believe, that all that conduces to blessedness shall be given him.[504]

But his most striking reflection in this area is one which neatly combines his personal sociability with his aching hunger to know *precisely* what this final life would be like: 'all the travellers in the world, if we could hear them all, all the libraries in the world, if we could read them all, could not tell us so much, as that friend, returned from the dead, which had seen the other world'.[505] Taken alone this is already remarkable. The closest parallel which springs to mind is the famous mutual agreement made with a friend some decades later by the Restoration poet and rake, Lord Rochester. Whoever died first, it was decided, would return from the next world – if possible – and confirm its existence to the survivor. Donne of course has no such scepticism, at least not consciously. Yet his unorthodox speculation is hardly less startling when set in precise context. He made the statement in a sermon on 25 March 1627. Exactly a week earlier, on 18 March, his closest friend, Henry Goodyer, had died. Could he possibly have been thinking of anyone else?

Heaven, then, promised Donne a fullness of self and of existence, rather than some token postscript to life. For, as he

377

explains in an undated sermon, 'I shall be all there, my body, and my soul, and all my body, and all my soul'. By contrast, at the moment of speaking,

> I am not all here, I am here now preaching upon this text, and I am at home in my library considering whether S. Gregory, or S. Hierome, have said best of this text, before. I am here speaking to you, and yet I consider by the way, in the same instant, what it is likely you will say to one another, when I have done.[506]

Perhaps it is no surprise that this remarkably astute sense of fragmented consciousness should come from that poet who so much excelled in capturing, on the wing and to the life, so many different, arguably irreconcilable moods and experiences. It was also in 1627 that Donne lost another longstanding friend, Lucy, Countess of Bedford, who died on 31 May. Yet it has been said that Donne did not exhibit any definite retirement from life, or obvious loss of energy or will in the later 1620s. Sometime in or after 1625 he in fact made a new friend, Bryan Duppa (and perhaps it struck him that the growing chance of death was all the more incentive to do so: one would keep friends in heaven, but might not be able to make any more.) Duppa is interesting because in a broad sense he looks remarkably well-suited to that role of 'another self' equated with true friendship by Cicero.[507] By being fifteen years Donne's junior he perhaps managed to offer something of Donne's earlier self; but he also mirrored Donne's life as a whole, having lived in very worldly terms before almost accidentally entering the Church in 1625, and later becoming a bishop. Again, as a letter of 1628 shows, Donne still carefully preserved a balance between personal and professional life by setting aside Saturday as 'my day of conversation and liberty'; and despite a quite widespread rumour of his death that same year, continued to preach and live with vigour up to and beyond the close of the decade.[508]

A curious moment in a sermon of February 1629, though, perhaps gives some hint of a changing stance toward death. Preaching on Matthew 6.21 ('For where your treasure is, there will your heart be also') Donne makes a remarkable attempt to evoke the otherworldly treasure of the committed Christian. Noting that he has 'seen minute-glasses' and that one of these would 'be enough to show the worldly man his treasure', he then imagines a glass which would 'run an age'. And, 'if the two hemispheres of the world were composed in the form of such a glass, and all the world calcin'd and burnt to ashes, and all the ashes, and sands, and atoms of the world put into that glass, it would not be enough to tell the godly man what his treasure, and the object of his heart is'.[509] Perhaps only Donne could imagine the world not just as burnt, but as burnt in this particular way. Those minutely distilled and self-sufficient spaces of 'The Sun Rising' or 'A Valediction: of Weeping' are here recreated with a bold apocalyptic ferocity. Is there, indeed, a certain growing impatience with worldly life behind this arresting image? And why an hour-glass? There may, indeed, have been one on the lectern as Donne spoke. That kind of exact material focus would certainly be typical of those other slight but highly-charged objects (compasses, teardrops, wreathes of hair) found in the secular poems. In the present case there are also three notable implications which aptly reflect the religious psychology of Donne's final years. As noted, at the last wild climax of earthly life, God would destroy not just all existing space as it had been known, but also time itself. It seems hard to deny, then, that with a certain familiar egotism Donne in fact imagines the total annihilation of the cosmos in four dimensions – space reduced, compressed and finally ebbing away, so that the last trickling grains of matter disappear simultaneously with human time, slipped to the bottom of a glass that will never be turned again. First of all, therefore, we might detect a similar impatience to that heard when the potential evangelists of Virginia were exhorted to strenuously pull the Christian future into the present by preaching the Gospel to 'all men'.[510] We have also seen, however, that these grand general aims for global evangelism frayed and shrank in the last months of Donne's life. And so we could be justified, secondly, in seeing this extraordinary miniature apocalypse (a kind of Renaissance version of the 'great collapse' posited by modern physics) as an indirect expression both of Donne's persistent egotism (the entire universe must die with him) and his unwillingness to quite 'die' at all. If he is called to heaven while still on earth, he may strictly expire for one instant, but will not suffer the slow crumbling of decay or revolutions of dust after burial. Thirdly and most generally, this almost surreal conceit can again be viewed as a (perhaps aptly violent) attempt to sweep the entire mass of a changing, fragmenting, dissonant cosmos within one definite compass of meaningful and safe Christian space. And, if any of Donne's listeners were convinced, we can certainly range them against Dr Johnson, with his misguided opposition to the minutely bounded truths of metaphysical poetry.

By late 1630, time was more definitely running out for Donne himself. He now fell seriously ill with a fever, and it may have been at this time that he lamented to Mrs Cokain: 'I am afraid that death will play with me so long, as that he will forget to kill me.' When he further resents 'a languishing and useless age, a life, that is rather a forgetting I am dead, than of living' the echo of *Biathanatos* is especially unmistakable.[511]

On December 13 of that year he made his will, and in January 1631 he noted to a friend with a little resentment that some parties had constructed his (alleged) illness as an excuse to escape preaching. This, he insisted, was 'an unfriendly, and, God knows, an ill-grounded interpretation'. Rather, 'it hath been my desire ... that I might die in the pulpit; if not that, yet that I might take my death in the pulpit, that is, die the sooner by occasion of my former labours'.[512]

This wish was effectively fulfilled. During his sickness Donne had been resting at Essex. He now returned to London, where he was again attended by eminent doctors. One of these, Simeon Fox, was in fact a friend. With Donne by this point apparently severely emaciated, Fox decided he must be built up, and told him 'that by cordials, and drinking milk twenty days together, there was a probability of his restoration to health'. Donne at first 'passionately denied' to drink any of this. Fox, who

> loved him most entirely, wearied him with solicitations, till he yielded to take it for ten days; at the end of which time, he told Dr Fox, he had drunk it more to satisfy him, than to recover his health; and, that he would not drink it ten days longer upon the best moral assurance of having twenty years added to his life: for he loved it not;

and was so far from fearing death, which to others is the King of terrors: that he long'd for the day of his dissolution.[513]

Like David Bowie, Donne made his own death into a work of art. It appears to have been shortly after Fox's failed attempt at restoration that Donne then kept an appointment to preach before the King at Whitehall, on 25 February 1631. Not surprisingly, the sermon came to be his most famous. It received the title 'Death's Duel', and the mesmerised auditors, watching the gaunt figure overcome his initial faltering to deliver one of his most insistently macabre performances, were supposed to have labelled it the Dean's 'own funeral sermon'.[514] In general terms, nothing could be more fitting than this last public and literary offering, from the writer who had peered over the shoulders of surgeons as they cut open his corpse, crept up behind the undertaker who shrouded him, and spied on the gravedigger who stood blinking down at that bracelet of bright hair about the bone. Still more precisely apt, though, is his return to the promiscuous indignity of dissolution. For, 'such are the revolutions of the graves' that one must be 'mingled in his dust, with the dust of every high way, and of every dunghill, and swallowed in every puddle and pond'. Now, though, Donne does not simply generalise upon the moral of death the leveller, but pinpoints just that undercurrent of special personal hostility to this loss of definition and integrity: 'this is the most *inglorious* and *contemptible* vilification, the most deadly and peremptory nullification, that we can consider.'[515]

I have tried to indicate what it was about this period of limbo and of imagined loss of control which peculiarly unnerved Donne. Perhaps another way of expressing the issue is to say that he was particularly repelled not just by the silence and selflessness of this uncertain time, but by the seeming inability to find in it even just one definite dramatic moment. Back in 1608, in the years of shapeless waiting and constricted stasis at Mitcham, he had telling remarked: 'I would not that death should take me asleep. I would not have him merely seize me, and only declare me to be dead, but win me and overcome me.'[516] By late February 1631 he had already made good something of this hope for a vigorously assertive, almost controlling, encounter with death, effectively staging his own funeral sermon. And, even at this late point, he still had one last gesture in hand. By early March it was clear that this was his last illness. He now seems to have been confined permanently indoors, but was for a time still moving between his bedroom and his study (a neat emblem, one might say, of his life as a whole). He was presently persuaded by Dr Fox to choose a funeral monument. A painter was appointed to make a drawing for what would later be sculpted to stand above his tomb.[517] And it was here that Donne finally decided not just that death should seize him, but that he should seize death. A carver made a wooden urn, large enough for him to stand on. Severely weakened and still further emaciated, he had charcoal fires lit in his study. He then undressed, and re-clothed himself in his burial shroud, knotted at head and foot as it would be in the grave, but opened sufficiently for his face to be seen. Standing on the urn, he was now drawn at life-size, and the drawing kept beside his bed, a fixed object of contemplation throughout all the following days.

This tale, for an era which has confronted so many taboos, but shrunk further and further from a realistic meeting with death, can now seem to verge on the fantastic. We perhaps need to pause for a moment to realise the kind of impressive single-mindedness which it involved. It may be that Donne never feared death for one moment during this last confinement. But it seems hard to believe that he did not need to overcome a certain basic charge of anxiety – if nothing else, a simple fear of the unknown. Where the modern hospital patient can rely on the effects of chemical painkillers which numb the horror of the mind as well as the suffering of the body, Donne had his period's own peculiar traditions available to him. His will shows that he in fact owned a picture of a skeleton; and he must

385

have walked under it day after day, year after year, in the hall of his London deanery.[518] This 'memento mori' was itself just one example of the whole attitude to death in a period where it was practically much harder to escape from, and intellectually not something which should be simply feared. The Renaissance explicitly recognised and cultivated the 'art of death'. 'Let a pious death determine a good life', Donne had emphasised in *Biathanatos*; and, elsewhere: 'Tis the end that qualifies all.'[519] Perhaps most tellingly, he remarked in a sermon some years before his death on how 'those pictures which are deliver'd in a minute, from a print upon a paper, had many days, weeks, months time for the graving of those pictures in the copper'. The first thing that springs to mind here is the familiar image of the globe and the teardrop. But this in fact is rather different. So, he explains, 'this picture of that dying man, that dies in Christ, that dies the death of the righteous, that embraces death as a sleep, was graving all his life; all his public actions were the lights, and all his private the shadows of this picture. And when this picture comes to the press, this man to the straits and agonies of death, thus he lies, thus he looks, this he is.'[520]

And thus he was. What enabled Donne to rise to that last challenge, quelling the most basic and durable of human fears, was his sense of self. Despite his implication that this last act was the summation of a life already lived, the act itself still remained to be accomplished. And Donne of all people would seize it. He would do so partly because this *was who he was*, and nobody would assert that sense of identity more fiercely. And he would do it because few things could repel him more than the idea of some shapeless, unmarked passage into death, a figure fading from sight into mist (as, of course, may more easily happen under the distorting blur of modern drugs). And finally, it is hard not to feel that in this gesture there was one ultimate dramatic flourish of unique personal invention, the signature signed across his skeleton, captured immediately as the frontispiece to the published version of *Death's Duel*, and still strangely affecting, in its stubborn composure, almost four hundred years on. But we must also be careful to remember that this beautifully apt piece of self-assertion was finally linked to a whole massive belief system. Donne was not some lone existential hero confronting the abyss. And it is only fair to leave him with what he himself clearly believed.

Back in *Biathanatos*, where he had first confessed his personal attraction to death as a kind of fulfillment, he had made a seemingly whimsical comparison. He noted the phrases of the Italian natural philosopher, Jerome Cardan, who said that 'metal is *planta sepulta*, and that a mole is *animal sepultum*'. So, Donne adds, 'man, as though he were *angelus sepultus,* labours to be discharged of his earthly sepulchre, his body'.[521] This last phrase seems logical enough. The 'buried spirit', the entombed angel of humanity yearns and labours to dig its way out of the flesh. But why did the first two images come to his mind? As we have seen, the period in general had an organic conception of metal – and especially gold – as slowly ripening like a plant within the ground.[522] The word 'perfection', with its dual meanings of both completion and of superior worth, captures this well. So humanity waits for the indestructible gleaming core of the soul to slowly alchemise itself from the evermore perished and frail body. And the mole? Initially puzzling, this is also in fact very apt. Here is a symbol of that compulsive digging of Donne's poems and sermons, not just down to some cold damp resting place of oblivion, but on and on, through shrouds, worms, decay, the revolutions of dust, further into dirt, silence, chill, a seemingly interminable loneliness, limbo and constriction – until, one unspecified day, a last crust tears softly upward, and dazzled eyes blink out at the eternal pastures of a summer meadow.

Of course, if we insist on taking a more secular view, we can simply say that all of us, in a subtle but very real sense, live an important dimension of our lives in the minds and memories of others. And in that case? Well, certainly he shall never die.

List of Abbreviations

Poems

John Donne: The Complete English Poems, ed. A.J. Smith (Harmondsworth: Penguin, 1971; repr. 1996).

Sermons

The Complete Sermons of John Donne, ed. George R. Potter and Evelyn M.

Simpson, 10 vols (Berkeley and Los Angeles: California University Press, 1953- 62).

Gosse

Edmund Gosse, *The Life and Letters of John Donne*, 2 vols (London: William Heinemann, 1899).

Eliot, *Essays*

T.S. Eliot, *Selected Essays* (London: Faber and Faber, 1972).

Lovelock, *Donne*

Donne: Songs and Sonets – a Casebook, ed. Julian Lovelock (London: Macmillan, 1979).

Mousley, *Donne*

John Donne, New Casebooks, ed. Andrew Mousley (Basingstoke: Palgrave, 1999).

Devotions

Devotions upon Emergent Occasions, ed. Anthony Raspa (Montreal and London: McGill-Queen's University Press, 1975).

Norton

The Norton Anthology of English Literature, 7th edn, vol. I, general eds. M.H. Abrams & Stephen Greenblatt (London and New York: W.W. Norton & Co., 2000).

Cover shows: Carlo Crivelli, *The Annunciation* (1486), oil on wood transferred to canvas.

The author wishes to express his thanks to the National Gallery, London, and to wikimedia contributor, Crisco 1492. His other images are highly recommended.

[1] We cannot be absolutely certain where Donne was in 1588 – a biographical obscurity which may itself be linked to the delicate religious situation of the period. A few months' study at Cambridge is the inference of Donne's biographer, R.C. Bald (*John Donne: A Life* (Oxford: Clarendon Press, 1970), p. 46).

[2] Gosse, I, 104-5. I will be giving dates and addressees for letters only where precisely relevant to the context of citation. Dates in square brackets are Gosse's hypotheses.

[3] Gosse, II, 59-60.

[4] 'Andrew Marvell' (1921), in *Selected Essays* (London: Faber, 1976), p. 293.

[5] For the varying reliability of Walton (1593-1683) see, for example, Bald, *Donne*, pp. 11-15.

[6] Gosse, I, 168-9; italics mine.

[7] Bald, *Donne*, p. 58.

[8] Bald, *Donne*, pp. 42-3.

[9] *Pseudo-Martyr* (1610), p. 46.

[10] See 'Donne and the Ancient Catholic Nobility', *English Literary Renaissance*, 19 (1989), 305-323, pp. 309-11.

[11] Bald, *Donne*, p. 63.

[12] Engraving by William Marshall, 1591 (see Bald, *Donne*, p. 54).

[13] See John Carey, *John Donne: Life, Mind and Art* (London: Faber and Faber, 1981), p. 23.

[14] For further discussion of this picture, see Dennis Flynn, *John Donne and the Ancient Catholic Nobility* (Indiana: University of Indiana Press, 1995), pp. 2-5.

[15] Flynn, *Donne*, 1995, p. 4.

[16] On the low graduation rate, see Kenneth Charlton, *Education in Renaissance England* (London: Routledge and Kegan Paul, 1965), p. 137.

[17] Bald, *Donne*, p. 55.

[18] *Sermons* IX, 325, VIII, 323. Cf. also *Poems*, pp. 213, 214.

[19] Satire 4, *Poems*, p. 169. Cochineal was used for making scarlet dye, and thus implies rouge.

[20] Satire 1, *Poems*, p. 155.

[21] Bald, *Donne*, p. 63.

[22] Bald, *Donne*, p. 63.

[23] Donne sailed with anti-Spanish raids to Cadiz, Faro, Corunna, and Ferrol in June and July 1596, and to the Azores in 1597 (see Bald, *Donne*, pp. 80-92).

[24] *The Stripping of the Altars: Traditional Religion in England c.1400-c.1580* (New Haven: Yale University Press, 1992).

[25] *The Birthpangs of Protestant England: Religious and Cultural Change in the Sixteenth and Seventeenth Centuries* (London: Macmillan, 1988), ix.

[26] Bald, *Donne*, p. 26.

[27] *Pseudo-Martyr*, B2^v, cited in Bald, *Donne*, p. 39.

[28] Flynn's claim (*Donne*, 1995, pp. 4-5), that even in the early 1590s Donne had powerful aristocratic and courtly connections, cannot easily be squared with the clearly real social and financial hardships Donne suffered after 1601.

[29] Gosse, I, 114-15.

[30] Gosse I, 219.

[31] Bald, *Donne*, pp. 148-54.

[32] Bald, *Donne*, p. 158.

[33] Gosse, I, 208-9.

[34] On periods of poetic composition, see *The Elegies and the Songs and Sonnets: John Donne*, ed. Helen Gardner (Oxford: Clarendon Press, 1965), li-lviii.

[35] Gosse, II, 215, [March 1625].

[36] Gosse, I, 219, [1609].

[37] Gosse, I, 190-1, September 1608.

[38] See, for example, Gosse, I, 263.

[39] See Gosse, I, 207-8.

[40] Gosse, II, 45. Gosse's dating here is not certain.

[41] Elizabeth was buried on 17 December, and it seems likely that Donne was commissioned before the year was out.

[42] *Notes of Ben Jonson's Conversations with William Drummond of Hawthornden*, January 1619 (London: Shakespeare Society, 1842), p. 3.

[43] Gosse, II, 41-2.

[44] The phrase 'to have the wall' was once a common expression, denoting someone sufficiently aggressive to force you to the outer side of the road as they passed you.

[45] For valuable studies of poverty in the Renaissance, see Piero Camporesi, *Bread of Dreams: Food and Fantasy in Early Modern Europe*, trans. David Gentilcore (Cambridge: Polity Press, 1989); William C. Carroll, *Fat King, Lean Beggar: Representations of Poverty in the Age of Shakespeare* (Ithaca: Cornell University Press, 1996).

[46] See *A History of St. Paul's Cathedral*, ed. W.R. Matthews and W.M. Atkins (London: Phoenix House, 1957), pp. 108-9, 150.

[47] For a recent guide to the minutest details of London life, see also Liza Picard, *Elizabeth's London: Everyday Life in Elizabethan London* (Orion, 2003).

[48] Eliot, *Essays*, p. 291. Although the phrase refers to Donne's poetry, it is arguably better suited to his sermons.

[49] For the more conservative viewpoint, see Winfried Schleiner, *The Imagery of John Donne's Sermons* (Providence: Brown University Press, 1970), p. 80. For the argument in favour of Donne's genuine originality, see Carey, *Donne*, p. 1. While Peter McCullough's recent essay, 'Donne as Preacher', is a valuable scholarly introduction to this area, it also seems to overly restrict the ways in which Donne's sermons can be read (see *The Cambridge Companion to John Donne*, ed. Achsah Guibbory (Cambridge: Cambridge University Press, 2006), 167-182, p. 169).

[50] *Conversations*, p. 3.

[51] Cf. Carew's 'A Rapture' (*Norton*, pp. 1661-4) with Donne's 'Elegies 18 and 19' (*Poems*, pp. 124-7); and also arguably lines 43-4 of Carew with 'The Ecstasy', ll. 49-76 (*Poems*, pp. 55-6).

[52] For Philips, see 'Friendship's Mystery' and 'To Mrs M.A. at Parting' (*Norton*, pp. 1681-2). For Killigrew, see *The Parson's Wedding* (1664), 2.1, 62. (The play was probably composed in 1639 or 40.)

[53] 'An Elegy upon ... John Donne', ll. 26-7, 49-50, 17, in *Norton*, pp. 1656-7.

[54] *Lives of the Poets – Abraham Cowley* (1779) cited in Lovelock, Donne, pp. 44-5. T.S. Eliot (*Essays*, p. 291) argued that Johnson directed most of his criticism here at the later 'metaphysicals', Cleveland and Cowley. But as will be seen that emphasis itself may be significant, given their later date.

[55] John Hoskins, *Directions for Speech and Style*, (1599), ed. H.H. Hudson (Princeton: Princeton University Press, 1935), p. 29. Bald (*Donne*, p. 43) thinks Donne knew Hoskins at Oxford.

[56] Johnson, in Lovelock, *Donne*, p. 45.

[57] See Lovelock, *Donne*, p. 106, p. 107.

[58] Lovelock, *Donne*, p. 109.

[59] These figures all died for their faith in the earlier or mid sixteenth century.

[60] *Essays*, p. 287. For one of the best discussions of Eliot's political and social agenda, see Terry Eagleton, *Literary Theory: An Introduction* (Oxford: Basil Blackwell, 1983), pp. 38-41.

[61] Lovelock, *Donne*, p. 107.

[62] *The Order of Things: An Archaeology of the Human Sciences*, trans. anon. (London: Tavistock Publications, 1970), pp. 50, 58.

[63] *Order of Things*, p. 54.

[64] *Order of Things*, pp. 50, 54.

[65] Verse Letter, *Poems*, p. 215.

[66] *Poems*, pp. 65, 47, 60, 75, 77, 51.

[67] For a revision of the relations between human subjects and material objects in the Renaissance, see *Subject and Object in Renaissance Culture*, ed. Margreta de Grazia, Maureen Quilligan and Peter Stallybrass (Cambridge: Cambridge University Press, 1996).

[68] Jacob Burckhardt, the nineteenth-century scholar who pioneered the notion of a new human subjectivity in the Renaissance, argued that the dominance of collective over individual identity was an essentially Medieval phenomenon (*The Civilization of the Renaissance in Italy* (1860), trans. S.G.C. Middlemore and Irene Gordon (New York: New American Library, 1960), p. 121). While it is true that Renaissance society was gradually shifting its class structure, in terms of both rank and economics this was clearly a slow and reluctant process. For a now classic study of how this very limited social mobility allowed some unusual individuals to explore their selves to a new degree, see Stephen Greenblatt, *Renaissance Self-Fashioning: from More to Shakespeare* (London: University of Chicago Press, 1980).

[69] For a brief introduction to Petrarch's life and work, see Nicholas Mann, *Petrarch* (Oxford: Oxford University Press, 1984).

[70] F. Scott Fitzgerald, *The Great Gatsby* (1926; repr. Harmondsworth: Penguin, 1972), p. 103.

[71] *Norton*, p. 1040.

[72] Helen Gardner argues that Donne's more cavalier poems were composed before 1600 (*Elegies and Songs and Sonnets*, li-lviii). *Twelfth Night* is thought to date from 1601 or 1602.

[73] Gosse, I, 306. This refers to his two *Anniversaries*, the poems for Elizabeth Drury, published that same year.

[74] See *John Donne, Coterie Poet* (Wisconsin: University of Wisconsin Press, 1986), p. 25; and 'The Social Context and Nature of Donne's Writings: Occasional Verse and Letters', in *Cambridge Companion*, 35-48. See also Ted-Larry Pebworth, 'The Text of Donne's Writings', *Cambridge Companion*, 23-34.

[75] On the relationship between blood and sexual fluids, see Michael C. Schoenfeldt, *Bodies and Selves in Early Modern England: Physiology and Inwardness in Spenser, Shakespeare, Herbert, and Milton* (Cambridge: Cambridge University Press, 1999), p. 4; and cf. Donne, 'The Progress of the Soul', *Poems*, pp. 183-4.

[76] Cited in Eliot, *Essays*, p. 301.

[77] Lovelock, *Donne*, pp. 44-5.

[78] Cf. also 'Love's Exchange' (*Poems*, p. 68).

[79] 'Sympathetic magic' (something broadly analagous to voodoo) supposedly enabled witches to harm their victims by inflicting damage on their picture, their hair, and so on. For a particularly intriguing case, see Anon., *The Most Cruel and Bloody Murder ... with the several witch-crafts ...* (1606), pp. 10-11.

[80] Recipe of Osvald Crollius, cited in Piero Camporesi, *The Incorruptible Flesh: Bodily Mutation and Mortification in Religion and Folklore*, trans. Tania Croft-Murray and Helen Elsom (Cambridge: Cambridge University Press, 1988), p. 15. For further discussion of mummy, see Richard Sugg, *Mummies, Cannibals and Vampires: The History of Corpse Medicine from the Renaissance to the Victorians* (2nd edn 2015).

[81] For plausible alternative readings of the final lines, see Smith, p. 384.

[82] For a probable echo in the Restoration, see John Oldham, *Satires upon the Jesuits* (1681), p. 148.

[83] 5.1, 121, *Norton*, p. 1099.

[84] 'To His Coy Mistress', *Norton*, p. 1691.

[85] For further discussion of this phenomenon, see chapter three, section five.

[86] See *Norton*, p. 1040.

[87] Gosse, II, 8.

[88] See Francis Bacon, *Sylva Sylvarum* (1627), pp. 191-2.

[89] See, for example, 'The Expiration', *Poems*, p. 56.

[90] See especially 'His Parting from Her', ll. 42-3, 50-2; 'A Tale of a Citizen and his Wife', ll. 13-14, 71 (*Poems*, p. 111, pp. 114-16).

[91] As regards youth, Smith thinks that most of the Elegies were written in the mid-1590s (*Poems*, p. 415).

[92] See, for example, Rosemond Tuve, *Elizabethan and Metaphysical Imagery* (Chicago: University of Chicago Press, 1947), p. 77, on the Renaissance idea of poetic 'decorum'.

[93] For Ovid's poetry of sexual adventure, see *The Erotic Poems*, trans. Peter Green (Harmondsworth: Penguin, 1982).

[94] Jarvis Cocker, 'I Spy', *Different Class* (Island, 1994). In this case, as the attentive listener will note, the persona is undercut by more than a hint of irony.

[95] Gosse, II, 192. In this case we can suspect reluctance on Constance's part, but probably little coercion from her father. For a comment on the problem of dowry, see Gosse, II, 169.

[96] Lawrence Stone, *The Family, Sex and Marriage in England 1500-1800* (Harmondsworth: Penguin, 1979), p. 111.

[97] Stone, *Family*, pp. 122, 260.

[98] Gosse, I, 106, 'from my chamber, whither by your favour I am come', 13 Feb 1602.

[99] *Poems*, p. 165.

[100] Lynda E. Boose, 'The 1599 Bishops' Ban, Elizabethan Pornography, and the Sexualization of the Jacobean Stage', in *Enclosure Acts: Sexuality, Property, and Culture in Early Modern England*, ed. Richard Burt and John Michael Archer (Ithaca: Cornell University Press, 1994), 185-200, p. 185.

[101] Ibid., pp. 187ff.

[102] On dating, see Smith, *Poems*, p. 469.

[103] See, for example, *Satires, Epigrams and Verse Letters* ed. W. Milgate (Oxford: Clarendon Press, 1967), or A.J. Smith's Penguin edition of the poems. A valuable and subtle guide is also offered by Thomas M. Hester's *Kind Pitty and Brave Scorne: Donne's Satyres* (Durham, NV: Duke University Press, 1982).

[104] See, for example, Satire III, ll. 1-12 especially, in *The Poems of Joseph Hall*, ed. Arnold Davenport (Liverpool: Liverpool University Press, 1969), p. 14. The first part of Hall's satires was published as *Virgidemiae* in 1597.

[105] Satire 4, p. 167.

[106] *The Acoustic World of Early Modern England: Attending to the O-Factor* (Chicago: University of Chicago Press, 1999), pp. 49-51.

[107] Londoners of the period were supposed to be particularly fond of prolonged bell-ringing as a form of exercise and entertainment (see Smith, *Acoustic World*, pp. 52-3).

[108] Pope compounded the mutilation by the misleading reference to 'Dr John Donne, Dean of St Paul's' – something neither Donne nor anyone else would have dreamed of in the 1590s (see Smith, *Poems*, p. 469).

[109] *Essays*, p. 289.

[110] That is, 'your only wearing' is interpreted as the speaker's only set of clothes, rather than as an aesthetic preference. The *OED* defines 'grogaram' as 'a coarse fabric of silk, of mohair and wool, or of these mixed with silk; often stiffened with gum'.

[111] See Wilfrid Hooper, 'The Tudor Sumptuary Laws', *The English Historical Review*, 30: 119 (1915), 433-49.

[112] *The Crisis of the Aristocracy 1558-1641* (Oxford: Clarendon Press, 1965), p. 61.

[113] On knighthoods, see Stone, *Crisis*, pp. 73-4. Stone sees the period 1580-1620 as the most unstable one prior to the Civil War (ibid., p. 15).

[114] Cf. Donne, Elegy 17, ll. 50-3 (*Poems*, p. 121).

[115] Cf., again, Donne's epigram, 'The Liar' (*Poems*, p. 152).

[116] Bald, *Donne*, p. 94.

[117] Cf. Bald, *Donne*, p. 94.

[118] Cf. Cain, 'Donne's Political World', *Cambridge Companion*, 83-100, pp. 88, 90.

[119] For the oppression of Catholics by such 'pursuivants', see also *Poems*, p. 172, ll. 61-8.

[120] *Norton*, p. 1035.

[121] *Donne*, pp. 39-41.

[122] On the intriguing cultural significance of London's 'liberties', see Stephen Mullaney, *The Place of the Stage: License, Play, and Power in Renaissance England* (Ann Arbor: University of Michigan Press, 1995).

[123] Gosse, I, 154 [?January 1607]. Donne's reference to 'this paper opposed to those, with which you trusted me' seems to indicate not his own letter, but a response to something (a religious tract?) which Goodyer had sent.

124 Ann Donne did indeed finally die, in August 1617, just five days after the especially difficult birth of a still-born child (Bald, *Donne*, p. 324).

125 For a similar elision of the female generative role, see 'Love's War', ll. 45-6.

126 See especially Jane Sharp, *The Midwives Book: or the Whole Art of Midwifery Discovered*, ed. Elaine Hobby (Oxford: Oxford University Press, 1999), xi-xxxii, esp. xiii. A male surgeon may occasionally have been present if there were particularly severe complications. The women in this community were known as 'gossips' – not in the later, narrower sense, but as derived from the term 'god-sibs' or 'god-sibling'.

127 *Poems*, p. 236. Donne's verse letters do not have formal titles. Smith lists them by their opening words.

128 Genesis 1.26, 2.7, 20-23.

129 '"Oh, let me not serve so": The Politics of Love in Donne's Elegies', in Mousley, *Donne*, 25-44, pp. 26-7 esp.

130 Guibbory, pp. 27-9.

131 See chapter two, section one.

132 *Poems*, p. 67.

[133] As regards sex, Smith (p. 421) is probably correct in suspecting the sense of sexual excitation in 'chafes' (cf. *The Progress of the Soul ... Metempsychosis*, l. 482 (*Poems*, p. 192)).

[134] Gosse, I, 168-9.

[135] *Sermons*, III, 19.

[136] Epistle, *The Progress of the Soul ... Metempsychosis* (*Poems*, p. 176).

[137] See Frank Lestringant, *Cannibals: The Discovery and Representation of the Cannibal from Columbus to Jules Verne*, trans. Rosemary Morris (Cambridge: Polity Press, 1997), p. 75.

[138] As Smith notes (p. 422), the 'chest' is both Proserpina's bosom and the box in which she kept a beautifying ointment.

[139] *Poems*, p. 96. Guibbory's view ('"Oh, let me not serve"', p. 29) that this may refer to 'the ageing Queen Elizabeth' seems difficult to prove, especially given the conventional nature of the poem. Indeed, the poem can be viewed as essentially *more* mysogynistic if one does not assume the presence of Elizabeth as a specific motivation.

[140] 'Husbands' puns on 'husbandmen', meaning farmers.

[141] 'Stews' were brothels. The biblical Joseph refused the advances of Potiphar's wife (see Smith, p. 417).

[142] See Smith, pp. 416, 421.

[143] See, again, Smith, p. 416, citing Helen Gardner.

[144] Cf. Stanley Fish, '"Masculine Persuasive Force": Donne and Verbal Power', in *Soliciting Interpretation: Literary Theory and Seventeenth-Century English Poetry*, ed. Elizabeth D. Harvey and Katherine Eisaman Maus (Chicago: University of Chicago Press, 1990), 223-52, p. 224.

[145] *Ways of Seeing* (New York: Penguin, 1977), p. 47.

[146] *Poems*, p. 87.

[147] *Sermons*, II, 261.

[148] For a glance at this, see Donne in Gosse, II, 260.

[149] See Thomas Laqueur, *Making Sex: Body and Gender from the Greeks to Freud* (Cambridge, Mass.: Harvard University Press, 1990). Laqueur's influential theory has been challenged by some critics as an oversimplification (see for example Hobby, *Midwives Book*, xxviii, n.38). For valuable discussions of Renaissance responses to the indeterminate sexuality of the hermaphrodite see, Ruth Gilbert, *Early Modern Hermaphrodites: Sex and other Stories* (Basingstoke: Palgrave, 2002); Cathy McClive, 'Bleeding Flowers and Waning Moons: A History of Menstruation in France c. 1495-1761', unpublished PhD thesis, Warwick, 2004, chapter six.

[150] 'De Anima', trans. J.A. Smith, *The Works of Aristotle*, ed. W.D. Ross, 12 vols (Oxford: Clarendon Press, 1931), III, 412a.

[151] See *John Donne: Selected Prose*, ed. Helen Gardner and Timothy Healy

(Oxford: Clarendon Press, 1967), p. 20.

[152] *Sermons*, IV, 241.

[153] Gosse, I, 166.

[154] Gosse, I, 170.

[155] *Poems*, pp. 50-51. Cf. also Elegy 16, ll. 3-5 (*Poems*, p. 118).

[156] See Stone, *Family*, pp. 78-9.

[157] Stone, *Family*, p. 77.

[158] On Pool, see Gosse, II, 14.

[159] Gosse, I, 296.

[160] *Life*, ed. Horace Walpole (London: Saunders and Otley, 1826), pp. 218-19.

[161] *Family*, p. 79. On his 'particular friends', see Donne in Gosse, II, 124.

[162] Nicole Castan, Maurice Aymard, Alain Coomp, Daniel Fabre, Arlette Farge, in *A History of Private Life* (general eds. Philippe Ariès and Georges Duby), *III. Passions of the Renaissance*, ed. Roger Chartier, trans. Arthur Goldhammer (London: Belknap Press, Harvard, 1989), p. 451.

[163] Gosse, I, 180, March 1608.

[164] *Essays* (1625) (London: Oxford University Press, 1966), p. 200.

[165] *The Friend* (Chicago: University of Chicago Press, 2003), p. 76. A good example of such 'danger' is found, as Martin Coyle kindly reminds me, in the friendship of Antonio and Bassanio, in *The Merchant of Venice*.

[166] Gosse, I, 122-3 [?1603 or 4].

[167] Gosse, II, 267.

[168] Gosse, I, 227.

[169] *Sermons*, VIII, 338.

[170] For Donne's disdain of careless speech, see *Sermons*, VIII, 292. On the high reputation of certain letters after Donne's death, see Dayton Haskin, 'On Trying to Make the Record Speak More about Donne's Love Poems', in *John Donne's 'desire of more': The Subject of Anne More Donne in His Poetry*, ed. M. Thomas Hester (London: Associated University Presses, 1996), 39-65, p. 45.

[171] Cited in Smith, *Acoustic World*, p. 38.

[172] *Acoustic World*, p. 39.

[173] Gosse, I, 170 [?July 1607].

[174] Gosse, I, 300 [Paris, 9 April 1612].

[175] Paul Hammond, *Love Between Men in Renaissance Literature* (London: Macmillan, 1996), p. 27.

[176] *Between Men: English Literature and Male Homosocial Desire* (New York: Columbia University Press, 1985), p. 1.

[177] For Bray's earlier work see *Homosexuality in Renaissance England* (London: Gay Men's Press, 1982). For the rituals, burials and tombs, see *The Friend*, pp. 13-42, pp. 42-3. Cf. also Theodore Zeldin on the 'camarada' of Guatemala, whose intra-male relationship involved its partners 'publicly embracing ... dancing together' and even saying they would willingly marry if the other were a woman (*An Intimate History of Humanity* (London: Minerva, 1995), p. 321. The last statement is remarkably like the sentiments of Shakespeare's sonnet 20.)

[178] *Poems*, p. 155.

[179] Any readers currently making university choices may like to know that Oriel College did not admit women until 1984.

[180] Gosse, II, 45.

[181] *Poems*, p. 201.

[182] Verse letter, *Poems*, p. 214.

[183] Gosse, I, 300, [Paris, 9 April 1612].

[184] Gosse, I, 224, from Mitcham.

[185] Gosse, I, 225.

[186] *Love Between Men*, p. 31.

[187] Gosse, I, 173, 9 October [1607].

[188] Gosse, II, 266 [?December 1630].

[189] Gosse, I, 154.

[190] Gosse, I, 168-9, 15 August 1607.

191 Gosse, I, 181, March 1607/8.

192 Verse Letter, *Poems*, p. 215. Cf. Donne's admission of 'unnecessary' writing elsewhere (Gosse, I, 122-3 [?1603 or 4]).

193 Cited in Bray, *Friend*, p. 19.

194 Gosse, II, 267. Italics mine.

195 *Autobiography*, trans. George Bull (London: Penguin, 1998), p. 219.

196 *Sermons*, I, 199.

197 See *Sermons* III, 148, VI, 57, VIII, 119-20, 240.

198 See Smith, *Poems*, p. 378.

199 See I Corinthians 13.12.

200 See Stone, *Family*, p. 170. William Shullenberger, 'Love as a Spectator Sport in John Donne's Poetry', in *Renaissance Discourses of Desire*, ed. Claude J. Summers and Ted-Larry Pebworth (Columbia: University of Missouri Press, 1993), 46-62, pp. 48-9, citing Stone, *Family*, p. 169.

201 *Love Between Men*, p. 26.

202 'Love as a Spectator Sport'.

203 In his *Timaeus* Plato tells of how the Creator made 'a moving image of eternity ... and this image we call time' (quoted in Bertrand Russell, *History of Western Philosophy* (London: Allen and Unwin, 1974), p. 158).

[204] Cf. Achsah Guibbory, 'Erotic Poetry', in *Cambridge Companion*, 133-148, p. 133.

[205] For an overview of this issue, see Haskin, 'On Trying ...', p. 43. For the poem's biographical context see also Marotti, *John Donne*, pp. 157-65.

[206] Gosse, II, 48.

[207] Gosse, I, 215 [1608].

[208] *Paradise Lost*, II, l. 148 (*Norton*, p. 1839).

[209] *Devotions*, p. 20.

[210] *Poems*, pp. 84-5.

[211] *Sermons*, IX, 175.

[212] *Sermons*, VII, 390.

[213] For the biblical origins of this belief, see John 5. 28, 29. For the biblical resurrection of certain saints during Christ's crucifixion, see Matthew 27. 52, 53.

[214] Gosse, I, 173.

[215] Caroline Walker Bynum, *The Resurrection of the Body in Western Christianity, 200-1336* (New York: Columbia University Press, 1995), pp. 97-8.

[216] *Sermons*, IV, 69, Easter day [1622]); *Poems*, p. 311.

[217] *Sermons*, IV, 75, Easter day [1622]. Cf. also IV, 65.

[218] *Hydriotaphia* (1658), p. 81.

[219] *Poems*, pp. 59, 125.

[220] *Essays in Divinity*, p. 50; *Sermons*, III, 196.

[221] Letter to Herbert Grierson, 1912, quoted in Lovelock, *Donne*, p. 99.

[222] *Sermons*, IX, 205.

[223] See James Cannon, 'Reverent Donne: The Double Quickening of Lincoln's Inn Chapel', in *John Donne's Professional Lives*, ed. David Colclough (Cambridge: D.S. Brewer, 2003), 207-14, p. 207.

[224] See, for example, Keith Thomas, *Religion and the Decline of Magic* (London: Penguin, 1991), and Piero Camporesi's *The Incorruptible Flesh*, and *Bread of Dreams*.

[225] Gosse, II, 124.

[226] Gosse, I, 226. For a more general relativism of belief, see also *Sermons*, VII, 97.

[227] For further discussion of this remark and its implications, see Alison Shell and Arnold Hunt, 'Donne's Religious World', *Cambridge Companion*, 65-82, esp. p. 65, pp. 75-6.

[228] Gosse, I, 171. For other, broadly similar instances, see Gosse, II, 78, [April 1615]; I, 196.

[229] Gosse, II, 176, 1623.

[230] Gosse, I, 288, 7 February 1611/12.

[231] Gosse, II, 246 [April 1627].

[232] See Bald, *Donne*, p. 206.

[233] Quoted in Bald, *Donne*, p. 298.

[234] Carey's construction of Donne's apostasy has been attacked for too negatively emphasising ambition and pragmatism (see Annabel Patterson, 'Misinterpretable Donne: The Testimony of the Letters', *John Donne Journal*, 1 (1982), 39-53, p. 39). In fairness to Carey, his point about the murky 'springs of human motivation' (*Donne*, p. 31) should be noted here.

[235] *Selected Essays*, p. 344.

[236] *Sermons*, X, 161.

[237] Cf. Shell and Hunt, 'Donne's Religious World', pp. 66-7.

[238] Gosse, II, 78 [April 1615].

[239] *Sermons*, VIII, 347.

[240] *Sermons*, II, 100.

[241] *Sermons*, VII, 114-115.

[242] *Sermons*, III, 228.

[243] *Sermons*, VII, 162.

[244] *Sermons*, III, 59.

[245] See Duffy, *Stripping of the Altars*, pp. 217, 279, 282. For two especially vivid instances of sin and judgement as conditioning the interpretation of events in Donne's lifetime, see John Field, *A Godly Exhortation* (1583); Thomas Goad, *The Doleful Even-song* (1623), B1^{r-v}; John Gee, *The Foot out of the Snare* (1624), pp. 6-7 esp.

[246] *Sermons*, IV, 330.

[247] Gosse, I, 190-1, September 1608.

[248] *Sermons*, IV, 55.

[249] *Sermons*, II, 356.

[250] *An Other Sermon before the King ... 26 March 1605* (1605), p. 1

[251] *Sermons*, I, 195.

[252] *The Sinfulness of Sin* (1631), p. 230.

[253] Gosse, II, 272.

[254] *Sermons*, III, 218.

[255] *Sermons*, I, 308. Cf., also, *Sermons*, I, 188

[256] See, for example, *Discipline and Punish*, trans. Alan Sheridan (London: Penguin, 1977), pp. 236-7.

[257] *Sermons*, X, 224.

[258] *Sermons*, IV, 329.

[259] See, for example, Duffy, *Stripping of the Altars*, p. 214. It is fair to say that for many believers such ritual practices probably had a magical aura.

[260] 'Consubstantiation' was originally a medieval theory. It was readopted by Martin Luther (1483-1546) and his followers. Notably, another influential Protestant, Ulrich Zwingli (1483-1531), promoted a still more dilute revision, arguing that the mass was a purely symbolic commemoration, with the bread and wine holding no physical presence of Christ at all.

[261] *Sermons*, VIII, 348.

[262] The already paradoxical quality of predestination is further complicated by the range of different attitudes existing outside the established English Church. Debate persists as to exactly what Donne's position was (for a concise survey of recent opinions, see Jeffrey Johnson, *The Theology of John Donne* (Cambridge: D.S. Brewer, 2001), p. 39). We know that he seems to have approved of both John Calvin and Theodore Beza, two of the most influential theologians of predestination (the former being the most often-cited Protestant authority in his sermons (see X, 375, IV, 25, 207, VII, 118, 207, 384)). The Arminians were the chief opponents of High Calvinist predestination, and Donne refers in a sermon to 'the Armenian heretics' (II, 115). For further discussion of Donne and predestination, see: Achsah Guibbory, 'Donne's Religion: Montagu, Arminianism and Donne's Sermons', *English Literary Renaissance*, 31 (2001), 412-39; Shell and Hunt, 'Donne's Religious World'; John Stachniewski, 'John Donne: the Despair of the "Holy Sonnets"', *English Literary History*, 48 (1981), 677-705, p. 689.

[263] Gosse, I, 185-6. Although the letter is not dated, a reference to the countryside (185) and to the writer's impotency (186) both suggest Mitcham.

[264] *Sermons*, I, 205. The remedy is the (restrained) conjugal love of marriage.

[265] For Donne's own comment on this danger, see *Devotions*, p. 10.

[266] *Sermons*, IV, 309.

[267] *Sermons* IV, 308.

[268] See Mary Morrissey, 'Narrative Authority in Spiritual Life-Writing: The Example of Dionys Fitzherbert (fl. 1608-14)', *The Seventeenth Century*, 15: 1 (2000), 1-17; Carola Scott-Luckens, 'Propaganda or Marks of Grace? The Impact of the Reported Ordeals of Sarah Wight in Revolutionary London, 1647-52', *Women's Writing*, 9: 2 (2002), 215-32, pp. 222-3. See, also, Collinson, *Birthpangs*, pp. 75-7; Arnold Hunt, 'The Lord's Supper in Early Modern England', *Past and Present*, 161 (1998), 39-83, pp. 41, 46, 47-9, 58.

[269] *Course in General Linguistics*, trans. Roy Harris (London: Duckworth, 1983), p. 110.

[270] *Sermons*, IX, 258.

[271] *Sermons*, II, 89; IX, 401.

[272] *Sermons*, IX, 256.

[273] For further examples from the *Sermons*, see IX, 172, 223.

[274] *Devotions*, p. 8.

[275] *Sermons*, VIII, 105.

[276] *Sermons*, IX, 195.

[277] *Sermons*, II, 86.

[278] *Devotions*, p. 11. For a discussion of the range of socially-influenced 'power relations' between the believer and God in this period, see Michael Schoenfeldt, *Prayer and Power: George Herbert and Renaissance Courtship* (Chicago: University of Chicago Press, 1991).

[279] *Holy Sonnets* 10, 13, 14 (*Poems*, pp. 313, 314, 314).

[280] *Essays*, pp. 344, 352.

[281] *The Poetry of Meditation: A Study of English Religious Literature of the Seventeenth Century* (London: Oxford University Press, 1954), pp. 43-53 especially.

[282] On Protestant use of such techniques, see Hunt, 'Lord's Supper', p. 60.

[283] 'The Relic', l. 6 (*Poems*, p. 76).

[284] For a discussion of how such imagery relates at least partly to an established tradition of amorous and marital devotional rhetoric, see William Kerrigan, 'The Fearful Accommodations of John Donne', in Mousley, *Donne*, 198-216.

[285] 'Despair of the "Holy Sonnets"', p. 689.

[286] *Poems*, p. 311.

[287] *Sermons*, VII, 82-3.

[288] *Sermons*, III, 371.

[289] *Sermons*, VI, 60.

[290] *Poems*, p. 330.

[291] *Sermons*, IX, 331. Cf. Proverbs 13.24, 19.18; Hebrews 12.6.

[292] *Sermons*, VIII, 62.

[293] *Sermons*, IV, 324.

[294] *Devotions*, p. 70.

[295] *Sermons*, IV, 150.

[296] *Sermons*, III, 218.

[297] *Sermons*, VIII, 368.

[298] *Sermons*, IX, 366.

[299] On gold, see 'A Valediction: forbidding Mourning', ll. 21-4, and *Sermons*, VIII, 119-20, 240; VI, 57. For a similar argument concerning change, religion and alchemy, see Kate Gartner Frost, '"Preparing towards her": Contexts of *A Nocturnall upon S. Lucies Day*', in *John Donne's 'desire of more'*, 149-171.

[300] *Poems*, pp. 348-9, ll. 6, 12.

[301] *Sermons*, II, 80.

[302] *Sermons*, II, 331. Cf. also *Sermons*, III, 303.

[303] *Sermons*, IX, 153.

[304] Part II appeared in 1615, with English counterparts coming in 1612 and 1620 (see *Don Quixote*, trans. Samuel Putnam, 2 vols (London: Cassell, 1953), I, xi).

[305] *Order of Things*, p. 46. For a more traditional, though arguably similar, version of Foucault's arguments about epistemic shift, see also Ernst Cassirer, *The Individual and the Cosmos in Renaissance Philosophy*, trans. Mario Domandi (Oxford: Basil Blackwell, 1963).

[306] *Order of Things*, p. 47.

[307] *Order of Things*, p. 47. For Mikhail Bakhtin's similar opinion on *Don Quixote*, see *The Dialogic Imagination*, ed. M. Holquist, trans. Caryl Emerson and M. Holquist (London: University of Texas Press, 1981), p. 324.

[308] In its narrowest sense typology is 'the doctrine that things in the New Testament are foreshadowed symbolically in the Old' (*Chambers Dictionary*). More generally it involves a desire to locate 'signs' in events or phenomena.

[309] *Sermons*, I, 186.

[310] That such a feeling belongs more to Donne than to Protestantism in general is confirmed when we find the fervent Protestant George Herbert echoing Neri (see esp. 'The Temper' I, l. 9, in *The Works of George Herbert* (Hertfordshire: Wordsworth, 1994), p. 46).

[311] For examples see: Jonathan Sawday, The Body Emblazoned: Dissection and the Human Body in Renaissance Culture

(London: Routledge, 1995); and The Illustrations from the Works of Andreas Vesalius of Brussels (Dover, 1973).

[312] *Andreas Vesalius' First Public Anatomy at Bologna: An Eyewitness Account by Baldasar Heseler, together with his notes on Matthaeus Curtius' Lectures on Anatomia Mundini,* ed. and trans. Ruben Eriksson (Lychnos Bibliotek, 18, Almqvist & Wiksells, 1959), p. 285. Hereafter 'Eriksson'.

[313] *Order of Things*, pp. 34, 81.

[314] *Order of Things*, p. 81.

[315] Preface to *De Fabrica*, quoted in K.B. Roberts and J.D.W. Tomlinson, *The Fabric of the Body: European Traditions of Anatomical Illustration* (Oxford: Clarendon Press, 1992), p. 133. Vesalius refers to the tradition whereby the lecturer sat reading some feet above the corpse and the surgeon (see Sawday, *Body Emblazoned*, Figure 3).

[316] For Donne's interest in the controversial, newly-revived 'atomistic' physics of the period, see David A. Hedric Hirsch, 'Donne's Atomies and Anatomies: Deconstructed Bodies and the Resurrection of Atomic Theory', *Studies in English Literature*, 31 (1991), 68-94. Donne owned a new work on atomism, Nicholas Hill's *Philosophia Epicurea, Democritiana* ... (Paris, 1601) (see Geoffrey Keynes, *A Bibliography of Dr. John Donne*, (Oxford: Clarendon Press, 1973), pp. 270-1). For atomistic references in Donne's letters, see Gosse, II, 300, 305.

[317] *Anatomy*, ll. 278-81, 387-88 (*Poems*, p. 278, p. 280); *Ignatius His Conclave*, ed. T.S. Healy, S.J. (Oxford: Clarendon Press, 1969), p. 7; *Sermons*, III, 210, 16 February 1621.

[318] *Sermons*, IX, 47, 90; *Biathanatos*, ed. Michael Ruddick and M. Pabst Battin (London: Garland Publishing, 1982), p. 140.

[319] Donne owned a copy of Kepler's *Eclogae Chronicae* (Frankfurt, 1615) (see Keynes, *Bibliography*, p. 271.) As the editors of *Biathanatos* note, Donne cites chapter 26 of Kepler's *De Stella Nova* in order to reinforce this criticism of conservative astronomy (p. 140.) On the meeting, see Wilbur Appelbaum, 'Donne's Meeting with Kepler', *Philological Quarterly*, 50 (1971), 132-4.

[320] Sermons, VII, 260.

[321] *Essays in Divinity*, p. 34

[322] *Dialogic Imagination*, p. 270. See, also, Bakhtin's *Rabelais and his World*, trans. Hélène Iswolsky (Cambridge, Mass.: M.I.T. Press, 1968).

[323] *Elegies and Songs and Sonnets*, li-lviii.

[324] Sawday, *Body Emblazoned*, ix.

[325] 'The Apparition', l. 12, Satire 2, ll. 81-4 (*Poems*, pp. 43, 160).

[326] 'The Dream', ll. 27-8 (*Poems*, p. 53); VIII, 223; Gosse, II, 112. Cf., also, Sermons, IV, 329.

[327] See *Lectures on the Whole of Anatomy*, trans. C.D. O'Malley, F.N.L. Poynter, and K.F. Russell (Berkeley and Los Angeles: University of California Press, 1961), esp. pp. 73, 79, 82, 104, 219, 44, 39. On Donne's evocations of the sensory world, see also Carey, *Donne*, pp. 135-40.

[328] *Sermons*, I, 273.

[329] *Sermons*, VIII, 255, IX, 385.

[330] For Donne's interest in it, see also *Essays in Divinity*, p. 94; *Sermons*, III, 105.

[331] 'Donne's Atomies and Anatomies'.

[332] Cf. David H.M. Woollam on Donne's elegy, 'The Bracelet' ('Donne, Disease and the Doctors', *Medical History*, 5 (1961), 144-53, pp. 150-1).

[333] *Sermons*, VIII, 220.

[334] *Sermons*, VIII, 231.

[335] For details, see, Richard Sugg, *Murder after Death: Literature and Anatomy, 1540-1642* (Cornell University Press, 2007), Appendix one.

[336] *Devotions*, p. 19. While Carey makes a similar point (*Donne*, p. 137) he is slightly too emphatic in his idea of Donne outrightly 'rejecting' an old relationship still in process of transition.

[337] *Sermons*, VIII, 146.

[338] For a similar example, see *Sermons*, IV, 159.

[339] Cold weather was required in this era to preserve the corpses used for demonstrations. Accordingly it was January, and many of these demonstrations took place in darkness.

[340] Eriksson, p. 220-1.

[341] Eriksson, pp. 220-1.

[342] Eriksson, p. 289.

[343] Eriksson, pp. 289-291. It is difficult to be sure exactly what Heseler did see and touch, but there are sufficient veins and arteries in that area to have satisfied someone predisposed to belief in the *rete*.

[344] *Microcosmographia* (1615), p. 470.

[345] 'Anima' is Latin for 'soul' or 'mind'.

[346] *Microcosmographia*, p. 516.

[347] *Microcosmographia*, p. 529.

[348] Eriksson, p. 220.

[349] For Vesalius' own later shame at this manoeuvre, see Charles Singer, *Vesalius on the Human Brain* (Oxford: Oxford University Press, 1952), p. 57.

[350] *Lectures*, pp. 228-229.

[351] Quoted in D.P. Walker, 'The Astral Body in Renaissance Medicine', in *Journal of the Warburg and Courtauld Institutes*, 21 (1958), 119-34, p. 130.

For the full story of body-soul relations c.1500-1700, see: Sugg, *The Smoke of the Soul: Medicine, Physiology and Religion in Early Modern England* (Palgrave, 2013).

[352] Gosse, II, 260.

[353] *Of the Progress of the Soul*, ll. 9-22, *Poems*, pp. 287-8.

[354] Gosse, I, 174-6, Mitcham, 9 October [1607].

[355] *Man's Mortality* (1643), pp. 12-13.

[356] *Sermons*, III, 235-6.

[357] For an evidently similar tendency, see *Sermons*, IV, 159.

[358] *ABC of Reading* (1934; London: Faber, 1991), p. 140.

[359] Cf. *Sermons*, VI, 116.

[360] *Science, Optics and Music in Medieval and Early Modern Thought* (London: Hambledon Press, 1990), pp. 177-78.

[361] Trans. Robert Burton, in *The Anatomy of Melancholy* (1621), ed. Thomas C. Faulkner, Nicholas K. Kiessling, Rhonda L. Blair, 3 vols (Oxford: Clarendon Press, 1989-1994), III, 89.

[362] Reginald Hyatte, 'The "Visual Spirits" and Body-Soul Mediation: Socratic Love in Marsilio Ficino's De Amore', *Rinascimento*, 33 (1993), 213-22; quoting *De Amore*, speech 7, chapter 8.

[363] *Sylva Sylvarum* (1627), p. 251.

[364] Carey, *Donne*, p. 138.

[365] *Sermons*, IX, 383.

[366] Similarly, Bacon believed that an envious glance could be physically dangerous (*Sylva Sylvarum*, p. 251).

[367] *Devotions*, pp. 51-2. Cf. *Sermons*, IX, 400.

[368] Lines 21-28, 37-40, 56, 57-60.

[369] *The Poems of John Donne*, ed. H.J.C. Grierson, 2 vols (Oxford: Clarendon Press, 1912), II, xlvii.

[370] Quoted by Joan Bennett, 'The Love Poetry of John Donne: A Reply to C.S. Lewis', in *Seventeenth Century Studies Presented to Sir Herbert Grierson* (Oxford: Clarendon Press, 1938), pp. 95, 94.

[371] Eriksson, p. 221.

[372] *Microcosmographia*, p. 516; Alexander Read, *A Manual of the Anatomy of the Body of Man* (1634), p. 161. (Although *Microcosmographia* was not published until 1615, Laurentius' *Historia Anatomica*, the source which Crooke was translating, had appeared in Paris in 1595.)

[373] I am very grateful to Gerald Hammond for suggesting this idea to me.

[374] *Sermons*, IX, 176.

[375] *Sermons*, VI, 75.

[376] *Sermons*, X, 125.

[377] *The Age of Reason* (1794-6).

[378] *Selections from the Work of Thomas Paine*, ed. Arthur Wallace Peach (New York: Harcourt, Brace and Co., 1928), p. 278.

[379] Or, in modern terms, Asia – 'Indies' or 'India' denoted the distant lands of both east and west.

[380] See *A Brief and True Report of the New Found Land of Virginia* (1588).

[381] See William Strachey, *The History of Travel into Virginia* (1612), ed. R.H. Major (London: Hakluyt Society, 1849), pp. 44-7.

[382] See José de Acosta, *Natural and Moral History of the Indies* (Seville, 1590), pp. 306-7.

[383] On Cham see Strachey, *History*, pp. 46-7; and Alderman Johnson in *The Records of the Virginia Company of London*, ed. Susan Myra Kingsbury, 4 vols (Washington, 1906-1935), II, 397.

[384] See Claire Jowitt, 'Radical Identities? Native Americans, Jews and the English Commonwealth', *The Seventeenth Century*, 10 (1995), 101-19.

[385] This ruling gave vastly more territory to Spain than to Portugal (Alexander himself was Spanish) and in 1494 the line was shifted in Portugal's favour. Even now, however, its only American possession was part of Brazil.

[386] Isabella's ruling of 1503 stated that her countrymen could legitimately enslave only cannibals. This itself of course prompted the invention of cannibals who did not exist (though some almost certainly did). In 1510 the unfortunately named Pope Innocent IV defined cannibalism as a sin whose forceful punishment was in fact the *duty* (rather than merely the right) of Christian soldiers.

[387] *Poems*, p. 213, l. 15.

[388] *Biathanatos* (1644), p. 40.

[389] See *The Black Legend in England: The Development of Anti-Spanish Sentiment, 1558-1660* (Durham, N.C.: Duke University Press, 1971), pp. 2-28 especially.

[390] *The Golden Dream: Seekers of El Dorado* (1967; repr. Athens: Ohio University Press, 1996), p. 37.

[391] *The Discovery of the Large, Rich and Beautiful Empire of Guiana* (1596), 'To the Reader', sig. 3^v, pp. 100-1. (All further references to this edition unless otherwise stated.)

[392] *Essays in Divinity*, p. 35.

[393] I am indebted here to Smith (*Poems*, p. 448) who notes that a chiming watch could be worn by women in this way.

[394] Gosse, I, 219.

[395] *Poems*, pp. 164, 204.

[396] See Silverberg, *Golden Dream*, pp. 32-7.

[397] On the relation between the ritual and the mythic city, see Silverberg, pp. 3-5.

[398] See, respectively, *Discovery*, pp. 70-1, 23-4.

[399] Cf. *The Discoverie of the Large, Rich and Bewtiful Empyre of Guiana*, ed. Neil L. Whitehead (Manchester: Manchester University Press, 1997), p. 71.

[400] *Discovery*, p. 95 (see also ibid., 'To the Reader', sig. 3^v).

[401] *Discovery*, pp. 48, 45.

[402] *Discovery*, pp. 67-8.

[403] On the generation of gold, see Charles Nicholl, *The Chemical Theatre* (London: Routledge, 1980), p. 27; *Discoverie*, ed. Whitehead, p. 71.

[404] *Sermons*, VI, 231.

[405] On metal as ripened into gold by the sun, see *Poems*, p. 141.

[406] See again section one, chapter three.

[407] Cf. *King Lear*, 4.6, 122-7.

[408] The 'remora' of the woman's tongue, for example, is especially telling. The former was a mythical fish which, though minute, could supposedly throw ships from their course if they encountered it.

[409] The reference to the Atlantic shows that this 'India' is indeed America, rather than the East Indies.

[410] On poison, see *Discovery*, p. 57.

[411] See, for example, letters to Magdalen Herbert, Gosse, I, 162-7.

[412] *Poems*, p. 238.

[413] For a discussion of this image, and of New World gender politics in general, see Louis Montrose, 'The Work of Gender in the Discourse of Discovery', *Representations*, 33 (1991), 1-41.

[414] See Aristotle, 'Politics', 1254a, 21-3, trans. A. Platt, in *The Complete Works of Aristotle*, ed. Jonathan Barnes, 2 vols (Surrey: Princeton University Press, 1984), I.

[415] For the debate, see Lewis Hanke, *Aristotle and the American Indian: A Study in Race Prejudice in the Modern World* (London: Hollis & Carter, 1959), pp. 38-73. Sepúlveda was an Aristotelian scholar and the historiographer of Emperor Charles V.

[416] *Sermons*, III, 274, italic mine. For more detail on 'res nullius', see Walter S. H. Lim, *The Arts of Empire: The Poetics of Colonialism From Ralegh to Milton* (London: Associated University Press, 1998), pp. 79-80.

[417] 'De Guiana, Carmen Epicum', in *The Poems of George Chapman*, ed. Phyllis Brooks Bartlett (New York: Russell and Russell, 1962), pp. 353-7, p. 354, ll. 26-8. 'Perfection' had, importantly, a precise sense of 'completion'. In Chapman's lines the plea is interestingly complicated by the fact that the power of 'forming' this primitive 'chaos' is given to Queen Elizabeth.

[418] Cf. Donne, chapter five, section five, on the need for the soul to 'actuate' a human individual.

[419] Gosse, I, 164-5, 11 July 1607.

[420] William Symonds, *Virginia. A Sermon Preached ... 25 April 1609* (1609); Keynes, *Bibliography*, p. 276.

[421] They died on 4 May and 4 August 1609 respectively (see Smith, *Poems*, pp. 573, 575).

[422] See 'John Donne and the Virginia Company', *English Literary History*, 14 (1947), 127-38, p. 128; and Gosse, I, 240.

[423] *Records*, II, 20.

[424] For Donne's attendance, see *Records*, II, 225, 231, 244, 300, 391, 422. For references, see *Sermons*, III, 357-9; IV, 59, 110, 181, 350-1; VI, 59.

[425] *Sermons*, III, 357-8, 1621.

[426] *Sermons*, III, 357-9. On Donne's attitude to the Koran in particular, see also Alison Shell and Arnold Hunt, 'Donne's Religious World', 65-82, p. 66.

[427] *Sermons*, III, 110.

[428] *Sermons*, IV, 181.

[429] *A Poem on the Late Massacre in Virginia* (1622), C1. Reference is to Brooke's (now very rare) poem as quoted in Johnson, *Donne*, p. 133.

[430] For a valuable discussion of Donne's positive stance, and its social and philosophical context, see also Tom Cain, 'John Donne and the Ideology of Colonization', *English Literary Renaissance*, 31 (2001), 440-76.

[431] *Sermons*, IV, 269.

[432] See, for example, *Devotions*, pp. 80, 118.

[433] *Sermons*, IV, 271.

[434] Mat. 24.14, Luke 24.47. Cf., also, Col. 1.5, Mark 13.9.

[435] *Sermons*, IV, 279.

[436] *Natural and Moral History*, p. 66. See also pp. 306-7.

[437] *Natural and Moral History*, p. 101.

[438] It was, moreover, readdressed by William Strachey, the Virginia Company secretary, in 1612, in his *History of Travel into Virginia*, an account much indebted to Acosta.

[439] *Sermons*, VIII, 371.

[440] *Sermons*, IV, 270, 271.

[441] *Sermons*, IV, 271.

[442] *Sermons*, IV, 280.

[443] *Sermons*, IV, 280-1.

[444] Some of the more precise and influential figures in this tradition included John Brightman, Joseph Mede, and the mathematician, John Napier (see Bernard McGinn, 'Revelation', in *The Literary Guide to the Bible*, ed. Robert Alter and Frank Kermode (London: Fontana, 1997), 523-41).

[445] *Sermons*, IV, 270.

[446] For a broadly similar approach, see John Goodwin, *Imputatio Fidei* (1642), B3^v-B4^r.

[447] *Sermons*, VII, 69.

[448] *Sermons*, VI, 59 [April, May or June 1623]. On dating see ibid., 1-2.

[449] *Sermons*, VII, 372-3.

[450] *Sermons*, IX, 207.

[451] *Sermons*, IX, 47, April 1629.

[452] Title quotation from *Sermons*, IX, 177, 12 February 1629; epigram from *Biathanatos*, p. 49.

[453] 'The Apparition', 'The Damp', 'The Legacy', 'The Funeral', 'The Relic' (*Poems*, pp. 42, 51, 63, 59, 75).

[454] For a convincing argument that the poem does very precisely commemorate Anne Donne's death, see Kate Gartner Frost, '"Preparing towards her"', in *John Donne's 'desire of more'*, 149-171, esp. pp. 154, 159. On the general acceptance that three broadly similar poems *were* written after Anne's death, see Achsah Guibbory, 'Fear of "loving more": Death and the Loss of Sacramental Love', in *John Donne's 'desire of more'*, 204, 227, p. 207.

[455] Quoted in Stone, *Family*, p. 82.

[456] Gosse, I, 189, August 10 [1608], II, 260-1, II, 89.

[457] Frost, ('"Preparing towards her"') argues for a more positive attitude underlying the poem's outer bleakness; but her reading arguably puts excessive weight on Donne's alchemical imagery.

[458] *Sermons*, II, 110.

[459] *Sermons*, IV, 333.

[460] *Sermons*, III, 105.

[461] *Sermons*, X, 233.

[462] *Sermons*, II, 197.

[463] *Sermons*, II, 83.

[464] *Sermons*, VIII, 106.

[465] *Sermons*, I, 273.

[466] Gosse, I, 173; *Sermons*, IV, 75.

[467] *Sermons*, IV, 75.

[468] *Sermons*, VIII, 98.

[469] *Sermons*, III, 302.

[470] *Sermons*, III, 105-6. Cf., also, IX, 63-4.

[471] *Sermons*, IX, 64

[472] *Sermons*, II, 66.

[473] Gosse, II, 270, 15 January 1630/1. Third comma my addition.

[474] Gosse, II, 261. Cf. I Corinthians 15.36.

[475] *Devotions*, pp. 13-14.

[476] *Sermons*, IX, 217.

[477] *Sermons*, VIII, 190.

[478] *Sermons*, VII, 105. Cf. St Jerome, as cited in Walker Bynum, *Resurrection*, p. 94.

[479] *Paradoxes and Problems*, ed. Helen Peters (Oxford: Clarendon Press, 1980), p. 59.

[480] See, for example, Bald, *Donne*, facing pp. 312, 382.

[481] See Bald, *Donne*, p. 158.

[482] *Biathanatos*, p. 18. For other references to or hints at suicide, see Gosse, I, 189 ('I flatter myself'), 190-1, 192 ('he is no safer'), 215.

[483] Gosse, II, 124.

[484] Gosse, I, 194 [1608?].

[485] Gosse, I, 181.

[486] Gosse, I, 291. Cf., also, I, 167, 171.

[487] Gosse, I, 191. See, also, I, 200.

[488] *Biathanatos*, p. 51.

[489] Gosse, I, 191.

[490] Gosse, I, 200.

[491] *Sermons*, X, 133-4, 222.

[492] *Sermons*, IV, 47.

[493] *Sermons*, III, 110.

[494] *Sermons*, III, 114, 118; VI, 73-4.

[495] Walker Bynum, *Resurrection*, pp. 97-8.

[496] It should, however, be emphasised that the resurrected body was often thought of as weightless (see Walker Bynum, *Resurrection*, p. 95).

[497] *Incorruptible Flesh*, p. 28.

[498] *Sermons*, IV, 129.

[499] Satire 1, ll. 2-4, *Poems*, p. 155.

[500] *Sermons*, III, 112.

[501] *Sermons*, VIII, 105.

[502] *Sermons*, IV, 128. Cf, also, *Sermons*, II, 87.

[503] Gosse, II, 15.

[504] *Sermons*, III, 118-19.

[505] *Sermons*, VII, 375.

[506] *Sermons* III, 110.

[507] See chapter three, section three.

[508] Gosse, II, 256.

[509] *Sermons*, IX, 173.

[510] See chapter six, section four.

[511] Gosse, II, 272, [Jan 1631].

[512] Gosse, II, 268, Jan. 7 1631.

[513] Walton, *Lives*, p. 75.

[514] Walton, *Lives*, p. 75.

[515] *Sermons*, X, 239, italics mine.

[516] Gosse, I, 190-1.

[517] The sculpture can still be seen in St. Paul's cathedral today. For the drawing, see Bald, *Donne*, p. 529.

[518] See Gosse, II, Appendix B, 359-363.

[519] *Biathanatos*, p. 55; *Sermons*, IV, 171.

[520] *Sermons*, VIII, 190.

[521] *Biathanatos*, p. 50.

[522] See, again, chapter six, section two.

Select Bibliography

Acosta, Jose de, *The Natural and Moral History of the Indies*, trans. Edward Grimston (London, 1604).

Alter, R. and Frank Kermode (eds), *The Literary Guide to the Bible* (London: Fontana, 1997).

Berger, John, *Ways of Seeing* (New York: Penguin, 1977).

Bray, Alan, *Homosexuality in Renaissance England* (London: Gay Men's Press, 1982).

Campbell, Mary Baine, *The Witness and the Other World: Exotic European Travel Writing, 400-1600* (Ithaca: Cornell University Press, 1988).

Camporesi, Piero, *The Incorruptible Flesh: Bodily Mutation and Mortification in Religion and Folklore*, trans. Tania Croft-Murray and Helen Elsom (Cambridge: Cambridge University Press, 1988).

-- *Bread of Dreams: Food and Fantasy in Early Modern Europe*, trans. David Gentilcore (Oxford: Polity Press, 1996).

Carey, John, *John Donne: Life, Mind and Art* (London: Faber and Faber, 1981).

Cassirer, Ernst, *The Individual and the Cosmos in Renaissance Philosophy*, trans. Mario Domandi (Oxford: Basil Blackwell, 1963).

Colclough, David, (ed.) *John Donne's Professional Lives* (Cambridge: D.S. Brewer, 2003).

Collinson, Patrick, *The Birthpangs of Protestant England: Religious and Cultural Change in the Sixteenth and Seventeenth Centuries* (London: Macmillan, 1988).

Duffy, Eamon, *The Stripping of the Altars: TraditionalReligion in England c.1400-c.1580* (New Haven: Yale University Press, 1992).

Eagleton, Terry, *Literary Theory: An Introduction* (Oxford: Basil Blackwell, 1983).

Flynn, Dennis, *John Donne and the Ancient Catholic Nobility* (Indiana: University of Indiana Press, 1995).

Foucault, Michel, *The Order of Things: An Archaeology of the Human Sciences*, trans. anon. (London: Tavistock Publications).

de Grazia, M., Maureen Quilligan and Peter Stallybrass (eds), *Subject and Object in Renaissance Culture*, Cambridge Studies in Renaissance Literature and Culture, 8 (Cambridge: Cambridge University Press, 1996).

Greenblatt, Stephen, *Renaissance Self-Fashioning: from More to Shakespeare* (London: University of Chicago Press, 1980).

Hadfield, Andrew (ed.), *The English Renaissance 1500-1620*, (Oxford: Basil Blackwell, 2001)

Hanke, Lewis, *Aristotle and the American Indian: A Study in Race Prejudice in the Modern World* (London: Hollis & Carter, 1959).

Hariot, Thomas, *A Brief and True Report of the New Found Land of Virginia* (London, 1590).

Harvey, Elizabeth D. and Katherine Eisaman Maus (eds), *Soliciting Interpretation: Literary Theory and Seventeenth-Century English Poetry* (Chicago: University of Chicago Press, 1990).

Hulme, Peter, & Whitehead, Neil L. (eds), *Wild Majesty: Encounters with Caribs from Columbus to the present day; an anthology* (Oxford: Clarendon Press, 1992).

Lestringant, Frank, *Cannibals: The Discovery and Representation of the Cannibal from Columbus to Jules Verne*, trans. Rosemary Morris (Cambridge: Polity Press, 1997).

McEachern, Claire, and Debora Shuger (eds), *Religion and Culture in Renaissance England* (Cambridge: Cambridge University Press, 1997).

Maltby, William S., *The Black Legend in England: The Development of Anti-Spanish Sentiment, 1558-1660* (Durham, N.C.: Duke University Press, 1971).

Martz, Louis, *The Poetry of Meditation: A Study of English Religious Literature of the Seventeenth Century* (London: Oxford University Press, 1954).

Mullaney, Stephen, *The Place of the Stage: License, Play, and Power in Renaissance England* (Ann Arbor: University of Michigan Press, 1995).

Montrose, Louis, 'The Work of Gender in the Discourse of Discovery', *Representations*, 33 (1991), 1-41.

Mousley, Andrew (ed.), *John Donne*, New Casebooks (Basingstoke: Palgrave, 1999).

Ralegh, Sir Walter, *The Discovery of the Large, Rich and Beautiful Empire of Guiana* (London, 1596).

Rivers, Isabel, *Classical and Christian Ideas in English Renaissance Poetry: A Students' Guide* (London: George Allen and Unwin, 1979).

Russell, Bertrand, *History of Western Philosophy* (London: Allen and Unwin, 1974).

Sawday, Jonathan, *The Body Emblazoned: Dissection and the Human Body in Renaissance Culture* (London: Routledge, 1995).

Scott-Luckens, Carola, 'Propaganda or Marks of Grace? The Impact of the Reported Ordeals of Sarah Wight in Revolutionary London, 1647-52', *Women's Writing*, 9:2 (2002), 215-32.

Sedgwick, Eve Kosofsky, *Between Men: English Literature and Male Homosocial Desire* (New York, 1985).

Smith, Bruce R., *The Acoustic World of Early Modern England: Attending to the O-Factor* (Chicago: University of Chicago Press, 1999).

Stone, Lawrence, *The Crisis of the Aristocracy 1558-1641* (Oxford: Clarendon Press, 1965).
-- *The Family, Sex and Marriage in England 1500-1800* (Harmondsworth: Penguin, 1979).

Sugg, Richard, *The Smoke of the Soul: Medicine, Physiology and Religion in Early Modern England* (Palgrave, 2013).

-- *Mummies, Cannibals and Vampires: The History of Corpse Medicine from the Renaissance to the Victorians* (2nd edn 2015).

Thomas, Keith, *Religion and the Decline of Magic* (London: Weidenfeld & Nicholson, 1971).
-- *Man and the Natural World: Changing Attitudes in England 1500-1800*
(London: Penguin, 1983).

Zeldin, Theodore, *An Intimate History of Humanity* (London: Minerva, 1995).

Printed in Great Britain
by Amazon

67796781R00265